Myron Eells and the Twana Indians of Skokomish

The Twana Indians of the Skokomish Reservation
in Washington Territory
and
Ten Years of Missionary Work Among the

Indians at Skokomish, Washington Territory

Myron Eells

Introduction
by
Peter N. Jones

Bauu Institute and Press
2012

Copyright © 2012

Library of Congress Cataloging-in-Publication Data

Eells, Myron
Myron Eells and the Twana Indians of Skokomish

p.cm

1. Native Americans. 2. Twana. 3. Skokomish. 4. Washington

ISBN 13: 978-1-936955-07-7

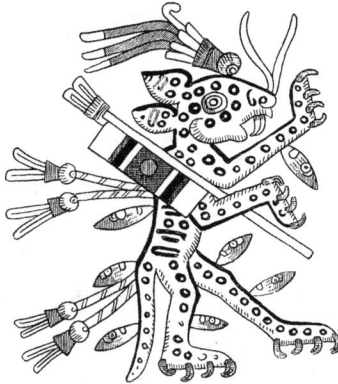

Bauu Press
Winter Park, Colorado
http://www.bauuinstitute.com

Myron Eells and the Twana Indians of Skokomish

The Twana Indians of the Skokomish Reservation in Washington Territory

and

Ten Years of Missionary Work Among the

Indians at Skokomish, Washington Territory

Myron Eells

Introduction
by
Peter N. Jones

Bauu Institute and Press
2012

INTRODUCTION

Myron Eells (1843-1907), the younger son of pioneer missionaries Cushing Eells (1810-1893) and Myra (Fairbanks) Eells (1805-1878), was born at the Tshimakain Mission near present-day Spokane, Washington. After missionaries Marcus and Narcissa Whitman were killed at the Waiilatpu Mission in 1847, near present-day Walla Walla, Washington, the Eellses relocated to the Willamette Valley of Oregon where Myron grew up. After graduating from Pacific University in Forest Grove, Oregon, in 1866, Myron worked on his father's farm in Walla Walla for two years until he began his studies for the ministry. He went East, graduated from Hartford Theological Seminary in Connecticut in 1871, and then returned to the Northwest. At first he led a Congregational Church in Boise, Idaho, but then shortly moved to the Skokomish Reservation, west of Puget Sound, where his brother Edwin was Indian Agent in 1874. Myron remained there for the rest of his life, working as a missionary among Native Americans and White settlers.

On the Skokomish Reservation, Myron conducted research on religious, historical, and anthropological topics, as well as conducting his missionary work. Beginning with a detailed ethnographic questionnaire (republished here) that had been sent to his brother from Otis T. Mason to gather information for the Centennial Exhibition in Philadelphia, Eells pursued "painstaking investigations into the written and unwritten records" of the people and history of the Northwest. Portions of an expansion of this work were later published as journal articles and as a monograph. His literary output included hundreds of articles for newspapers and magazines, some 50 pamphlets, four books, and a number of unpublished manuscripts. Although his attempts to interpret Native culture are circumspect, the picture he gives of contemporary Native life during the late nineteenth century are unparalleled, and his account of his missionary work (republished here) is the most important published source on the origins of the Indian Shaker Church.

The people of the present-day Skokomish Reservation are primarily composed of Twana Indians, a Salishan people whose aboriginal territory encompassed the Hood Canal drainage basin in western Washington State. The first recorded direct contact with European culture came in 1792 when the British expedition under George Vancouver explored Puget Sound and Hood Canal. At the time, there were nine Twana communities, the largest being known as the Skokomish, or "big river people." The Twana subsisted on hunting, fishing and gathering activities, practicing a yearly seasonal cycle that involved movement to resource and trading camps during warmer weather with a return to permanent village sites during the winter. In 1854 and 1855 the Southern Coast Salish people, including the Twana, became parties to the Treaties of Medicine Creek, Point Elliott, and Point No Point, which reserved for them seven tracts of land, which in time came to form today's present-day reservations, including the Skokomish Reservation.

The two works by Myron Eells republished here, *The Twana Indians of the Skokomish Reservation in Washington Territory* (first published in 1877) and *Ten Years of Missionary Work Among the Indians at Skokomish, Washington Territory* (first published in 1886) were both written shortly after the formation of the reservation and during a period of great change for the people of Skokomish. *The Twana Indians of the Skokomish Reservation in Washington Territory* provides an unparalleled ethnological account of contemporary Native life during this period of change, while *Ten Years of Missionary Work Among the Indians at Skokomish, Washington Territory* not only builds on the previous work, but also provides the most important published source on the origins of the Indian Shaker Church. Not only does the republication of these two complete works provide important sources for those interested in Twana culture, society, and religion at a pivotal point in history, but also for the comparative anthropologist and ethnologist.

Peter N. Jones
Winter Park, Colorado 2011

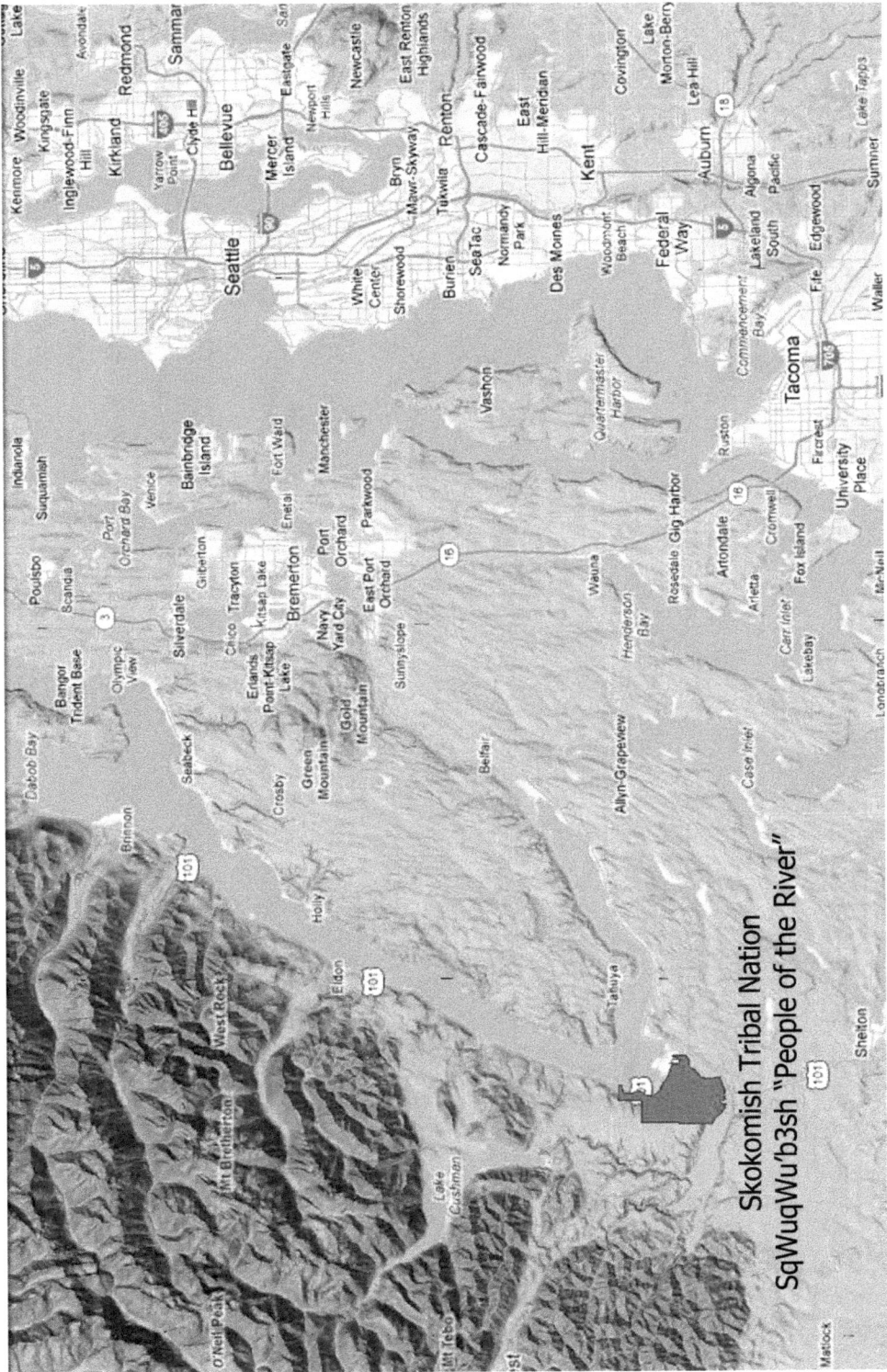

Skokomish Tribal Nation
SqWuqWu'b3sh "People of the River"

DEPARTMENT OF THE INTERIOR.
UNITED STATES GEOLOGICAL AND GEOGRAPHICAL SURVEY.
F. V. HAYDEN, U. S. Geologist-in-Charge.

THE

TWANA INDIANS

OF THE

SKOKOMISH RESERVATION IN WASHINGTON TERRITORY.

BY

REV. M. EELLS,

MISSIONARY AMONG THESE INDIANS.

EXTRACTED FROM THE BULLETIN OF THE SURVEY, VOL. III, No. 1.

WASHINGTON, April 9, 1877.

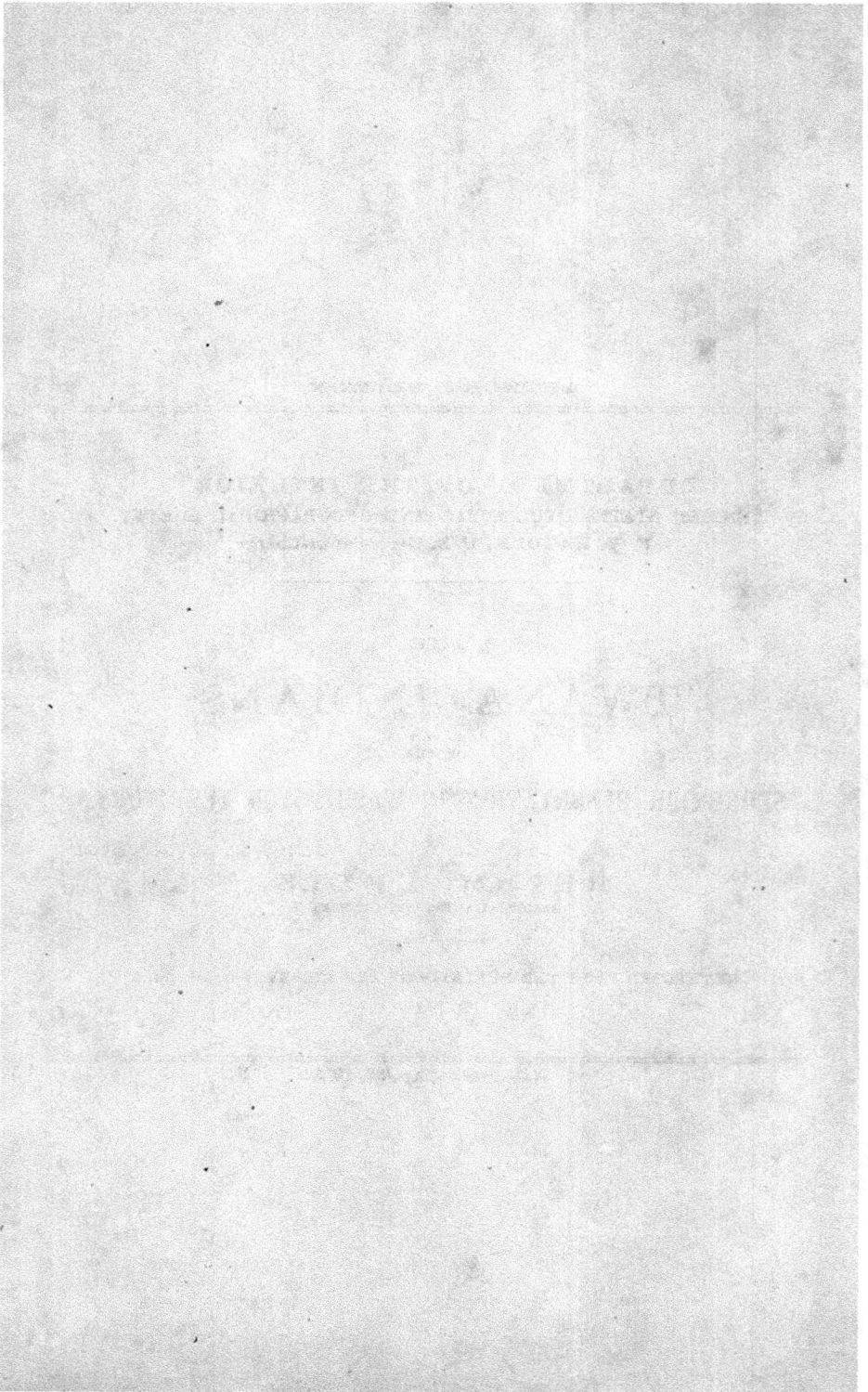

ART. IV.—THE TWANA INDIANS OF THE SKOKOMISH RESERVATION IN WASHINGTON TERRITORY.

BY REV. M. EELLS,
Missionary among these Indians.

PLATES 23-25.

INTRODUCTION.

The following account has been written in answer to questions asked[*] by the Indian Bureau, for the Centennial Exhibition and the Smithsonian Institution. If it is of any value, it is not altogether because it describes the Indians under their old native habits and customs, but because it gives an account of them in a state of *transition* from their native wildness to civilization. For the past sixteen years, a United States Indian agent and Government employés have been on the reservation. Previously to that, there were American settlers in this region for ten or twelve years, and previously to that, the Hudson's Bay Company were trading in the country for thirty years or thereabouts. They have therefore had contact with civilization for a long time, during which they have been adopting civilized customs more or less rapidly, and may be called about half-civilized. Hence, transition is marked in every department of their lives—in food, dwellings, clothes, implements of use, manners, customs, government, and religion; therefore it is very difficult to describe their primitive customs, especially in regard to their ancient ornamental dress, war and hunting customs, stone-work, adornment, secret societies, and tamanamus. There are very few, even of the old men, who know all these customs thoroughly.

The families have not all made equal advancement in civilization, and hence what applies to some will not apply to others, even at the present time; the younger, as a general rule, being further advanced than the older ones. On this account, it has also been difficult to describe all truthfully. On looking over the list of individuals, which number about sixty-five, forty-two of them are at least half-civilized in regard to eating-customs and houses, while of the remaining twenty-

---

[* In the publication entitled " Ethnological Directions relative to the Indian Tribes of the United States.—Prepared under direction of the Indian Bureau, by Otis T. Mason.— Washington : Government Printing Office, 1875."—8vo, pp. 32. The article is in the form of answers to the questions there asked, following the printed heads of subjects of inquiry very closely.—ED.]

three fourteen are either so old or so weak that they cannot work and earn money and obtain civilized food, and so are obliged to live more according to their old ways.

I have only been here about one year and a half, but I desire to say that I have been assisted very materially by the present agent, Mr. E. Eells, who has been here four and a half years, and by Mr. J. Palmer, a native Indian, who both reads and writes English, and has been interpreter here for about six years. Dr. R. H. Lansdale, the resident physician for the past two years, has written paragraphs A and B in Part I, B, C, and D in section 14, Part III, and a part of B in section 15 of Part III.

PART I.—MAN.

A.—PHYSICAL NATURE.

Measurement of the body with reference to each other and to a standard.—Eleven men were weighed and measured, with their clothes, and the following table is the average, both before and after deducting what we think to be right on account of clothes, hair, &c., and also the extreme limits under each head:—

	Before deducting.		After deducting.	
	Average.	Extremes.	Average.	Extremes.
Weight	151 7-11 lbs	124½ lbs.—174½ lbs.	142 lbs	114 19-22 lbs.—164 19-22 lbs.
Height	5 ft. 6 in	5 ft. 3¾ in.—5 ft. 9 in.	5 ft. 5 in	5 ft. 2¾ in.—5 ft. 8 in.
Circumference of head	21 8-11 in	21 in.—23 in	21 in	20 3-11 in.—22 3-11 in.
Circumference of chest	35 3½-11 in.	32 in—38 in	34¼ in	31 2-11 in.—37 2-11 in.
Circumference of pelvis	35 2¼-11 in.	33½ in.—37 in	34 in'	32 3-11 in.—35 8½-11 in.
Circumference of arm	10 2-11 in	9 in.—11 in	10 in	8 9-11 in.—10 9-11 in.
Circumference of forearm	9 5-11 in	8½ in.—11 in	9 3-11 in	8 2½-11 in.—10 9-11 in.
Circumference of thigh	18¾ in	17 in.—20 in	17 in	15¼ in.—18¾ in.
Circumference of leg	13½ in	12 in.—14¼ in	13 in	11½ in.—14 in.
Length of upper extremities			27 8-11 in	26 in.—30 in.
Length of lower extremities			31 3-11 in	29 in.—34 in.
Length of trunk			23 7-11 in	22 in.—25 in.

Color of hair.—Black.

Color of eyes.—Black.

Blushing.—The same as white people, though not so sensitive.

Muscular strength.—Quite inferior to that of white men.

Characteristics of speed.—Not equal to that of white men.

Characteristics of swimming.—Superior to that of white men.

Characteristics of climbing.—Inferior to that of white men.

Senses.—They are a little inferior to those of white men.

Growth and decay.—Their growth is attained early in life, and their decay also begins early.

Child-bearing.—Very easy.

Reproductive power.—Much less than with whites.

Sterility.—This prevails to a large extent. They cause it early in life by various kinds of abuse.

Puberty.—In males at the age of fourteen, and in females about the age of thirteen.

Crosses.—They cross with all races.

Dentition.—The teeth come about the same as in white children, but they wear down early in life. They attribute it to eating dry salmon, though this is not the cause.

Loss of power.—It is lost sooner than with white persons.

Growing gray.—There are very few gray people among them. They do not grow gray as soon as white persons, owing to the freedom from mental care and strain, their out-door life, and the bareness of the head from covering.

Longevity.—I think it is ten years less than with white men.

B.—Pathology.

Diseases.—The principal ones are scrofula, consumption, bleeding at the lungs, scrofulous swellings and scrofulous abscesses, all of which are grafted on a scrofulous diathesis; also acute and chronic bronchitis, all forms of catarrh, diarrhœa, dyspepsia, conjunctivitis, skin diseases, all forms of syphilis, gonorrhœa, toothache, and chronic rheumatism. There are others, but they are not common.

Physical effect of diet, habit, and climate.—These have been the means of producing a scrofulous diathesis from generation to generation, and thus of shortening their lives, as previously stated. The dampness of the climate also produces rheumatism and consumption.

Pain and healing.—They are not sensitive to pain. Cuts and wounds heal easily. Scrofulous diseases are very difficult to cure.

Abnormalities and natural deformities.—There are no natural deformities.

C.—Psychical Phenomena.

Mental capacity for acquiring, remembering, generalizing, volition.—In school, the Indian children acquire on an average as rapidly as the white children in the same school, who have had the same advantages in the primary studies, but do not progress as well in the more advanced studies. The younger ones reason a little, and the older ones more, sometimes quite sharply. The strength of will in some of the older ones, who become leaders, is quite great, but that of the common people is not very great. Their memories are good.

Sagacity in tracking game, following bees, and other occupations.—They have no bees; but in tracking game, they will notice very little things, and follow generally until they find it. In obtaining fish, they have also a large amount of patience and good habits of observation. The greater portion of them have, however, of late years, left these pursuits as their principal means of support, and follow American forms of labor, chiefly logging and working for the whites, making gardens, and raising hay. At these things they are quite industrious, and on most pleasant days a trip over the reservation shows most of them, both men and women, busy in some way. They still hunt some, and fish more; but the majority of them do not follow these occupations as the principal means of support.

Moral ideas.—Formerly quite low, in regard to theft, lying, murder, and chastity, but of late years they have been elevated very much. Formerly they would say it was wrong to steal; but if not found out it was all right. Now, both among Indians and whites, there are very few who accuse any of them of stealing. Lying is much more common. Murder of late years has been almost unknown on the reservation. In regard to chastity, they have improved very much, though there is still room for improvement.

Emotions and passions.—Generally strong; sometimes lasting and sometimes not.

D.—TRIBAL PHENOMENA.

Name.—Twana, spelled in the treaty between the tribe and the United States, made at Point-no-Point January 26, 1855, Too-an-hooch; but I much prefer Twana as being simpler and the one most in use here.

Their own account of their origin and relationships.—God made them soon after he made the world, and he placed them here, as they think he did the different tribes and peoples in the different countries. They believe in different centres of creation for themselves and all other tribes and peoples. God made them at first man and woman.

History of their increase, migrations, growth, and decay.—There is no reliable information about their increase, growth, or any migrations. Twenty years ago, when the treaty was made with them, they numbered about twice as many as they do now, although for the past four years their births have equaled or exceeded their deaths. According to the record of the physician, the deaths for two years previous to July 1, 1875, have been only sixteen. It has been impossible to keep any record of the births. As far back as there is any reliable information, they have always lived in this region. They have a tradition that at the time of the flood, which was only a few generations ago, one great mountain, Mount Olympus, was not wholly submerged, and that on it the good Indians were saved; that as the flood subsided a number of canoes with those in them broke from their fastenings on the mountain, and were carried away to the east and north, which accounts for there being but few people left here now.

Population, male, female, children, and causes affecting.—January, 1875, men, 80; women, 95; boys, 50; girls, 39; total 264. Till within about five years, they have been decreasing, owing chiefly to syphilitic diseases.

Invention, conservatism, and progress.—But little invention. Are generally more than medium about progress. Improving very much in dress, houses, names, food, and habits of industry, though but slowly in Christian ideas; learning more from example than from precept, but in both ways. They have had instruction in Christianity only about four years, and in the other matters for fifteen years, which accounts partly for the difference in regard to this. In almost all things, however, as they see the superiority of the white man, they are ready for progress, especially the younger ones; the old ones being more conservative.

PART II.—SURROUNDINGS OR ENVIRONMENT.

A.—INORGANIC.

Outline and size of Territory—Elevation and Water-systems.—Reservation near the head of Hood's Canal on Puget Sound, in Washington Territory, and at the mouth of the Skokomish River. It is nearly square, and comprises about 5,000 acres; two-thirds of it but a few feet above tide-water, the other third mountainous and several hundred feet high. The Skokomish is the only river which, coming from the north in the Olympic range of mountains, flows east on the south side of the reservation and north on the east side, when it empties into Hood's Canal. There are several sloughs running from the river to the canal across the reservation.

Geological environment, both stratigraphical and economic.—The stratigraphical environment has not been thoroughly studied. Both lava and granite evidently lie at the bottom; the granite I think to be the oldest. Since the granite, evidently there has been a long washing her by salt-water or fresh, I do not know which, but presume it was salt, as the upland is mostly a gravel-bed. As the sea then went down, the river formed most of the soil good for cultivation.

Economic.—The soil of about two-fifths of the reservation is black, rich bottomland, very excellent for cultivation when cleared of the timber which covers it. One-fifth of the land is swampy, and 1,800 acres, nearly two-fifths, is gravelly and covered with fir timber, and is almost useless except as timber-land.

Climate.—Chiefly a dry and wet season, as in Western Washington and Oregon; but little snow or cold weather generally during the winter, but a large amount of rain, which continues at intervals during the summer. The spring is generally backward, as the Olympic Mountains, some of which are snow-capped most of the summer, are but twenty miles distant to the north. Frosts in the fall generally not early, coming from the 1st to the 25th of October usually.

Remains of plants and animals found with relics of extinct tribes.— There are two shell-beds, which as yet have not been opened, at Eneti, on the reservation; one is near the north line of the reservation, and is about 450 feet long, from 3 to 20 wide, and a foot or two thick; the other, half a mile south of it, 300 feet long, and about the same width and thickness. They are both just above high tide, and are evidently of recent formation, the shells being chiefly clam-shells. There is also said to be one at Big Jackson's place, eight miles up the canal, and another at Humhummi, 15 miles down the canal; and I think it very probable that there are such, and perhaps others about, as these are old camping-places of the Indians.

NOTE.—The vegetable and animal resources of the country being all mentioned under other heads, there is no necessity for a detailed enumeration here.

C.—SOCIAL.

Contact with civilized and uncivilized tribes, and its influence.—There are no civilized tribes of Indians with whom they have any contact. There are a number of tribes of half-civilized Indians, with whom they are in contact more or less, chiefly the Squaxons, Nisqually, Clallams, Snohomish, Lummi, and Chehalis tribes. Their relations are peaceful with them all, and their influence is to keep them in about the same condition, neither particularly elevating nor depressing.

There is much contact between them and white civilization, and has been for twenty-five years, and a little for twenty years previously. Its influence has been both good and bad; good with reference to food, clothes, houses, and habits of industry, and against theft, murder, and lying; bad with reference to chastity and temperance.

PART III.—CULTURE.

§ 1.—*MEANS OF SUBSISTENCE.*

A.—FOOD.

Methods of procuring.—Their food is a mixture of old Indian and civilized food, but principally the latter, varying, however, in different families; the younger and middle-aged using chiefly civilized food, and the old and poor ones a large amount of old Indian food.

Most of them have gardens, where they raise chiefly potatoes, corn, peas, onions, turnips, beets, carrots, parsnips, beans, and cabbages, and some fruits, as the raspberry, strawberry, gooseberry, and apple. Potatoes, however, are the principal crop. In the cultivation of their gardens, they do not equal the white man. They seldom plow the ground, as they have been accustomed to clear small patches of land, often too small to plow, and where also too many roots remain. The first season they dig it up with a spade or large hoe, but afterward do not always every year, but sometimes plant the seeds in the old ground, and cultivate with the hoe. As a general thing, they cultivate less than Americans.

They gather many wild berries, chiefly the wild raspberry, gooseberry, currant, sallalberry, strawberry, cherry, cranberry, blackberry, elderberry, salmonberry, thimbleberry, and red, blue, and black huckleberries. Most of these are eaten at once, both cooked and uncooked, but some are dried for future use, chiefly the huckleberry, sallalberry, and black-berry, the last of which is pounded up and made into cakes, which are then dried.

They also gather fern-roots and three other kinds without English names, which grow in swamps, the sprouts of the thimbleberry and salmonberry, rush-roots, Indian onion, and hazelnuts.

They are fond of kamass; none, however, grows near them. Formerly they made long journeys in order to obtain it, but having other food now they have used but little of late years. Most of the roots named are eaten in their season, but few being kept for future use.

They have a few cattle, from which they get a little beef, but prefer to keep most of them in order to raise more cattle to use as work-oxen. They do but little milking, not seeming to think that it pays. They buy some pork, bacon, and hams, and hunt and obtain chiefly venison, bear-meat, pheasants and grouse, ducks and geese, rabbits and squirrels. Most of the hunting is done with the gun, the bow and arrow being entirely out of use, except as a plaything for children. At certain times of the year, ducks are very abundant, yet they have been shot at so often that they are very much afraid of canoes. The Indians, therefore, cover their canoes with green boughs, standing some upright. Hiding among these boughs, they paddle quietly among the ducks, which are not frightened at such things, when they are easily shot.

They fish and obtain salmon, salmon-trout, dog-salmon, herring, silver trout, rock-cod, flounders, smelt, halibut, and skates. Salmon-eggs and the eggs of all large fish are used for food. They fish with the hook, spear, net, and build traps across the Skokomish River. Their fish-spear is three-pronged generally, but sometimes they are only two-pronged. These are about two feet long, and made of iron, old rasps being preferred. When iron cannot be obtained, they are made of very hard wood. These prongs are tied to a very slim pole, from fifteen to twenty-five feet long, with strings or tough bark; and when a fish is still they are easily thrust into it by the Indian in his canoe. Their traps across the river are built of small sticks about an inch in diameter and six feet long, very close together, leaning down stream, which prevent the salmon going up, when they are easily caught and killed. They dry some of the fish, especially large quantities of the salmon, for winter use.

They dig for clams, which they dry in the smoke, and also obtain mussels and oysters.

Formerly they obtained oil from seals and porpoises, and bought whale-oil from the Makah Indians, but of late years they have ceased to use oil for food.

They use no grasshoppers, crickets, or insects for food.

They buy chiefly flour, sugar, rice, beans, coffee, tea, butter, yeast-powders, saleratus, salt, lard, spices, sirup, dried apples, and crackers, according to their means.

Division of labor, concerning.—The men and women both work in the

gardens. The men hunt and do most of the fishing; the women get a
large share of the clams, mussels, berries, and roots, and do the cooking.

Amount eaten and frequency of eating.—They generally eat three times
a day, and about the same amount as white people. Formerly they
were very irregular, eating a large amount at times, and very often, and
again very little for a long time.

Eating customs and rites.—Many of them have tables, chairs, and
stools, plates, bowls, knives and forks, and eat in the American way.
Sometimes they cook in a large pot, and a number sit around it and take
out what they wish with spoons, knives, and their fingers. At feasts
where there are a very large number present they spread mats upon the
ground, in the open air or in a large house, place the food upon them,
and sit on the ground around them while eating.

B.—DRINKS.

*Methods of preparing decoctions and intoxicating drinks; occasions for
their use, and their effects.*—They make no intoxicating drinks. They
sometimes get them of white people, drink secretly, and the effect is
very bad—physically, pecuniarily, mentally, and morally.

There is a temperance society among them, and about one hundred
have joined it, pledging themselves to abstain from all intoxicating
drinks. Within the last year and a half since its organization a few
have broken this pledge; but it is not known that any more have done
so than when the same number of white people join such a society.
The fact is also to be taken into consideration that in earlier years,
when there was less restraint, the greater portion of them would get
drunk.

They are very fond of tea and coffee, and use them as Americans do;
and also make teas of cranberry-leaves and young blackberry and hem-
lock leaves.

C.—NARCOTICS.

Methods of using, and effects.—Tobacco is quite generally used. The
older ones generally smoke; the younger ones both chew and smoke.
A few of the women also use it. It makes them somewhat dizzy at
first. No other narcotics are used to my knowledge. Tobacco is used
much as Americans use it, and not to my knowledge as a calumet of
peace.

The leaves of the killikinick, a small bush which grows a foot or two
high, dried, and of laurel, dried, also the dried bark of ironwood, are
used, when they are short of tobacco, to mix with it, but are seldom if
ever used alone.

D.—SAVORS, FLAVORS, ETC.

They use salt, pepper, and some other American spices as Americans
use them, but have no native ones.

E.—MEDICINES, POISONS, ETC.

Medicines, preparation and administration of.—Usually by old men or women, but by any one who is supposed to know. There is no class of physicians.

List of diseases sought to be cured, the medicine for each, and the effect.—Colds and biliousness: Eat alder-buds, and afterward drink salt water for an emetic.

To strengthen general debility: Heat rocks, throw water over them, place skunk-cabbage leaves on them, then get over the steam.

For a physic and tonic: Cherry-bark; grind it in water and drink the water.

For a tonic: Alder-bark; in same way as cherry-bark.

To purify the blood: Barberry-bark; in same way as cherry-bark.

Skin-diseases: Oregon grape root and bark; in same way as cherry-bark.

Burns and scalds: Potatoes; scrape and put them on.

Sore eyes: They make a cold tea from crab-apple bark, and wash the eyes with it.

This is a partial list, but is the best I can give, as they do not tell all they have.

Effect.—All of them cure sometimes, and at other times do not. At present, the Government furnishes them with a physician, who uses American medicines entirely. If, however, they are not cured immediately by him, they often cease to take the medicine sooner than he orders, and use their own. They sometimes also buy patent medicines. Thus their medicines are a mixture of American and Indian.

Poisons.—They have no native poisons which they now use, and very seldom obtain any from the whites. Formerly it is said that matter from sores was used, especially where there were two wives, one of whom became jealous. When this was so, the jealous one gave this matter to the other with her food.

§ 2.—HABITATIONS.

A.—DWELLINGS.

Are they permanent or movable?—Nearly all permanent; only occasionally one which is movable.

Natural refuge and habitations of degraded tribes.—These Indians cannot be called degraded, but about half-civilized. All have houses of some kind.

Location and laying out.—There is no order. Most of their houses are on their farms, which consist of from ten to forty acres. In a few places, there are quite a number of houses together, and where this is so they are generally near the water, in a single row facing the water.

Labor of construction.—The men build the houses with the help of the Government carpenter, when they can have his assistance.

Plans of interior arrangement; structures at different seasons.—The best houses, which are built by Government help, are on their farms, most of them on the Skokomish River bottom, which is liable to overflow in the winter. Hence the houses are built on blocks about two feet from the ground, which renders them cold in the winter. Owing to this, most of them leave them in the winter, and go to some large houses at Eneti, that part of the reservation which is on Hood's Canal and is not liable to overflow.

The summer houses are mostly about 16 by 22 feet, and generally divided into two rooms, one for a bed-room and the other for a kitchen and eating-room. Sometimes there is only one room, and sometimes there are the two and a shed-kitchen added. A few of the rooms are papered, and most of the houses have a cook-stove, one or two bedsteads, a cupboard, a few chairs and trunks, &c.

Their winter houses are much larger, four times as large often, or larger, generally 25 or 30 by 40 or 50 feet, and are for several families, but with no partition. There is no floor but the ground, excepting against the wall all around for about 6 feet from it. Above this floor there are bunks all around about 3½ feet wide, on which they sleep. The doors are either in the middle of both ends of the house, or in the middle of one side, and in each of the four corners one or more families reside, building their fire on the ground, and letting the smoke escape through holes in the roof. Their trunks, provisions, &c., are stored on the small board floor. The workmanship of these houses is much poorer than of the summer houses. Each house is owned by one man, and he allows his friends to live in a part of it, but they pay him no rent. I shall speak of these two different kinds of houses as summer and winter houses, although they are not strictly such, as a few use each kind all the year round, and during the coming winter most of them expect to live in their new, better houses, which I have termed summer houses.

Ancient structures.—They were small, movable, and generally made of split cedar boards, poles, and mats. Occasionally, when they are off fishing, or away from home for a time, they build such now. They are 5 or 6 feet high, 14 by 18 feet or less; the door is a mat, and all the property is stored in this house, consisting of a single room, where they also eat and sleep. The fire is in the middle of the house, and when they are fishing, the fish are hung overhead, where they dry in the smoke. There is no floor but the ground, or sometimes a mat.

Out-buildings.—(1) A barn for hay, as they use no other kind of feed. This is either a shed made by setting posts in the ground, and covering it with split cedar boards, varying in size, according to the amount of hay, which is usually not more than three or four tons; or it may be one of their houses, for they sometimes store hay in a part and live in the other part, or they fill the house with hay and go away for the summer, either at work in a logging camp or fishing.

(2) A stable for work-oxen. This is generally built similar to the sheds for hay, or that is built larger, and answers for both.

(3) A few have stables for horses, when they have one, which they prize very highly, as a race-horse. Most of their horses and cattle, however, are not sheltered; the timber, according to their ideas, being sufficient for this.

Structures for observation, memorial, defense, burial, and ceremony.— There are none for any of these things except for burial, which are described under chapter III, section 15, B, " Manner of disposing of the dead."

Public buildings.—There are none, except when a potlatch is to take place, which may be only once in ten or twenty years or more. The last one took place seven years ago, a few miles off from the reservation. A large house, about 50 feet wide and more than 300 long, was erected. It was a frame building, inclosed with boards. The best part of the material was removed soon after, and the rest has gone to decay.

Sweat-houses.—These are used much as among most other Indian tribes. They are 3 or 4 feet in height, and a little more in diameter, being conoidal. Sticks are first driven into the ground, rather close together, which are covered with large leaves, as the maple, and these are covered with mud.

B.—APPURTENANCES TO DWELLINGS.

Doors.—For their best houses these are a plain American door, made by the Government carpenter. For their large winter houses, they are made by themselves, are smaller, and much rougher.

Fireplaces.—For their large winter houses and their fishing-houses, they have been described under the previous section. Most of their summer houses have no fireplaces or chimneys, but are furnished with cook-stoves, a part of the annuity goods of last year. A few have a rough chimney built of sticks and mud at one end of the house, and on the outside of it, and a few have cut a hole in the middle of the floor, filling it up with earth to the floor, on which they build the fire, cutting a hole in the roof, where the smoke escapes.

Windows.—Their winter houses have none. Their summer ones have one or two American windows.

Roofs.—These are made of split cedar boards. For some of their better houses, they are dressed smooth, something similar to shingles, and some are covered with shingles.

Fastenings, such as locks and latches.—Their winter houses are generally fastened with a wooden latch, which is worked with a string, and when they leave the house for the summer the door is usually nailed fast. The summer houses are provided with American locks and door-knobs.

Water-tanks.—They have none; but when they live some distance from good water, which is not often the case, they generally carry their water in kegs and small barrels.

Totem-posts.—In the potlatch house which they began to build at Eneti more than a year ago, but which was not finished on account of the death of the principal man connected with it, there are five totem-posts, or tamanamus-posts, as they are called, which are about 8 feet long, about 1 foot through, some being round and some being about 6 inches through by 1 foot. They are intended to support the ridge-pole, as shown in Fig. A, Plate 23, and are 8 feet long, of the shape shown in Figs. B–E of the same plate, though there is not really much more art to them than there is to a wooden turned bedstead-post. They are not painted.

At the old potlatch house (see III, 2, A, "Public-houses"), there were originally twenty-six large cedar slabs set in the ground, which support the cross-pieces, thirteen on each side. Ten of these have been removed, and on four more there are no figures. Five were originally painted, but the weather has worn the most of the paint off. They are about 9 feet long above ground, $1\frac{1}{2}$ to $2\frac{1}{4}$ feet wide, and 5 or 6 inches thick. These posts are delineated on Plate 24, Figs. F–K, where the dark shading indicates figures in red paint on the inside of the posts.

The first four of these figures are simply painted on a smooth surface, but the last is carved, the darkest parts being raised the highest. These posts have been left exposed to the weather for seven years, but are still considered tamanamus-posts, and probably would be even if they should remain there until they should rot down.

Materials for building.—Everything is built of lumber, or occasionally split cedar boards are used, except some temporary structure of mats.

C.—FURNITURE AND UTENSILS.

Hammocks, beds, bedsteads.—They have no hammocks. Most of their summer houses are furnished with plain, unpainted bedsteads made by the Government carpenter. Those in the winter houses have been described in A of the present section. For beds they have straw, feathers, the head of the large mat-rush—sometimes called catstail—several thicknesses of mats or blankets. A few use sheets. For the covering they use blankets and quilts.

Pillows and head-rests.—They have feather-pillows or roll up their mats.

Cradles and pappoose-cases.—They have no cradles, but for young infants they have a small board about the length of the child, on which they place cedar bark, which is beaten up very fine, and on this they tie the child a large portion of the time. When the child is a little older, but not strong enough to hold on to its mother's neck, she wraps a blanket or shawl around it and herself, and thus carries it on her back.

Chairs, stools, and benches.—Last year a number of chairs were furnished them among their annuity goods. Previously to that they had

Fig. A.

 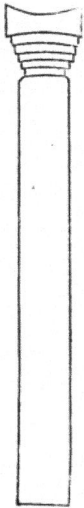  

Fig. B.   Fig. C.   Fig. D.   Fig. E.

Fig. L.   Fig. N.   Fig. O.

Fig. M.

Appurtenances of dwellings, and implements, of the Twana Indians.

very few, but used home-made stools and benches or sat on the ground. The women especially are very much accustomed to sit on the ground, or on their mats, or on the floor.

Matting, carpet, and floor-coverings.—They use nothing in the form of carpeting. They often lay their mats on the floor or ground, on which they store their things, eat, or sit, but do not use them as carpeting.

Racks and other protections for food.—Most of them have a small cupboard five or six feet high and two or three feet wide, without any door. Their flour is generally kept in the sack, the salmon in bundles or baskets, and much of their other food in baskets or sacks, or small amounts in cupboards. Their dishes are generally kept in the cupboards.

Tables.—The Government carpenter has made plain, unpainted tables for most of the summer houses, on which they eat, seldom, if ever, using a table-cloth. In their winter houses they use very few tables, either placing the food on a mat or eating from the vessel in which it is cooked, sometimes eating singly and sometimes together.

E.—MISCELLANEOUS—FURNITURE.

Brooms, fly-brushes, urinals, others not mentioned.—A number of them have American brooms, and a few use them considerably, becoming somewhat neat, but with most of them there is very much room for improvement. They also sometimes make a temporary broom from fir and cedar boughs. There is nothing else under this head of any importance which is used.

§ 3.—*VESSELS AND UTENSILS.*

a.—*Natural material.*

Mineral material.—They make no pottery or wares from clay, nor am I aware that they make any utensils from stone or of metallic material.

Vegetable material.—Maple and laurel are used in making spoons, cedar roots in making water-tight baskets, cedar boughs in making common carrying-baskets; also, one kind of swamp-grass forms the chief material for one kind of carrying-basket. Small grasses of black, yellow, and slate colors are used for beauty in the water-tight baskets. Rushes or cattail are used in making mats.

Animal material.—Cattle-horns are used in making large spoons, and clam-shells are occasionally used as drinking-dishes or spoons without any manufacture.

A.—VESSELS FOR HOLDING AND CARRYING WATER, FOOD, ETC.

Gourds, dug-outs, bladders, and funnels.—None.

Bottles, jugs, jars, bowls.—All of these are used, and are of American manufacture.

Boxes.—Boxes of all shapes and sizes are in use, chiefly of American manufacture, both of tin and wood. They like also those of Chinese make. They do not use them for carrying water, and but little for holding food, but usually for holding other things. Cheap trunks of American manufacture are very common, in which they keep their best clothes, and other things which they wish to save from the smoke and dirt.

Tight baskets.—Water-tight baskets which are inflexible are very common, holding from a quart to half a bushel. They make them of cedar roots split, sew them very firmly together, and ornament them with grasses of various colors, yellow, black, slate-color, &c.

Mats.—Their mats, which are often spread on the ground, and on which their food is placed, are made of the swamp-grass sometimes called cattail. The women gather the material in the summer, dry it, and make them in the winter. The grass is first cut as long as is to be the width of the mat, usually about three feet, but sometimes five feet. The ends are then fastened together in the shape of the mat, and strings made of the same grass torn to pieces and twisted are run through lengthwise of the mat and about four inches apart. In doing this, a needle is used, which is about three feet long, a half an inch wide, and three cornered, with an eye in one end, in which the string is placed. After the string is run through, a small piece of wood with a crease is run over the mat where the string has been sewed to render it firm and of good shape. The edges of the mats are fastened by weaving the grass firmly together. These mats are also used for beds, several thicknesses of them being quite soft, for making temporary houses, and for lining wooden houses to make them warm.

Mat-baskets.—A basket is sometimes made of grass, which is quite strong, but their principal flexible basket is made of cedar limbs, split and dressed. These pieces, some with the bark on and some with it off, are arranged quite regularly and tastily. They are strong, and are used for carrying apples, potatoes, fish, clams, mussels, indeed are of almost universal use for carrying purposes. They hold from half a bushel to a bushel. A rope is fastened into the handles of the basket, which passes around the forehead of a woman, and thus they usually carry the load by the strength of the neck. I have seen one carry a basket full of apples, and two babies one and two years old. Where the rope presses against the forehead it is changed to a braid of cloth, about three inches wide, which is soft, and does not hurt the head. The colors in this braid are often woven in quite fancifully.

B. VESSELS AND UTENSILS FOR PREPARING FOOD.

Troughs and baskets for stone boiling.—None are in use now. Formerly their water-tight baskets described in A of this section were used for this purpose.

Pots of clay, stone, &c.—None of clay or stone are used. Iron pots of

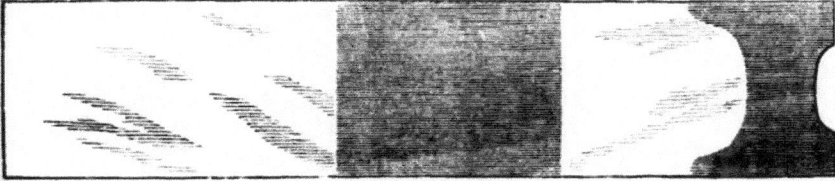

Fig. F.

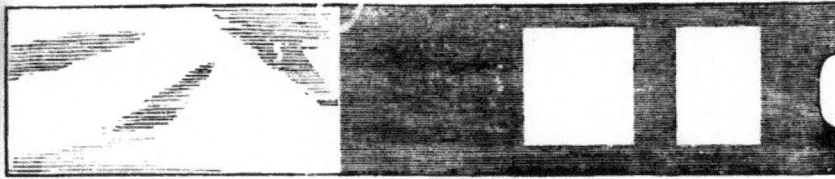

Fig. G.

Fig. H.

Fig. I.

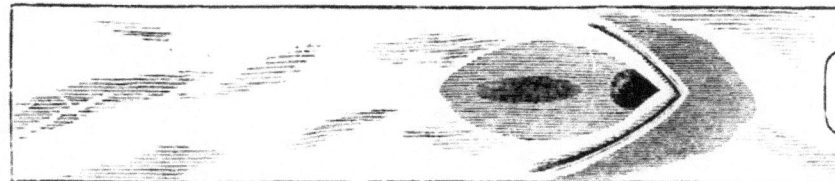

Fig. K.

Appurtenances of dwellings of the Twana Indians.

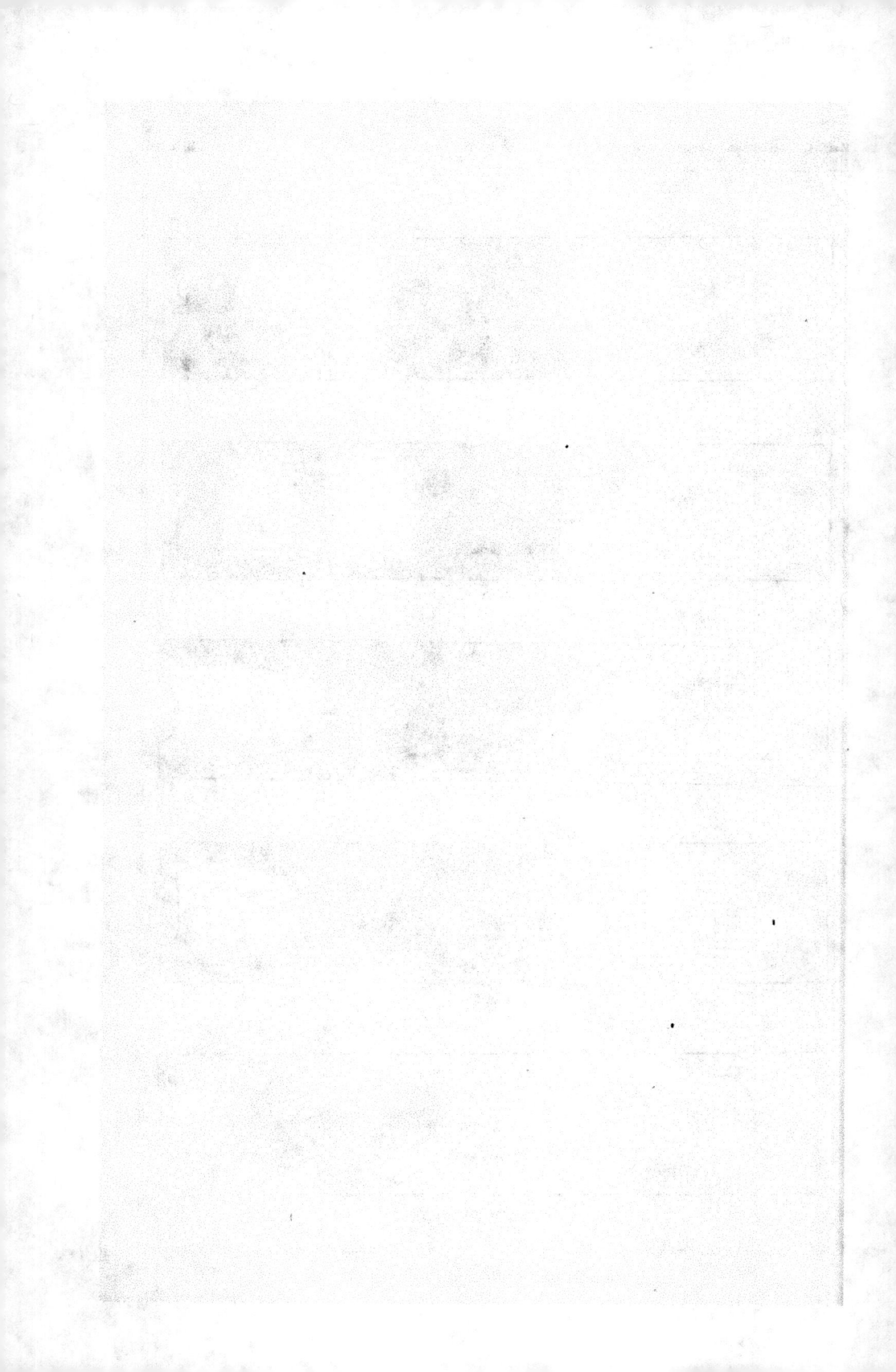

American manufacture are very common for boiling food, whether they cook by a stove, fireplace, or on the ground.

Pans.—Tin pans of American manufacture are very common for various cooking purposes.

Spits and other contrivances for roasting.—A very common spit for roasting fish is made by splitting a stick about three feet long and an inch in diameter two thirds of its length, and then tying it with grass to prevent its splitting farther; all the ends are sharpened, the meat being stuck on the parts that are split, and the other end placed in the ground before the fire.

Bowls for mixing food.—They use American ones of earthenware quite generally.

Churns and dairy-vessels.—They have none, as they use but very little milk, and make no butter.

Coffee-mills.—American coffee-mills are used for grinding coffee.

C.—VESSELS AND UTENSILS FOR SERVING AND EATING FOOD.

Bread-trays, mush bowls, meat-trays.—There is nothing made specially for these things.

Plates and dishes, pitchers.—Those of American manufacture, chiefly earthen, but some of tin, are almost universally used.

Drinking vessels.—Earthen tea-cups, bowls, tin cups, and dippers, are commonly used, and glasses are sometimes in use.

Knives and forks.—Common ones of American make are quite generally in use.

Spoons, ladles, and dippers.—Common American tea and table spoons and tin dippers are used quite often. They also make a spoon both of horn and hard wood, the handle of which is 4 inches long, the bowl of the spoon 6 inches long, 4 wide, and 1¼ deep, which is quite common, though sometimes they are much smaller and sometimes larger.

Pipes, pipe-stems, pouches.—Common American pipes and stems are generally used; sometimes they make stems of wood; generally they carry their tobacco in their pockets or in a common bag; a few of the older ones have pouches adorned with fancy work and beads and similar to a shot-pouch.

D.—ORNAMENTAL AND MISCELLANEOUS VESSELS, ETC.

Lamps and the like.—Quite often they use American coal-oil lamps. Candles were used a few years ago, and are to some extent now; but as lamps have become cheap they prefer them. Some also use American lanterns, and torches of pitch-wood are very common. However, they use neither candles nor lamps as much as Americans, as they cannot read or write during the evening.

Pails, basins.—For wash-basins they commonly use American tin wash basins, or tin pans, or sometimes earthen bowls; they use both tin and wooden water-pails.

§ 4.—CLOTHING.

A.—RAW MATERIAL.

Skins, sinews.—Formerly, clothes were made of dressed deer-skins sewed with sinews. I, however, have seen only one pair of pants here made of this material, and they were bought of the Chehalis Indians. A few moccasins are made of deer-skins. They dress a few deer and elk skins and catch a few beaver and seals, but sell most of the skins to the whites.

Wool and hair.—Formerly, a blanket was made of dogs' hair and feathers, but not now. They have no sheep, but buy a little wool, which they card, spin into yarn, and knit into socks and stockings.

B.—FABRICS IN DIFFERENT STAGES OF MANUFACTURE.

Dressed skins and furs.—Nothing except what is spoken of in the preceding section.

Woolen, cotton, and linen stuffs.—They buy a large amount of these kinds of American goods, which they make into dresses, women's underwear, shirts, children's clothes, and the like, and articles of household use.

C.—SUITS OF CLOTHING.

Of dignitaries.—There are none; neither the chiefs nor the medicine-men dressing differently from others.

Of male adults.—They generally dress with plain American clothing of all kinds during the week, though they do not keep it very clean. For Sunday, Fourth of July, and public days, most of the men have good pants, broadcloth or linen coats, according to the season, white bosom-shirts, collars, neckties, shoes and boots, socks, vests, hats, and caps.

Of females.—They dress very much as American women, with plain clothes. For more particulars, see the following paragraphs.

Of children.—At home, those just able to run around sometimes have little more than a long shirt, but generally they have more, especially as they grow older; very seldom, however, wearing shoes during the week-days. They have good clothes, like American children, for Sundays. Nearly all of school-going age are in the boarding-house, where they are provided with plain, strong American clothes as American children, Government furnishing the cloth, and the matron or her assistant making the clothes.

For special occasions.—Nothing except that both men, women, and children have better clothes for Sunday and prominent days than their common every-day wear.

Of special castes or crafts.—None.

D.—HEAD-CLOTHING.

Head-cloths, hoods, &c.—The women often tie handkerchiefs around their heads, or wear their shawls over their heads; very often also they go bareheaded. Very few have hoods, hats, or bonnets. About a dozen have American ladies' hats, though but few wear them much. The school-girls all wear hats.

Caps, hats.—The men wear always American hats or caps, some wearing one and some the other; but hats are more generally worn. There are a very few hats which are made by the Makah Indians which are worn by the old Indians. They are strong and water-proof.

Head-dress of ceremony.—They wear none now.

E.—BODY-CLOTHING.

Clouts, cinctures, smocks.—They wear none now. Formerly they had a clout around the waist made of cedar bark, it being a band with a fringe extending nearly down to the knees. After the English came, they made them of blankets.

Aprons.—The women sometimes wear plain ones.

Breeches.—American ones are always worn by the men and older boys, except occasionally a very old man does not.

Shirts.—The men commonly undershirts and woolen overshirts; but on Sunday many appear with white ones.

Jackets, blouses, parkas, and tunics.—A few jackets and blouses are worn; almost all have coats of some kind; and, for rainy and cold weather, a few have cloaks, all of American make. Vests too are common.

Women's underwear.—They buy American material, and make their own clothes. First a chemise, and second a petticoat, and sometimes two or three.

Gowns.—A few of the very old ones are seen without dresses, stopping with the skirt; but almost all wear gowns made by themselves of American calico and woolen dress goods, according to the season.

Mantles, capes, and the like.—A very few have cloaks.

Shawls.—American woolen and "Dolly Varden" shawls are very common. Often they have several.

Blankets.—Occasionally blankets are worn in the winter, but not often, except by very old persons.

Robes of state and ceremony.—None are worn now.

F.—ARM-CLOTHING.

Gloves and mittens.—Occasionally, when well dressed, a few men and women wear cotton gloves, and in cold weather a few wear woolen mittens. All of American make.

G.—LEG AND FOOT CLOTHING.

Moccasins.—` very few are worn, but the climate is too wet to admit of their ~. ~ us l much.

Shoes, boots.—Both are very common, of American make. Thick p
heavy ones are generally worn; but sometimes they have lighter ones d
for Sunday. The men, except the old ones, wear them constantly; the c
women but little in the summer, except on Sundays, and the children u
are barefoot a great portion of the time. Even the Indian school-chil- n
dren are barefoot in the summer, but not in the winter.

Stockings.—Socks and stockings are very common, both of native and
American manufacture.

Leggings.—Very seldom worn.

H.—PARTS OF DRESS.

Collars.—They are not usually worn, but sometimes the men wear
American paper ones, and the women American paper and linen ones.

Pockets and reticules.—They have no reticules. Pockets are common
in coats, vests, pants, overshirts, and gowns.

Needle-work and quill-work.—I have seen no quill-work. They do
plain sewing very well, and a large amount of it, making their dresses
and underclothes, and sometimes men's white shirts.

Bead-work.—There is not very much bead-work among them. Their
gowns and shot-pouches are sometimes trimmed with them.

Fastenings.—A large brass pin of native manufacture, about five
inches long, is used for fastening the shawl together; and when this is
lacking, one made of hard wood and in similar shape is used. American
buttons, pins, a few buckles, hooks and eyes, are used.

Belts.—The men and women both wear belts, as American men and
women do.

Others not mentioned.—Of late years, suspenders are slowly taking the
place of belts among the men.

I.—RECEPTACLES FOR DRESS.

Nets, knapsacks, and skin-bags.—Very few, if any.

Trunks, chests, &c.—Trunks are very common for this purpose. See
sec. 3, A, " Boxes." In their better houses, some of their clothes are
often hung up on the walls. There are also a few American valises
among them.

§ 5.—*PERSONAL ADORNMENT.*

A.—SKIN ORNAMENTATION.

Painting, patterns, and apparatus.—During their games, festivals, and
at special times, a few of the men paint their faces, but it is more common among the women, not only on such days, but on other days.
They use American red paint chiefly, but sometimes the juice of berries; formerly they obtained a red paint in the mountains. The women
paint to prevent their being tanned by the sun; and also, if they have
done anything which will make them blush when in company, they

paint to prevent their blushes being seen. They paint their faces very
differently—sometimes in streaks on the cheeks, sometimes the whole
cheek, or other parts of the face. There is no order about it. They
use their fingers for brushes. Formerly there was much more of it than
now, it being almost universal in time of war.

The native red paint was obtained from a tree in the mountains,
and apparently has the grain of the bark; but from their description
of it I think it is a parasite of the tree, and is prepared in some way,
which certainly, from the specimen I have seen, does not destroy the
grain of the plant, which is very coarse.

Tattoos and apparatus.—A little of this is done, but much less than
formerly, and chiefly now among the children. In doing it, they use a
needle and thread, blackening the thread with charcoal, and drawing it
under the skin as deeply as they can bear it.

Scarring lancets and flint.—There are none now. Probably there were
formerly, but I cannot learn definitely about them.

B.—HEAD ORNAMENTS.

Plumes and the like.—It is very seldom now that they wear native
plumes in their hats. Formerly they were quite common, eagle's and
hawks' feathers being preferred. Occasionally now in play the boys
put a feather in their hats. Two or three of the men have their caps
trimmed with a band of fur or red velvet. The few women who have
hats have an ostrich feather in them, bought with them.

Hair-pins.—Some of the women braid the hair and put it up with
pins; a few put it up in nets, but generally it is left to hang down un-
braided.

Tucking-combs.—Very few are used.

Ear-rings and pendants.—They wear both native ear-rings and American cheap jewelry. One kind of native ear-ring is about an inch square,
green, and made of a large oyster-shell. Another is their ancient money,
obtained, as they say, far off in the ocean, probably north. They are
white, about an inch and three-fourths in length, three-sixteenths in
diameter at the larger end, and tapering toward the smaller end and
slightly curved. Small bits of black or red cloth are thrust into the
large end of them. About ten of them are worn in each ear. They
also buy of other Indians, one made of silver, about two inches long,
one-half an inch in diameter at the lower end, and tapering toward the
upper end. I have also seen money used as a child's ear-ring. Except
in the cases of a few old ones, the men wear none. The old women
more commonly wear the shells, and the younger ones American cheap
jewelry.

Head-bands were also made of the second kind of shell, used for ear-
rings (see ear-rings of present section); also used for money, and called
dentalia. Enough of these were strung to go around the head, but
often ten or fifteen were placed side by side, making a wide head-band

Check-studs, mouth-pegs, labrets, nose-ornaments, teeth mutilations, and ornaments.—None are used now. Formerly they bored holes in the nose, into which they inserted quills or shells, the second described among the ear-rings in this paragraph.

C.—NECK-ORNAMENTS.

Necklaces.—Those of beads are often worn, the blue color being preferred, the second kind of shells spoken of under the previous paragraph. Ear-rings were formerly sometimes used for this purpose. American cheap jewelry is also sometimes worn now. All of these are worn chiefly by the women.

D.—BREAST AND BODY ORNAMENTS.

Gorgets and ornamental chains ; nipple-studs.—There are none in existence now, nor have they been used as far as I can learn.

Ornamental girdles, sashes, &c.—There are none now, but they formerly were used.

E.—ORNAMENTS OF THE LIMBS.

Armlets.—There are none now, and I do not know that they have been used.

Bracelets.—American ones are often worn by the women, of copper, brass, silver, and gutta-percha.

Finger-rings.—Those of American manufacture are often worn, chiefly by the women, made both of silver and gold.

Anklets.—There are none worn now, but those of copper and brass were formerly used.

F.—TOILET-ARTICLES.

Cosmetics.—None except paint.

Pomades for the hair.—Hair-oil is very often used, and formerly they used bear and other oils, but nothing for coloring the hair.

Soaps and substitutes therefor.—American soaps are very common. They also use a kind of sugar-colored clay, and the leaves of some trees.

Combs.—American ones are in common use. Formerly they made them of wood. I have one with teeth about two and a half inches long, and five of them to the inch, but they vary in size.

Brushes.—American hair and clothes brushes are often used.

Tweezers for removing hair and beard.—They make them of steel and tin, and sometimes pull out the beard between the finger and a knife.

Mirrors.—Small American ones are very common.

Perfumes.—All kinds of American perfumes which they can obtain they use. They also use sweet-scented roots.

G.—OTHER PERSONAL ORNAMENTS.

Fans.—Boughs of trees are used for fans, also birds' wings and tails, especially those of eagles and hawks.

Parasols, shades.—None are used to protect them from the sun. A few have American umbrellas for rainy weather.

Artificial flowers.—The few women who have American hats have artificial flowers in them. They use no others.

Beads.—They are common for necklaces; a few also use them for trimming dresses. A few children have their dresses trimmed with dimes, on the shoulders.

§ 6.—IMPLEMENTS.

I.—Of general use.

Knives.—American eating, butcher, and pocket knives are in common use. They also make one of steel, with a wooden handle. It is about six or eight inches long, and curves at the end, as shown at Fig. L, Plate 23.

Chopper-knives.—They use none. Formerly they made one similar in shape to a chopping-knife, of tin, for opening salmon.

Axes and hatchets.—All use American ones, as they do a large amount of logging.

Adzes and wood-scrapers.—They make a small hand-adze of a large file, sharpening it at one end and fastening the other to one branch of a forked stick with rawhide, while the other branch is used as the handle. Each branch is about six or eight inches long.

Wedges and mauls.—Both are in use. The mauls are made by themselves, as Americans make them, or with the help of the Government carpenter. Old ax-heads are also often used for wedges. They were formerly made of elk-horns, pieces a foot in length being cut off from the base where they are two and a half or three inches in diameter. Wooden ones are also used.

Chisels, gouges, and the like.—They have American chisels.

Sawing-tools.—American hand and cross-cut saws are in common use, the latter chiefly in logging.

Hammers.—They use American ones chiefly. A few have the old stone ones, made in the shape of a pestle.

Drills and perforators, embracing awls, reamers, hand and bow drills.—American awls and augers are in common use.

Clamps and nippers.—They have American nippers.

Rasps and other smoothing-tools.—They have American drawing-knives for smoothing boards, and some of them are able to use a plane, but they own none.

Whetstones and other sharpening tools.—They have American whetstones, and some own grindstones. They use American files, large and small, for filing saws.

Levers, &c.—They use wooden levers and cant-hooks for rolling logs. They also have some American blocks and tackle.

Tool-boards and boxes.—They have no tool-boards. Any common box answers for holding the smaller tools, and the large ones are kept any-where about the house.

II.—*Implements of war and the chase.*

A.—STRIKING.

Clubs of various forms and material.—Formerly they made such of wood and stones large enough to be handled easily.

B.—THROWING-WEAPONS.

Slings and shots or stones.—Slings and stones are used as playthings by the boys, and formerly by the young men in killing ducks.

Fire-pots.—Those filled with pitch-wood were formerly used to set on fire houses into which an enemy had fled. A part of the besieging force would attack one side of the house in order to draw the attention of the besieged away from the opposite side, when the party with these fire-pots would approach, set on fire the pitch-wood, throw it on the roof, and as the besieged attempted to escape they were killed with spears, clubs, knives, or were shot.

C.—WEAPONS FOR CUTTING AND STRIKING.

Battle-axes, tomahawks, and the like.—None are in use now. Formerly they had them made of stone, and, after they were able to obtain them, hatchets were used, though not to throw.

D.—THRUSTING-WEAPONS.

Lances and lance-heads.—These, about eight feet long, were formerly used in both war and the chase. The points were stone, iron, bone, yew, or ironwood.

Harpoons and points.—These were formerly used in fishing. See be-yond, under "Fishing-implements."

Daggers.—They formerly made them of files or other suitable iron which they could obtain, and they are used some now.

Spears and points.—A duck-spear, which is fifteen or twenty feet long, with four or five prongs at the end, so far apart that a duck may be caught between them. At the end of each prong is a piece of steel about six inches long, made from an old file, with a few very coarse teeth, which are on the outside so that they will not injure the body of the bird, and yet will catch among the feathers. They use these spears by night, going in their canoes, making a kind of dark lantern, so that the duck will not see the men. (See Fig. M, Plate 23.)

E.—PROJECTILE WEAPONS.

Bows and arrows, arrow-heads, and quivers.—At present, they are used only as playthings for children, and are very poor; but formerly they were very common. The bows were about three feet long, and were made of yew-wood; the strings of sinew, or the intestines of raccoons. The arrows were about two and one-half feet long, were made of cedar, with feathered shafts, and points of stone, and of nails after they obtained them; and the quiver of wolf-skin. Arrow-heads are sometimes made of brass or iron, two or three inches long, half an inch wide, and very thin, and of very hard wood, five inches long, and round. Sometimes, for birds, they are made of ironwood, about five inches long, with two prongs, one of them being half an inch shorter than the other.

Fire-arms and outfit.—Rifles and muskets are very common, the men often owning several. Their shot-pouch is made either of cloth or leather, and their powder carried either in the flask or horn. A very common sheath for the gun is made of a piece of a blanket, sewed so that the gun will fit into it.

Poison for missiles.—None, as far as I can learn, has been used. Formerly, they sometimes burned their spear-points a little, both before and after wounding an enemy, superstitiously thinking it would hurt worse, or poison that into which it had been or would be thrust.

F.—DEFENSIVE WEAPONS.

Parrying-sticks, shields, helmets, visors, mail, greaves, fetters, snares, pitfalls, stockades, earthworks, and other fortifications.—None are in use now, nor do I learn that they ever were, in war. In hunting, they formerly sometimes used pitfalls, and also made stockades of sticks in the form of a V, at the small end of which was a net made of string. The deer being driven into the V would attempt to escape, but not seeing the net, would catch his horns in it, and then was killed. The string for the net was made of nettlestalk fiber twisted.

G.—BESIEGING AND ASSAULTING CONTRIVANCES.

The only one of which I learn has been described in B of the present section, "Fire-pots."

H.—ARMORIES.

They had none.

I.—TROPHIES AND STANDARDS.

Scalps and the like; tomahawks of ceremony and other standards-trophies erected to commemorate victories.—As far as I can learn, none of these have ever been in use.

Skulls.—The heads of the enemy were formerly brought home as emblems of triumph.

K.—OTHER WEAPONS.

Deadfalls were formerly used in hunting, some of them very large with weights so heavy that they would kill large animals. As they have had no war either with the whites or other Indians for eighteen or twenty years, it is almost impossible to describe minutely their weapons or mode of war. They are now a very peaceful tribe. If by any chance a war should occur, it is probable that an observer would learn many things of which we now have no report.

III.—*Implements of special use.*

A.—FLINT AND STONE WORK, EMBRACING ALSO WORKING IN IVORY AND OTHER HARD MATERIALS.

Quarrying, flaking by fire and otherwise, chipping, pecking, grinding, sharpening, polishing, perforating, carving.—They do no such work now, and hence have no such implements. I have been told that they never did much such work, but bought their stone implements of other Indians; but I am inclined to think they did make some stone hammers, pipes, and arrow-heads, but if they did it was so long ago that it is impossible to describe the process or the implements.

B.—IMPLEMENTS FOR FIRE-MAKING AND UTILIZING.

Hand-drills and fire-sticks, bow-drills, flint and steel or other pyrites, moss, punk, and tinder-tongs, bellows, other fire-tools, and special fuels.—I do not learn that they ever used tongs or bellows. Formerly a fire was made with two sticks, holding one perpendicular to the other, letting one end of it press on the side of the other, and rubbing it briskly between the hands. Fire was then very valuable, and was often carried very carefully long distances from one camp to another by inclosing it closely between two sticks, so that very little air should strike it. This process was used twenty or twenty-five years ago. Afterward, when they obtained flint-lock muskets, they struck fire with them. Of late years, they use matches almost entirely. Fir pitch-wood is also very common in helping to start the fire, and also for a light out-doors, especially when fishing in the night. They frequently bring small bundles of it to the whites for sale.

C.—IMPLEMENTS FOR BOW AND ARROW MAKING.

Bow-dressing, bowstring-making, arrow straightening and polishing; cement and sticks.—As at present, bows and arrows are only used as playthings by the children; the making of them is of no special importance. They are made with a knife, and any common strong string is used. A straight cedar stick is split for arrows, a few common feathers tied on, the point split, and a nail tied into it. For further particulars see sec. 6, II, E.

D.—FISHING-IMPLEMENTS OTHER THAN WEAPONS.

Hooks and lines.—They buy American lines, also some American hooks. They make a large number from steel and bone, which they prefer, as they say they are stronger than American ones. By heating and filing the steel, they bring 't into the proper shape. One kind of salmon-hook is made of a straight piece of steel, about six inches long, and sharp. On each side of it pieces of bone are tied. A line is attached to it, and also a pole fifteen or twenty feet long, in such a way that by means of the pole it may be driven into the fish, the pole drawn out, and the hook remain, held by the string, when it is drawn in.

Gigs, harpoons.—Harpoons are sometimes used for seal-fishing. The point is of iron, and the spear and line used as with the salmon-hook just described.

Spears.—For one kind, see sec. A, of the present chapter. A herring-spear or rake is made about fifteen feet long, and on the lower end for three feet sharp iron points, often made of nails, are driven in about an inch apart.

Nets.—They generally buy American twine and make them. For one kind, see the following description of weirs. There is one net on the reservation about four or five hundred feet long and forty feet wide, made of twine, buoyed with blocks made of cedar, and used for catching salmon in salt-water.

Probes. ice-breakers, stools, skewers, &c., for seal-fishing.—They have none. In catching them, they shoot them or spear them at night. For spear, see harpoons.

Weirs and traps of every kind.—Weirs are made across the river. They are of small sticks, about an inch in diameter and six feet long, fastened closely together, so that a fish cannot run up between them. A number of nets are made of twine, about eight feet across, and in the shape of a shallow bowl, the rim being of wood bent around. These are let into the water at night below the weir, and closely watched. A few strings, one end of which is tied to them and the other end above, indicate when a salmon is in it, when it is hauled up, and the fish killed.

E.—HUNTING-IMPLEMENTS OTHER THAN WEAPONS.

Traps and snares.—American steel-traps are often used in catching mink and beaver.

F.—LEATHER-WORKING TOOLS.

Butchering and flaying.—For this an American knife, commonly a butcher-knife or large pocket-knife, is used.

Scrapers, tanning.—The deer or elk hide is soaked for two days, and the hair removed by scraping it with a rough iron. It is then soaked a half a day with the deer-brains, in hot water, over a fire; the deer-brains being rubbed over, something like soap. It is then stretched, a rubbed with rocks until it becomes soft and pliable, when they dig hole in the ground, build a fire of rotten wood or cedar bark, stret the skin over it, and cover it with blankets, thus smoking it, aft which it is fit for use.

Leather-working, crimping, sewing, shoemaking, fringing, braiding, mal ing babiche, &c.—There is very little of this now, as has already bee stated. They sell most of their tanned deer and elk skins to Amer cans. In sewing into moccasins, they use a needle and awl, thread an sinew. I have not seen any of the other kinds of work mentioned.

G.—BUILDERS' TOOLS.

Tent-making.—They have no real tents, only mat houses, in the makin of which they use an ax, hatchet, hammer, and a few nails.

Felling trees.—American axes are always used.

Making planks.—They are bought at the American saw-mills. Fo merly they were split from cedar-trees with wedges.

Smoothing wood.—The knife, ax, hand-adze, and drawing-knife, an a few use Government planes, though they own none.

Hollowing and carving wood.—The knife, ax, hatchet, and hand-adz are commonly used.

Painting.—Generally this is done with the fingers or a cloth; seldom if ever, using a brush.

Boat-building.—They make no boats except canoes, in the making o which an ax and the hands are the principal implements used.

I —POTTERS' TOOLS.

As has been already stated (sec. 3, A), they do no work of this kind and hence have no tools.

J.—TOOLS FOR MINING AND METALLURGY.

Sledges for breaking ore, hammers and anvil-stones for cold metal, smel ing and molding apparatus, smithing-tools, implements for gold and silve working.—They do no stone, gold, and silver working, and hence hav no tools. In working iron for making spear-points and fish-hooks, the use an ax and hammer and file and fire.

K.—TOOLS FOR PROCURING AND MANUFACTURING FOOD.

Root-diggers.—Sharp-pointed sticks and iron tools are used.

Gathering-baskets and fans.—Their common baskets, of all kinds an sizes, are used; the water-tight ones more especially for berries and th larger ones for roots. (See sec. 3, A.)

Pounding-baskets and pestles.—Their water-tight baskets are used i which to pound the food, and any rough rock or the hand for pounding

L.—AGRICULTURAL IMPLEMENTS.

Spades, shovels, hoes, rakes.—All of these of American manufacture are in constant use, a large share of which they have received among their Government annuities.

Plows.—Generally they dig their gardens with the hoe or spade. When they wish to plow, which is seldom, they borrow a Government plow, as they own none.

Harvesting-tools, granaries.—As they raise no grain, they have none. For cutting hay, they use American scythes; forked sticks in the shape of forks, and American forks for putting it up, and haul it in with oxen on a sled.

M.—BASKET-WORKING TOOLS.

Tools, ornamentation patterns.—They use but few tools in doing this; a knife in cutting and splitting the material, and an awl in sewing the water-tight baskets. The rest of the work is done with the fingers. For ornamentation, see sec. A of the present chapter. There is no particular figure in this ornamentation, nor does it mean anything, but is done simply for beauty.

N.—TOOLS FOR MAKING AND WORKING FIBER.

Carding and hackling.—They have none for hackling now. Formerly when they made string out of nettle-stalks, they scraped them with a shell or knife. Some of them use American cards for carding-wool very well.

Spinning, twisting.—Some of them roll the wool on their laps with their hands, and make a coarse yarn. A more common way is to use a native hand-wheel, eight or ten inches in diameter, through the center of which a spindle twelve or fifteen inches long is inserted at right angles. This is rolled by one hand on the lap and the wool held by the other. This year a few American spinning-wheels have been introduced among their annuities, and are well liked.

Knitting.—This they do with American knitting-needles.

Weaving, matting.—These have been described under section A of the present chapter.

Ornamenting.—The needle is chiefly used in ornamenting common work.

Sewing embroidery with beads.—American needles are used.

For braiding.—The hands are used.

For dyeing.—Dark mud is used in dyeing black; the grass which they use in ornamenting their baskets and the root of the wild Oregon grape in coloring orange.

O.—IMPLEMENTS OF NOMADIC AND PASTORAL LIFE.

Tools for marking cattle.—They have but few cattle, which they readily know, and do not mark them.

Whips.—Generally any common stick is used. A few have whips, with wooden handles, about a foot and a half long, and a lash of raw hide inserted into the end.

Tethers, halters, lassos, lariats.—For these they use chiefly American hemp ropes. Formerly they used those made of rawhide.

P.--IMPLEMENTS OF SPECIAL CRAFTS NOT ENUMERATED.

Logging is a very prominent business among them, as they sell the logs to the different saw-mills on the sound. After the road is built, they cut the timber. As they wish to cut the trees much higher than they can when they stand on the ground, they cut notches in the tree, and insert therein a plank, about 4 or 5 feet long, and 6 or 8 inches wide, with the end ironed, on which they stand and cut with an ax. When the tree has fallen, they measure it with a pole, saw it with a cross-cut saw, and take off a part of the bark, so that it will slide easily. This is done with an ax, or a heavy iron made for the purpose, about 3 feet long, widened and sharpened at the end. They then haul the logs to the water with three yoke of oxen. For a whip they use a small stick about 5 or 6 feet long, with a small brad in the end, with which they punch the cattle. They use American yokes and chains. When the saws are dull, they file and set them with American files and saw-sets. When the boom is full, a steamer from the mill comes for it and tows it to the mill. The money being received, they first pay the necessary expenses of running the camp, including the provisions, and divide the rest among themselves according to the amount of work done by each. They mess together, some of their wives generally cooking for the camp.

§ 7.—*MEANS OF LOCOMOTION AND TRANSPORTATION.*

A.—TRAVELING BY WATER.

Dug outs, canoes.—They do a large amount of traveling by water, chiefly in canoes. These are dug out of a single cedar-tree and vary in size. The largest are about 30 feet long and 5½ wide and 2 deep, and the smallest about 10 feet long, 2¼ wide, and 8 inches deep. They make but few here larger than those 22 feet long, 4 wide, and 1½ deep. The larger ones are bought of the Clallam Indians, who in turn buy them of the Indians of British Columbia.

Boats built from logs or of planks.—There is one small sloop owned by one of the Indians, which was bought from an American.

Sailing-crafts.—The larger canoes and sloop carry sails.

Bridges, ferries, &c.—Bridges are made with log stringers, and covered with logs, or split cedar. In crossing a large river where there is no bridge, they swim their horses, and take their things over in canoes.

B.—APPURTENANCES TO THE FOREGOING.

Poles for propelling, pushing-sticks.—None.

Paddles.—There are two kinds, each about four or five feet long, the blade two and a half to three feet long, and five or six inches wide, and a second handle three or four inches long at the end of the main handle, and at right angles to it. The blade of one kind is straight; that of the other kind curves (see Plate 23, Figs. N and O). The first is most generally used, but the latter is used in the river for pushing off from logs, the point being made for that purpose, and there being many in the river. They are generally made of maple or yew.

Oars.—A very few are used, generally six or seven feet long, and made of cedar.

Sails.—All the larger canoes are made to carry sail, and the largest two or three, which are of cloth. Formerly they were of cedar-bark mats, made by the Makah Indians.

Rudders.—Very few are used, as they generally steer with a paddle.

Anchors.—Generally a large stone, or piece of iron of any shape, answers for these.

Cables and tackle, cleats for various uses, dead-eyes.—None, except in the American-made ones in the sloop.

Outriggers.—Booms and sprits are used for spreading sail.

C.—TRAVELING ON FOOT.

Carrying-straps, baskets.—The common water-tight and mat baskets are used for this purpose. For a description of them and straps see sec. 3, A, of the present chapter. In addition to these, others of the same shape are made, but the material is bark, and they are also used in carrying loads of wood and bark. They are used almost entirely by the women and very old men.

Staff for mountain-travel, scrip or haversack, canteens, carrying-nets and yokes, sedan for carrying travelers, skates, ice-creepers, and the like, and snow-shoes.—I do not know that any of these things are used. There is but little snow and ice here during the winter, therefore they have no special means of traveling in that way.

D.—LAND CONVEYANCES AND OTHER MEANS OF TRANSPORTATION.

Saddles and their parts.—American saddles and their rigging are used. No womens' saddles are used, the women riding like the men on men's saddles.

Bridles and halters of all kinds.—American bridles are used, but often a rope is put in the animal's mouth for a bridle. American leather halters and hemp ropes are used for tying.

Packs, panniers.—Sometimes they pack on American pack-saddles, and sometimes on riding-saddles, often carrying large loads on the horses which they ride.

Harness for horses.—This year a number of American harnesses hav been furnished them among their annuities. Previously to that, a fe ropes and bands roughly put together generally answered the little u they had for them. American ox-yokes are used always with the oxe

Trappings, tassels, saddle-cloths, fringes.—Hardly anything of this kin is used.

Sledges, embracing sliding vehicles of all kinds.—Sleds are in commo use for hauling hay, lumber, &c. Some are very roughly made an slender; others are quite strong. As the reservation is not three mile square, with water on two sides of it, and the greater portion of the houses not far from the water, they do most of their transportation i canoes.

Road-making and tools.—Roads for common traveling are simple, . trail sufficiently wide for walking and traveling on horseback being cu through the timber with an ax. A few roads are wide enough for sled, drawn generally by oxen. Their logging roads are more expen sive. Of necessity in hauling long logs there cannot be short turns i them, they must be tolerably level, and also must go through heav timber. Large trees must be cut down, large logs cut out of the way roots dug out, holes filled up, and small banks dug down. This is don with axes, saws, spades, and shovels. Then skids, about a foot in diam eter and eight feet long, are placed across the road, at intervals of abou ten feet, on which the logs are hauled. Where it is very muddy, espe cially over the salt-water marsh, corduroy road and bridge are made On one road there is more than a thousand feet of this work. The skid are kept constantly oiled with dog-fish oil, so that the logs may slide easily.

Postal apparatus for sending messages, means of signaling, public convey ances.—None. When they wish to send a message, some one goes i person, or occasionally they get some one who can write to write fo them and send by mail.

§ 2.—*MEASURING AND VALUING.*

A.—COUNTING.

The extent and character of their numeral system :—

1. Da'-kus.	10. Ō'-pah-dich.
2. Es-sa'-le.	11. O'-pah-dich-klo-de-dakus.
3. Cho'-us.	20. Tsub-klak'.
4. Boo'-sus.	30. Chah-dahk'-klak.
5. Tsa-whess' (whisper first sylla- ble).	40. Shtib-oo'-sus.
6. E³pah'-chy.	50. Tsitss-a-whus' (whisper first syl lable).
7. Tu-khos'.	60. Stee-a-pah'-chy.
8. T-kah'-chy.	70. Stich-tu-kōs.
9. Hwi'-lea.	80. St-tu-kah'-chy.

90. St-tu-hwile.
100. St-tu-pahl-owlse'.
200. Esab-li-tu-pahl-owlse.
300. Cho-us-tu-pahl-owlse.
400. Boo-sus-tu-pahl-owlse.
500. Tsa-whess-tu-pahl-owlse
    (whisper first syllable).

600. Ee-a-pah-chist-tu-pahl-owsle.
700. Tu-kos-h-tu-pahl-owlse.
800. Tu-kah-chish-tu-pahl-owlse.
900. Hwilish-tu-pahl-owlse.
1,000. O-pah-dieh-tu-pahl-owlse.

Having no written language, all their counting is verbal.

Methods of calculating.—None, except mentally.

System of notation, if any exists.—None, except sometimes by cutting notches on a stick, or the like.

B.—MEASURING.

Linear and other standards.—They use the American foot, yard, mile, &c.; formerly the two arms' lengths. For cubic measure, they use pint, quart, gallon, bushel; formerly a basket-full.

Divisions of the month and year.—Now they use the American hour, day, week, and month. Formerly they divided the year into moons, or lunar months, and months into days. Many of them have clocks, and a few have watches.

Names of days, months, year, heavenly bodies, and points of the compass.

Moon,	Slo-khwill'-um.	*June,*	Täh-kä-chid.
Star,	Kla-kla-chīs'.	*July,*	Kwī-o-wät-id.
Sun,	Klo-kwät'.	*August,*	Klä-läch'-rid.
January,	Hä-hät.	*September,*	Kä-ka-bat.
February,	Stäh-kwäl'-deb.	*October.*	Kwä-lä-kwobe.
March,	Sī-ai-kwûdst.	*November,*	Kwä-kwa'-chid.
April,	Stä-ko'-lit.	*December,*	Yä-shutl.
May,	Stä-klä'-chid.		

These are the names as well as I can find out. They are nearly out of use, and the young men who understand English do not know them. The older ones can only begin at the present month, November, and count backward and forward, and hence they may be a little inaccurate as to the order. The beginning and end do not exactly agree with ours, but are nearly as indicated.

There are no names for the points of the compass; but the following are the names for the winds:—

    North wind, Tō-lō'-tsäd.
    South wind, To'-lä-chūl'-lä.
    East wind, (No word.)
    West wind, Tōz-bä'-dit.

Before the Americans came, they had no weeks, but simply num-

bered the days in each moon. Since that time they have used the f me‍
lowing: —

Sunday,	Hä-ha-ät'-lis.
Monday,	Tslä-pät'-lis.
Tuesday,	Tsib-bī-äs'-sab.
Wednesday,	Chä-da-kwi-sub.
Thursday,	Būs-sä-tlī'-sub.
Friday,	Su-kus-tlī'-sub.
Saturday,	Sä-chub-its.

The first means literally holy day; the second, past, *i.e.*, one day past
the third, second day; the fourth name, third day; the fifth, fourth day.
the sixth, fifth day; and the last, alongside, *i. e.*, of, Sunday.

Number of generations, moons, hunting-seasons, &c., to which memory
runs back.—How far tradition runs back they do not know.

C.—VALUING.

Means of establishing value, valuing, obligations, liens, transfers, money,
&c.—Formerly they had a kind of shell-money, the second described
under ear-rings, sec. 5, B. At present, they use the American standard
coin, both gold and silver, not having much to do with currency, as they
cannot read, and cannot tell the difference in the value of currency.
Their obligations, liens, transfers, &c., were, and are, all verbal, and
are sometimes broken.

§ 9.—*WRITING.*

None of the older Indians write, and none of the others, except those
who have been in our schools. I send, in connection with Part I, some
specimens from the school. They are generally as good as that of the
children of the white employés, who attend the same school and have
written for the same length of time. During the last four years, the
school has increased from an average attendance of five to thirty-five.
which is all that the Government funds will support; for, in order to
secure anything like regular attendance and cleanliness, it is necessary
to keep most of them at the boarding-house, where Government sup-
ports, feeds, and clothes them; also paying the teacher $1,000 in cur-
rency and the matron $500 per annum. Thus far, the children have
studied only reading, spelling, writing, geography, arithmetic, and gram-
mar, all being taught in the English language, their own language never
having been reduced to writing. In the winter, they attend school six
hours a day, and in the summer three hours, working half of the day,
under the teacher, getting wood, in the garden, and the like.

§ 10.—*SPORTS AND PASTIMES.*

A.—GAMBLING.

Number of games and mode of playing and effect.—There are three methods: with round blocks or disks, with bones, and the women's game.

(1) *With round blocks.*—The men's game more generally, though sometimes all engage in it. There are ten blocks in a set. All but one have a white or black and white rim. Five of them are kept under one hand on a mat, and five under the other, covered with cedar bark, ground up fine. After being shuffled round and round for a short time, the opposite party guesses under which hand the one with the black rim is. If he guesses aright, he wins and plays next; but, if wrong, he loses, and the other continues to play. The players are ten or twelve feet apart. Generally they have six or more sets of these blocks, so that if, as they suppose, luck does not attend one set, they try another. They generally have from twelve to twenty-four sticks, a few inches long, lying on a board or frame, with which they keep tally. When one party wins, a stick of the opposite party is moved to his side, and when he loses, it is moved back again. If fortune attends each party evenly, or nearly so, it naturally takes a long time to finish a game, sometimes three or four days. Sometimes two persons merely are interested, one on each side; but on special occasions nearly the whole tribe engage in it, being attached to one side or the other. When one player is tired, or bad luck attends him, another takes his place. When many are engaged, they are accompanied by a kind of drum, and those belonging to the party playing halloo and sing in regular time to keep up the spirits of the player. Sometimes they play for fun, but in large games sometimes for $300 or $400; generally, however, for only a small amount. as a dollar or a dinner. There is a tradition in regard to the disks, that when the Son of God came, a long time ago, he told them to give up all bad habits and things, these among others; that he took the disks and threw them into the water, but that they came back; he then threw them into the fire, but they came out; he threw them away as far as he could, but they returned; and so he threw them away five times, and every time they came back; after which he told the people that they might use them for fun and sport.

(2) *Game with one or two small bones.*—The young men and older boys play this most. The players sit opposite each other, about six feet apart, from one to six or more on a side, each party in front of a long pole. Then one person takes one or both of the bones in his hands, and rapidly changes them from one hand to the other. One person on the opposite side guesses in which hand one is. If only one bone is used, he guesses which hand it is in, and if both are used he guesses in which hand a certain one is. If he guesses aright, he wins and plays next; but if not, he loses, and the other continues to play. While each one is playing, the rest of his party beat with a small stick upon the larger one in front of them, and keep up a regular sing-song noise in regular time. Small sums are generally bet in this game, from 50 cents to $1.50. Different ones play according as they are more or less successful. Sometimes

they grow so expert, even if the guess is right, that the one playing can change the bone to the other hand without its being seen.

(3) *Women's game.*—The dice are made of beavers' teeth generally but sometimes from muskrats' teeth. There are two pairs of them, and generally two persons play, one on each side; but sometimes there are two or three on each side. The teeth are all taken in one hand, and thrown after the manner of dice. One has a string around the middle. If this one is down and all the rest up, or up and the rest down, it counts four; if all are up or down, it counts two; if one pair is up and the other down, it counts one; and if one pair is up or down and the other divided, unless it be as above when it counts four, then it counts nothing; 30 is a game; but they generally play three games, and bet more or less, money, dresses, or other things. They sometimes learn very expertly to throw the one with the string on differently from the others, by arranging them in the hand so that they can hold this one, which they know by feeling, a trifle longer than the others.

The general effect of gambling is bad, because it teaches them to lie and cheat, and many other evils attend it besides the common ones of loss of money, and the excitement. It is very common among them, though less so than formerly. Regular dice, chess, and checkers are not used, and cards but very little.

B.—FIELD SPORTS AND PASTIMES.

Horse-racing and sometimes foot-racing are common. Bets are made on them, generally small, but occasionally amounting to $300, and are said to have amounted occasionally in former times to $1,000.

Dancing is another amusement, which was formerly very much practised, but now very little. There are no partners chosen, but men and women both dance; the men generally being together, and the women by themselves, holding on to each other's hands, in the same room. Their dancing is chiefly a jumping up and down, keeping time to the music, which consists of singing, hallooing, pounding on a drum, on sticks, or on the wall, &c., while rattles, either in their hands or hung around their waists, are being continually shaken. These rattles are simply deer-hoofs dried and hung on a string.

C.—SPORTS AND TOYS OF CHILDREN.

The extent to which they are taught to mimic the occupations of their seniors.—They are continually taught to do so from youth until grown.

Their toys and games as above.—Formerly the boys played at shooting with bows and arrows at a mark, and with spears throwing at a mark, with an equal number of children on each side, and sometimes the older ones joined in; but of late years there has been but little of this. They now mimic their seniors in the noise and singing of gambling, but without the gambling; also play ball, jump, and run races. The girls play with dolls. The girls and boys both play in canoes, and stand on half of a small log six feet long and a foot wide and paddle around in the water with a small stick an inch in thickness, and in fact play at most things which they see their seniors do, both whites and Indians.

§ 11.—MUSIC.

The character and frequency of their music, both vocal and instrumental.—Vocal: Love songs, tamanamus or medicine-men songs, war and gambling songs, and baby songs. All but the war songs frequent, but with no regularity. Instrumental: A kind of rough drum to accompany tamanamus and gambling songs.

The classes who practice it.—All classes practice all kinds.

The existence of minstrels or special musicians.—None.

The occasions, with copies of the melodies and score, if possible.—War songs in war time; tamanamus songs at the medicine-men's work; gambling songs at gambling, and love songs very irregular, but often, especially when in company, traveling, or at work, and more especially by the women and younger persons; baby songs when taking care of their children. Their own native songs as yet I have been unable to obtain.

The following are songs in Chinook, which they have been taught during the past two years at church and Sabbath-school. The Chinook is the language which they use in their intercourse with the whites, except when an interpreter is used, although the Twana is their own language, and used in the intercourse between themselves.

TUNE.

1. Ahukuttie nika tikegh whiskey, (Repeat twice.)
   Pe alta nika mash.
         Alta nika mash (Repeat twice.)
   Ahukuttie nika tikegh whiskey, (Repeat twice.)
   Pe alta nika mash.

2. Whiskey has cultus,
   Pe alta nika mash.

3. Whiskey mimoluse tillicums,
   Pe alta nika mash.

4. Cultus klaska muckamuck,
   Pe alta nika mash.

These all repeat as the first verse.

(*Translation.*)

1. Formerly I liked whiskey,
   But now I throw it away.

2. Whiskey is very bad,
   And now I throw it away.

3. Whiskey kills the people,
   And now I throw it away.

4. They drink that which is bad,
   And now I throw it away.

Song 2.—Tune: *Come to Jesus.*

1. Chaco yakwa, (Repeat twice.)
   Okoke sun (Repeat once.)
   Chaco yakwa, (Repeat once.)
   Okoke suu.

2. Halo mamook
   Okoke sun.

3. Halo cooley
   Okoke sun.

4. Iskum wawa
   Okoke sun.

5. Saghalie tyee
   Yaka sun.

(Repeat as in verse 1.)

(Translation.)

Come here (*i. e.*, to church).
To-day (*i. e.*, Sunday).

Do not work
To-day.

Do not play
To-day.

Get the talk
To-day, *i. e.* Sunday.

God,
It is his day.

Song 3.—Tune: *John Brown.*

1. Jesus chaco copa Saghalie. (Repeat
   Jesus hias kloshe.   [twice.)
   Jesus wawa copa tillicums. (Repeat
   Jesus hias kloshe.   [twice.)

2. Jesus wawa wake kliminhoot.
   Jesus hias kloshe.
   Jesus wawa wake kapswalla.
   Jesus hias kloshe.

3. Copa nika Jesus mimaloose.
   Jesus hias kloshe.
   Jesus klatawa copa Saghalie.
   Jesus hias kloshe.

Repeat as in verse 1.

4. Alta Jesus mitlite copa Saghalie.
   Jesus hias kloche.
   Yahwa Jesus tikegh nika klatawa.
   Jesus hias kloche.

(Translation.)

1. Jesus came from Heaven.
   Jesus is very good.
   Jesus preached to the people.
   Jesus is very good.

2. Jesus said, Do not lie.
   Jesus is very good.
   Jesus said, Do not steal.
   Jesus is very good.

3. For me Jesus died.
   Jesus is very good.
   Jesus has gone to Heaven.
   Jesus is very good.

4. Now Jesus lives in Heaven.
   Jesus is very good.
   There Jesus wishes me to go.
   Jesus is very good.

Song 4.—Tune: *Greenville.*

1. Copa Saghalie conoway tillicums,
      Halo olo, halo sick,
   Wake kliminhoot, halo solleks,
      Halo pahtlum, halo cly.
Chorus:
   Jesus mitlite copa Saghalie
      Kunamoxt conoway tillicums kloshe.

2. Yahwa tillicums wake klahowya,
      Wake sick tumtum, halo till,
   Halo mimoluse, wake mesachie,
      Wake polaklie, halo cole.
Chorus:
   Jesus mitlite, &c.

3. Yahwa tillicums mitlite kwanesum.
      Hiyu houses, hiyu sing.
   Papa, mama, pee kloshe tenas;
      Oacut yakachikamin pil.
Chorus:
   Jesus mitlite, &c.

4. Jesus potlatch copa Siwash.
      Spose mesika hias kloshe,
   Conoway iktas mika tikegh,
      Copa Saghalie kwanesum.
Chorus:
   Jesus mitlite, &c.

(Translation.)

1. In Heaven all the people
      Are not hungry, are not sick,
   Do not lie, are not angry,
      Are not drunk, do not cry.
Chorus:
   Jesus lives in Heaven
      With all good people.

2. There the people are not poor,
      Have no sorrow, are not tired,
   Do not die, are not wicked,
      There is no darkness and no cold.
Chorus:
   Jesus lives, &c.

3. There the people live always.
      Many houses, much singing. [dren;
   There are father, mother, and good chil-
      The road is of gold.
Chorus:
   Jesus lives, &c.

4. Jesus will give to the Iudians,
      If you are very good,
   Everything you wish,
      In Heaven forever.
Chorus:
   Jesus lives, &c.

Instruments for beating.—A rough drum is made about a foot and a half square and four or five inches deep. This is covered with rawhide on one side, and used in their gambling and tamanamus songs. One of the school-boys has a small American snare-drum, which he beats tolerably well. No clappers, bells, sounding bars, tambourines are used.

Blowing instruments.—One of the school-boys owns and plays on a flageolet. There are no pan-pipes, flutes, nose-flutes, clarionets, reed instruments, or whistles. American tin horns are used for calling the people together, especially the people of a logging camp, to their meals, but not as a musical instrument.

§ 12.—ART.

The classes of men called artists, if there are any, and are they separated from the artisans ?—There are no special artists.

The first efforts of rude tribes to carry out art ideas.—I know of none except as under the next head.

The sources from which they draw their models, mythical, imaginary, and natural.—A figure similar to an alligator is painted on some of their canoe-heads, said to represent lightning. There are no alligators near here which they have ever seen. These figures are chiefly on those which have come from British Columbia. The face of a man is painted on one door. The figure of a man's head roughly carved from wood, and painted, with the body dressed with clothes, is placed inside of a few of their grave-inclosures. I have also seen two figures roughly carved, representing an English man and woman, about eight and eleven inches tall. There are no specimens of art-work in pottery or on stone, ivory, bone, shells, or gourds, no feather-work purely artistic, no mosaics or stucco-work, nor do I know of any cloth or leather embroidery or bead-work for art purposes, except that spoken of under sections 4, H, and 5. Their powder-horns are sometimes ornamented with figures marked in the horn and with brass tacks driven in.

§ 13.—LANGUAGE AND LITERATURE.

Vocabulary.

Man.	Stē'-bāt.
Woman.	S'khlāl'-dai.
Boy.	Ts'-chai'-āts.
Girl.	Sl'-hāl-do.
Infant.	Ts'-chai'-āts (same as boy).
My father (said by son).	Dō-bād.
My father (said by daughter).	Dō-bād.
My mother (said by son).	Dis-kō'-yā.
My mother (said by daughter).	Dis-kō'-yā.
My husband.	D-kwit-tā-bāts.
My wife.	Dl-cho'-wash.

My son (said by father).	L'is-bŭd'-dā.
My son (said by mother).	Dis-bŭd'-dā.
My daughter (said by father).	Dis-klā'-da-ale.
My daughter (said by mother).	Dis-klā'-da-ale.
My elder brother.	Dis-sīl'-klā-du-chat.
My younger brother.	So-so'-kwi, (or) Tī-ŭ-hwa-tāl-la-bdis so-kwi.
My elder sister.	Tsī-tsī-klā-dŭ-chush.
My younger sister.	Tsī-u-hwa-tal-lāb dŭ-chush.
An Indian.	Klā-wâl'-pīsh.
People.	Klō-klā-wâl'-pīsh.
Head.	Sō-hōtes-h īs.
Hair.	Tā-bate'-kwob.
Face.	Būs.
Forehead.	Skŭ-pōs'.
Ear.	Kwŭl-lād-dī.
Ear.	Kwŭl-lād'-y.
Eye.	Dō-klais'-á-bŭt.
Nose.	Bŭks'-sŭd.
Mouth.	Tsūts-tsīd'.
Tongue.	Dukt'-sāch.
Teeth.	I'-ē-dīs.
Beard.	Kwī-dūts'-a.
Neck.	St'stsa-hāps'-ud.
Arm.	Chāl-lāsh'.
Hand.	S'khā-sŭk'-kāh-gy.
Fingers.	S'khā-suk'-kāh-gy (same as hand).
Thumb.	Sī-dā-kuls-chy.
Nails.	Kwow-hŭ-chy.
Body.	Dow'-ŭt-sy.
Chest.	Skŭp-pō-bade.
Belly.	Khl-ach'.
Leg.	Shī-ā shud.
Foot.	Ī-á-shud.
Toes.	Skā-shŭk-ā-sīd.
Bone.	Skā'-wā.
Heart.	I'-á-dū-wŭs.
Blood.	Sīd-dŭk'-kōle.
Town, village.	No word; they use town.
Chief.	Sō'-wīl-lūs.
Warrior (literally brave).	Schā-lah-kāh.
Friend.	S'to-bā'-ted.
House.	Sī'-ā.
Kettle.	Tsŭk-sta'-kīd.
Bow.	Stāt'-pt-sĕd.
Arrow.	Tă-ăt-sĕd.

Ax, hatchet.	Kŭb'-băd, kŭb-băd-dŏtl.
Knife.	Dä-whĭk'-bŭd.
Canoe.	Klä-ī-ŏ-latl.
Moccasins.	Ĺ-ŏ-shĭd.
Pipe.	Päh-äk'-u.
Tobacco.	St-ĭsp'-whŭ-ub.
Sky.	Sklä'-tl.
Sun.	Klo-kwätl'.
Moon.	Slo-kwill'-nm.
Star.	Klä-kla-chĭ'-us.
Day.	Slŭ-khēt'.
Night.	Chä-äl'.
Morning.	Cha'-lŭ.
Evening.	Hŭ-ät'-kd.
Spring.	Sī-ai-kwatst, or petl'-ko-säb, or säl'-läl-äb (the first a name, the last two literally getting warm).
Summer.	Spĭt'-käp.
Autumn.	Pet-tŏ ŭl las (literally getting cold).
Winter.	Spät-chĭ'-ä (literally cold weather).
Wind.	Spō-hōbe'.
Thunder.	Kwä-ä-hwŏd.
Lightning.	Chŭl'-lä-kwob.
Rain.	Stŭts.
Snow.	Sä-ŭk'-kwä-kwä.
Fire.	As-kwot'-tä.
Water.	Kä'-ä.
Ice.	Skab'-ŭ.
Earth, land.	Tä-bī-hu.
Sea.	Sī-dä'-kwä.
River.	Kä'-ä (same as water).
Lake.	Kwä-lä'-ät.
Valley.	Bä-kwäb.
Prairie.	Bä-kwäb.
Hill, mountain.	S'bä-tay-chab, s'bäh-date.
Island.	S'tē-chä.
Stone, rock.	S'chäl-täs'.
Salt.	Salt (having no word).
Iron.	Pay-tä-dĭ'-up.
Forest.	Chē-säb.
Tree.	Tsä'-ko-pay.
Wood.	Sī-ä-wis'.
Leaf.	Kwa'-la-oy.
Bark.	Pä-läd' (whisper first syllable).
Grass.	Skwil'-la-ai.
Pine.	Tuk-tuk'-la-hoi.
Maize.	Have no word; use *corn*.

Squash.	Have no word; use *squash*.
Flesh, meat.	Bai'-yăts.
Dog.	Skwâ-bai-yä.
Buffalo.	Have no word.
Bear.	Stsa-ñ'-ŏl.
Wolf.	Dŭ-eh-shŭ'-eh-yai.
Fox.	Have no word.
Deer.	Swhē-shĭd.
Elk.	Kwäh-kwa'-chid.
Beaver.	Stŏ-pŏ-hwob.
Rabbit, hare.	Kwĭch-i-dy.
Tortoise.	Have no word.
Horse.	Stĭ-ā-kĕ'-ō.
Fly.	Ŭh-hwai'-ŭh-hwai'-ŭh.
Mosquito.	Chĭ-chĭ'-ats.
Snake.	Bŭts'-ai.
Rattlesnake.	Wät-push.
Bird.	Späpts'-ho.
Egg.	Kaw'-kŭ-ba-lich.
Feathers.	St'klŭkʰ'-el.
Wings.	Same as feathers.
Goose.	Pi-sak.
Duck, mallard.	Hăh-hob-shud, or bâk.
Turkey.	Have no word.
Pigeon.	Hŭ-bĭp.
Fish.	Sbe-lăch'-sŭd.
Salmon.	Slaw-awb.
Sturgeon.	Have no word.
Name.	Tsō-bât'.
White.	Päk.
Black.	Ais-klâl'.
Red.	Ȧst-sa-uk.
Light blue.	Äs-kwa-ŭh.
Yellow.	Ȧs-kwa-kä.
Light green.	Ähs-pap-kwak-do-kureb (whisper last syllable).
Great, large.	Sĭ-sĭd'.
Small, little.	Kä-käp, or kä-kăm-el.
Strong.	Sto-bish.
Old.	Has-pōt'-ŭl.
Young.	T'chay-shul, tchai-ăts.
Good.	Ai'-y.
Bad.	Ki-lŭb.
Dead.	Ais-klai'-hul, äs-at'-to-bit.
Alive.	Hăh-lay'.
Cold.	S'chay'-ŭh.

Warm, hot.	Us'-say-lăb, us-kwil-lok-kho.
I.	Dits-ŭ.
Thou.	Dŭ'-I.
He.	Tsud-dĭ-ŭl.
We.	Dĭ-ă-bătl.
Ye.	Wil-la-wŏl lup.
They.	Tsood-tsud-dăl.
This.	Tee-tli-ă.
That.	Klă-tsăh-ĭ-ă, taw-o-y.
All.	Pĭ-ase'.
Many, much.	Haw-haw'.
Who.	Wŭ-ăt.
Far.	Kwă.
Near.	Chate.
Here.	Ech-tel-ya'.
There.	Klay-tsă-ĭ-a, taw o-y.
To-day.	Tel-es-lŭ-kha' it.
Yesterday.	Ŭt-sŭs-wŭd-it.
To-morrow.	Tsŏ-ŭt-chă'-ŭl.
Yes.	A.
No.	Hwă'-kă.
One.	Dă'-kus.
Two.	Es-să'-ly.
Three.	Cho'-ŭs.
Four.	Bu'-sŭs.
Five.	Ts-whess'.
Six.	Ĭ-ă-pa'-chy.
Seven.	Tŭ-khōs.
Eight.	T-khă'-chy.
Nine.	Hwail-e-a.
Ten.	Ŏ'-pă-dich.
Eleven.	O'-pă-dich-klō-dy-dă-kŭs.
Twelve.	O-pă dich-klō dy-es-să'-by.
Twenty.	Tsub-kh-lăk'.
Thirty.	Chă-dăk-klōk.
Forty.	Sh'tib-bŭ-sus.
Fifty.	Tsitss-a-whŭss' (whisper first sylla-ble.)
Sixty.	Stĕ'-ă-păh'-chy.
Seventy.	Stich-tŭ-khōs.
Eighty.	St'-tŭ-kă'-chy.
Ninety.	St'-tŭ-hwal'-ē-a.
One hundred.	St'-tŭ-păl-owlse.
One thousand.	Ō-pă-dich-tŭ-păl-owlse.
To eat.	Sŭ-ĭ-klăd.
To drink.	Skŏh.

7 BULL

To run.	Wĕ-chñ′-chun.
To dance (Indian dance).	Skwates.
ing.	S'il-lāl.
To sleep.	S'tō-păd′.
To speak.	S-lay-ăl-kwob.
To see.	Sil-lā-lap.
To love.	S-hāt′-l.
To kill.	Āt′-to-bid.
To sit.	Āb′-būt.
To stand.	Us-sāh-tăd′-u-bit.
To go.	S'ōl.
To come.	Tsī-ñ′, hai-ñ.
To walk.	Wōh′-chab′.
To work.	Sū-ā-chib.
To steal.	S'chā-lo-ăl.
To lie.	Skwai-yup′.
To give.	Sbī-hwâ.
To laugh.	Sbī-hwâ-wa (whisper last syllable).
To cry.	Il-lal.

I have obtained these words by asking three or four individuals, and where they differed, continually asking until I found which was right. They are the native Twana. Quite a number talk the Nisqually language entirely; a large number understand, and it is said that during the last few years more and more individuals are learning to speak it. The great majority, however, talk the Twana language in their conversation among themselves. All except the old persons talk also the Chinook in their intercourse with the whites and some other tribes of Indians, and quite a number understand English.

Their knowledge of their own affairs.—Of their history they know very little except what the oldest remember.

Their theories of natural phenomena, as sunrise and sunset, the origin and motion of the heavenly bodies, thunder and lightning, wind, rain, &c.— They supposed that the sun really rose and set, and not that the world turned over as they have been told.

Wind they supposed was caused by the breath of a great being, who blew with his mouth. In this they reasoned from analogy, as a man can with his breath cause a small wind.

Cold they supposed to be caused by our getting farther away from the sun in the winter, for they suppose that the sun is much farther off when it is low than when it is high, and that the cold regions are away from the sun, hence that we are near these cold regions in the winter.

Thunder and lightning some supposed were caused by a great thunder-bird flapping its wings, an idea which is prevalent among nearly all of the Indians on the sound. Others suppose that a wicked tamanamus, or medicine-man, very strong, caused it by his tamanamus when angry with some one.

I have heard of two legends of the origin of the sun; both, however, being legends, more than a matter of real belief.

First. A woman had a son who ran away from home. After a little she went after him, but could not find him. Her people went after her, found her, and brought her back. They did not know what became of her son until a short time afterward they beheld him, having been changed into the real sun, coming up from the east. This is the origin of the sun.

Second. A woman having no husband had a son, who, being left in charge of its grandmother, who was blind, was stolen away by two women who carried him very far away, where they brought him up, and he grew very fast and became their husband. His children were the trees, the cedar-tree being the favorite one. His mother in the mean time sent messengers, the cougar, panther, and some birds, who went everywhere on the land searching for him except to this place, where they could not go on account of a very difficult place in the road, which was liable to come together and crush whatever passed through. At last, the blue-jay made the attempt, and was almost killed, being caught by the head, nearly crushing it, and thus causing the top-knot on it. It however found the son, a man grown, and induced him to leave his present home and return to his mother. When they came to this difficult place in the road, he fixed it, and did good wherever he went. When his mother found that he was lost at first, she was very sorry, and gathered his clothes together, pressed from them some water, wished it to become another boy, and, being very good, her wish was granted. He was a little boy when his older brother returned. They were both somewhat like God, in that they could do what they wished. The older brother said to the younger one, "I will make you into the moon to rule the night, and I will be the sun to rule the day." The next day he arose in the heavens, but was so hot that he killed the fish in the sea, causing the water to boil, and also the men on the land. Finding that this would not do, he retired, and his brother tried to be the sun and succeeded, as the sun is at present, while the older brother became the moon, to rule the night.

Orations.—The following are taken from the minutes of a council held with them by Commissioner F. R. Brunot, September 4, 1871:

By BIG FRANK, the present head chief:

I am the only one who was at the treaty at Point-no-Point. I heard what Governor Stevens said; and thought it was good. I am like a white man, and think as the white man does. Governor Stevens said all the Indians would grow up and the President would make them good. He told them all the Indians would become as white men; that all their children would learn to read and write. I was glad to hear it. Governor Stevens told them, "I will go out and have the land surveyed, and it will be yours and your children's forever." I thought that very good. He said a doctor and carpenter and farmer would come. The chiefs thought that was all good; they thought the President was doing a kindness. I never spoke my mind to any one. I talk to you because you come from Washington. All the agents talk differently. You talk as Governor Stevens did. I hear what you say. Every agent who comes here, I don't know them. I thought all Governor Stevens said was very good. Perhaps the President thinks all the Indians are good, as they were to be under the treaty; but they are not, they are Indiâns still. I think there was plenty of money sent by the President, but I think much did not come here. Perhaps it gets scattered. I really think it does not come. When it comes, it is in calico. But I know more is sent than gets here.

By SPAR, the chief at that time, since dead:
When I came here I was young, and did not know much. I was here when the reservation was opened, and know what was done. When the agents came, they never taught us anything; never said, "Go and fix your places." All they think of is to steal, to sell the reservation cattle and reservation hay; to sell the fruit and get all they can; to go and log and sell them. That is all every agent has done. They never advised us what to do, never helped us. After I had seen all this, I was sorry. Did the President send men for this, to come and get what money they could out of the reservation and their pay? I know the Indians lose all their cattle. When they get the money, where does it go? When I ask about it, they say they will punish me. I thought the President did not send them for that. I got very poor, and wanted to borrow the reservation team. You know what I have done. They refused me the use of the cattle.

By DUKE WILLIAMS:
I am glad to see you. All our folks are very poor. Our planting grounds and logs and apples and hay are taken from us, and I felt sad, and wanted to go and see the President. I know I will not live long. I asked the Indians to give me the money, and I would go and see the President. I would have gone if you had not come here. Did the President send men here as agents to log and get all the benefits? That is what I wanted to go and ask the President.

By BIG JOHN, a subchief:
You come to get the Indians' hearts. You ought to take time. You are the great chief, and we want you to hear us. When we talked before, it was put down, and they said it would go to Washington. We do not know what became of it. We don't think the President saw it. We think it don't go far from here. I am a poor man. You are making all of these young men and women happy. I thought, when a boy, that we would get all of the money that was promised. White men don't give things away. They don't take a shirt or a blanket for lands. They get gold and silver. The Indians don't get money for their country.

These are samples of their orations on this subject, and enough to show their style. I have heard them speak on other subjects; on temperance and religion; but those orations have not been preserved. We do not get their real style, however, when they talk through an interpreter. They are natural orators, and their looks and gestures, which are numerous, speak eloquently.

§ 11.—DOMESTIC LIFE.

A.—MARRIAGE.

Including courtship, betrothal, and wedding ceremonies.—Formerly courtship extended for a long time, and the couple were engaged for some time before marriage, though secretly. The husband purchased the wife of her parents, the price generally being a hundred or several hundred dollars, a large part of which was returned at the wedding. At the wedding there was a large feast at the house of the wife's parents, to which all the friends were invited, and after this there was often more feasting for a long time, alternating between the families of the husband and wife. There is but little of this now. At present when they are married in Indian fashion they generally simply take each other without any ceremony, though a few marriages in ancient form have taken place lately among the more uncivilized.

Within two and a half years, a dozen marriages in American Christian form have taken place, and when this is done they consider the relations far more binding, so much so, that they are generally unwilling to have it done unless they have been married six months or more in Indian fashion, to learn whether they will like each other sufficiently.

Conditions of both parties as to relationship.—The wife is not so elevated as white women, doing much more rough work, but is by no means a slave, and is highly prized.

Dowry.—The wife receives at marriage a large share of the property which the husband gave her father for her before marriage, and also some other things, but there is no regular rule.

Polygamy, rank of wives, &c.—Polygamy has been practiced quite commonly among them, the number of wives depending on their ability to purchase, and their wishes. But this custom is going out of existence, only four of them having more than one wife and only one having three now.

Laws about marrying in and out of the tribe.—They may do with the consent of the parents. The children of those wi of the tribe belong to the tribe of the father; and a number of persons have married out of the tribe.

Sacredness and permanency of marriage.—Quite sacred, there being trouble when the marriage-vow is violated by either party; but not permanent, divorces occasionally taking place, though much less often now than formerly.

B.—CHILDREN.

Accouching.—The woman attends to herself.

Seclusion of mother.—They are secluded as unclean about one week.

For a long time, the mother is not allowed to touch fish, fowl, or game, the gun, fishing-apparatus, or anything by which any of these are taken, as they think it will bring ill luck.

Naming.—They are named after deceased friends often, and when this is done, a little potlatch is made.

Cradling.—The cradle is described in chap. III, sec. 2, C. The cradle often lies down, but sometimes is hung on a small stick, a few feet high, which is fastened in the ground or floor, in a slanting direction, and acts as a spring. A string is fastened to it, and the mother pulls the string, which keeps the stick constantly moving, and the cradle and child constantly swinging. This is done with the foot when the hands are busy at work.

Deformations.—The only one is the flattening of the head, which is done in infancy.

Nursing.—This is done longer than among the whites.

Child-murder.—This is unknown.

Adoption.—This prevails a little, but is not common.

Education or treatment while growing up.—The Indians educate them only in Indian customs. For school, see sec. 9.

C.—WOMEN.

Standing in family and society.—Inferior to whites.

Peculiar duties.—Waiting on her husband, preparing meals, getting wood and water, preparing fish, the large game being dressed by the men, spinning, sewing, knitting, making of clothing, and washing are her chief duties.

General appearance.—Unattractive, with coarse features.

Growing old.—Early in life, they begin to have a wrinkled and aged appearance.

D.—RIGHTS AND WRONGS.

Chastity.—Very many are unchaste.

Immoralities.—Almost universal.

Prostitution.—It is rather common by both sexes.

Schoopanism and Sodomy.—Unknown.

Divorce.—They are easily obtained, but growing less.

    Conditions of.—If a man puts away his wife, he gives her a present; but if she leaves him, he does not.

    Results of.—Morally they are evil, but socially, among others, neither party is lowered.

Celibacy.—Not known.

Inheritance.—See sec. 16, B, of present chapter.

Rights of parents and guardians.—Parents exercise authority over their children fully equal to that of white parents over theirs, but over adopted children they have less.

§ 15.—*SOCIAL LIFE AND CUSTOMS.*

A.—ORGANIZATION OF SOCIETY.

Classes of men and professions.—Chiefs, sub-chiefs, headmen, medicine-men, common people, slaves.

Military, political, and religious castes.—None in the proper sense of the term.

Secret orders.—Black Tamanamus. I cannot learn that there has been any of it for eight years. If it is practiced at all now, it is done very quietly, and in a very different manner from formerly; but as near as I can learn, the society is entirely broken up. I have not been able to learn the entire ceremony, but am told that it was similar to the Makah ceremony, which has been given by Mr. J. G. Swan in his description of that tribe, though the ceremonies varied somewhat in the different tribes on the sound. I, however, learn that the candidate was starved for a long time (one man saying that he did not eat anything for eight days), but he or she (for both men and women were initiated) was closely watched inside a large tent, and what else was done in it I cannot learn; but occasionally the candidate was let out and pursued by two or three others with all their might, and sometimes he himself pursued others, and if he gave out in the race or other exercises he was not considered worthy to become a member. If he did not, he was taken back to the tent and watched and starved, and the same scene repeated every day or two. At last he was brought out perfectly rigid, and taken by several men and thrown up as high as they could into the air, sometimes eight feet, and caught, and this was continued until he apparently came to consciousness and screamed. There was also very much cutting of the body and limbs quite deep, so that the candidate became quite bloody, but he did not seem to take any notice of it. After these ceremonies, he would sometimes sit, in his house or lodge, looking like an idiot, for two or three months, and speak to no one, even to a husband or wife, but simply wind something on a stick and unwind it again day after day.

Slaves.—Those taken in war or bought, always originally captives, however, were slaves. Formerly they were very much oppressed, but now they have considerable liberty, and there are only two in the tribe, as there has been no war for a long time, and the treaty by the Government provides that there shall be no slavery.

B.—CUSTOMS.

Personal habits.—Not neat in their houses, and not very neat in their clothes, though growing much more so. Very much accustomed to bathe. In dress, quite showy and clean on public days.

Salutation, etiquette, hospitality.—Not much form in salutation, only a word or two, and sometimes shaking of hands, which they have learned from Americans. Not much etiquette. Very hospitable to friends.

Feasting and festivals, manner of observing, and meaning.—When friends come on the 4th of July and Christmas, or because of a potlatch, *i. e.*, distribution of gifts. On the 4th of July, Christmas, or when friends come, they simply cook a large amount of food, spread it on mats, which are on the ground, and they gather around the different mats in companies. Sometimes when friends come, they bring a large amount of food with them, both for themselves to eat and those whom they come to see, expecting that there will be much over, which will be given to the friends whom they visit. At a potlatch, one man, or a few persons, give notice that they will give away a large amount of money and provisions, and they invite not only their own tribe, but also the neighboring tribes. Food, clothes, and money, and other things, are then given away, sometimes to the amount of $5,000, the persons doing so immortalizing themselves for life by this means. The potlatch lasts from three days to three weeks, and is accompanied by feasting, gambling, visiting, &c.

Sleeping customs.—The more civilized class have a bed-room partitioned off, and very many have bedsteads. Often men, women, and children sleep in the same room, and sometimes on the floor with mats, feather-beds, straw-beds, skins, blankets, and quilts, more or less as they are able to procure them. A few use sheets. Formerly they all slept in the same room and on the ground, but are now slowly adopting American customs.

Charities, &c.—There is nothing organized, and formerly there was much suffering among the sick and old; but of late years, as they have earned money, the friends of the sick and poor care for them, so that there is but little real suffering because of poverty. The agent also provides extra food for the sick and poor from Government supplies.

Initiation into manhood or into the tribe.—There is no ceremony now, and has not been, as far as I can learn.

Social vices.—Intemperance, gambling, and filthiness.

Healing.—See sec. 1, E, of present chapter.

Bleeding, extracting teeth, amputation, trepanning.—These were unknown among them before a white physician came.

Customs when about to build a house, to go on a hunting or fishing expedition, to make a journey, or to engage in any new pursuit.—Formerly, as now, when about to build a house, they did nothing special, as their houses were so small and often removed, that it was an event of no great importance; but when about to go on a hunting or fishing expedition, to make a journey, or engage in anything special, they would tamanamus, their way of invoking the presence of the Great Spirit, so that they might be successful. They do very little of this now.

Customs when about to engage in war.—They would consult together in an assembly where those who wished would speak, and then do as the chiefs said. After this they would tamanamus in order to be successful, and paint themselves with black and red, making themselves as hideous as possible. They have had no war for many years.

Treatment of the captives and wounded.—Wounded enemies were generally killed. Captives were made slaves or sold; but sometimes prominent men were ransomed.

Customs around the dying and dead.—They will tamanamus (see III, 17, D, Exorcism) for the removal of the evil spirit. When a person is about to die, they remove the person from the house, supposing that if a death takes place in a house the evil spirit who killed the deceased will kill every one who shall afterward live in the house. If it is unpleasant weather, a mat house is built in which they may die, and being immediately torn down, it allows the evil spirit to escape. If a person dies in a house, they will not live in it afterward, and generally tear it down. After death, there is a great deal of crying and mourning and noise.

Funeral and burial customs.—The dead are placed in coffins, and many things are also placed with them in the coffins, as good clothes and other things, which they will be supposed to need in the next world. Occasionally, Christian services are held over them, after which they are taken to the graveyard. The number of these Christian services has increased considerably during the last two years. If no Christian service is held at the convenience of the friends, they are taken to the grave, but generally much sooner after death than with the whites, often as soon as the coffin can be made. They are quite superstitious about going near the dead, fearing that the wicked spirit who killed the dead will enter the living who go near. They are most fearful of having children go near, they being more liable to be attacked than older persons. They are very slowly overcoming these prejudices as they see the customs of the whites, but are more slow in regard to this than to adopt most other American customs.

Manner of disposing of the dead, by cremation, in coffins, embalming, in graves, in lodges, on scaffolds.—No cremation, no embalming, not in lodges. They are placed in coffins, which are made by the Government carpenter, or in a rough box, if the former cannot be easily procured, and then in a grave. Formerly they were placed on scaffolds, but there is very little of this now. Over the grave is an inclosure generally in the shape of a small house, shed, lodge, or fence, and with some the sides are quite open, and with others entirely closed, or with a window. Both outside and within the inclosure are various articles, as guns, canoes in miniature, dishes, clothes, blankets, sheets, and cloth mats, and occasionally a wooden man, carved and painted in the face, and dressed. On some graves, these things are replenished every year or two, as they are destroyed by the effects of time. Some graves have nothing of this kind. In this respect, they are adopting American customs more and more.

Ossuaries and public cemeteries.—There are no ossuaries. They have two cemeteries, both on Hood's Canal, one on the reservation and the other a little ways from it. They are not regularly laid out, but face the water, generally extending back only one or two rows of graves.

§ 16.—*GOVERNMENT AND POLITICAL ECONOMY.*

A.—ORGANIZATION.

Authorities in time of peace, claims, and treatment of.—The United States Indian agent is almost supreme with them, and hence the chiefs have but little real authority. The officers are a head chief, four sub-chiefs, headmen, and a policeman. The honor of chieftainship is, however, considerable, so much so that the place is sought after. The chiefs, sub-chiefs, and headmen have, however, considerable influence, and on court-days, while the agent acts as judge, they act as jury, and they also are supposed to have more influence with the agent than others. They also settle some of the minor cases.

Assemblies and public deliberations.—They generally assemble on the sabbath for religious worship and sabbath-school, on court days for court, at feasts and tamanamus, and when Government annuities are distributed; also when any event of importance takes place. The chiefs and headmen do most of the talking, but any one who wishes has the privilege of speaking.

Military organizations, war chiefs.—The same persons who are chiefs in time of peace are also chiefs in time of war. They are the commanding officers of the army, which, in battle, is a very irregular one, each man fighting as seems best to him.

Authority of privileged classes.—The chiefs are honored, and have some authority, but not much, especially when they disagree with the Indian agent. The medicine-men are feared.

The common people, what part of them have a voice in the assembly.—Any one speaks who wishes to do so.

B.—REGULATIONS, LAWS, ETC.

Concerning labor, trades, and castes.—There is no law about labor or the trades. There is no caste. When one wishes to labor, he does so in the way which suits him best. Logging has been their principal business. A number work together, from six to fifteen, and when the boom is sold and the amount deducted which their food cost, the rest is divided among them according to their labor. They have farms and work on them, also work for white persons as they find employment. None have learned the trades to any extent. It has been difficult to teach the older ones the trades, as, while they are able to earn but little, they wish full pay. A few, however, have learned to handle tools quite well. Many of the women wash and iron for the whites.

Personal and communal possessions, debtors.—Their possessions are personal wholly; hardly anything is held in common. Common custom says debtors must pay, though seldom is property taken by force for debt.

Oaths and trials.—The United States Indian agent acts as judge sometimes; in regard to small cases, the chief and subchiefs decide: but generally the cases are brought to the agent, who, after hearing all the evidence, decides the case, or else refers it to five or six of the principal men as a jury for decision. Witnesses and jury are not put on oath; but when persons join the temperance society, they are sworn in the presence of God and all present.

Slavery.—There are a very few slaves; but as there has been no war for a long time, slavery is dying out, and the few which there are are not treated as harshly as they formerly were.

Inheritance.—Property of deceased parents goes to their children, or, if there are no children, to their friends; sometimes, with the consent of the friends, it being given to everybody, strangers even. The oldest child generally receives most.

Torture and punishment.—There is no torture among them now, nor has been, except when captives tried to run away or were contrary, when they cut the soles of their feet. The punishment is generally by fines or imprisonment for a few days, seldom more than two weeks. Generally murder is settled by the payment of from $300 to $600, though occasionally blood revenge is practiced.

Revenue—The only revenue is that the convicted persons pay the sheriff or policeman; the chiefs and jury give their time.

Census.—They take no census. All that is done is taken by the agent, as given under I, D.

Declaring and conducting war, truces, treaties, &c.—For declaring war, see III, 15, B. When a truce takes place, one man, who is favorably known, is sent to the opposite party to arrange the terms of peace; and if a treaty is made, then, sometimes, they prepare a feast, to which the principal men on both sides are invited, and of which they partake together. In their later truces, they used the white flag, or something white as a sign of the truce.

Commerce, foreign and domestic.—There is nothing deserving the name of commerce among themselves; they simply trade for different articles as they wish. To the Americans they sell boom-legs chiefly, and buy provisions, clothes, ornaments, &c. They have very little trade with other tribes, sometimes trading horses with the Nisqually Indians, and buying canoes of the Clallams.

Succession to rank.—Formerly the chieftainship descended from father to son; now the head chief is elected, generally annually, on the Fourth of July, the custom having changed within ten years. The subchiefs are chosen by the people to serve during good behavior, subject to the will of the people and agent. The sheriff or policeman is appointed by the agent to serve during good behavior.

Public property, provisions, and stock.—There is none.

§ 17.—RELIGION.

A.—OBJECTS OF REVERENCE AND WORSHIP.

Angelic spirits and demons.—Many angelic spirits. (See Tamanamus.) Sometimes it is believed that they do fear the devil and demons so much that their medicine-men try to gain their favor so that they shall not be injured by them.

Shamans.—As above, under head of demons.

Gods.—They worship a Great Spirit, who they believe made the world and all in it, and who preserves and governs it. See nothing of a Trinity in their ideas.

Totems.—Each person has his own guardian spirit, called his tamanamus. On the door of one house is an image painted with white paint (see Fig. P, Plate 25),—the tamanamus of the owner of the house.

On the door of another is one of the shape shown at Fig. R, Plate 25, the heavy shading immediately around the human figure indicating red paint. At the head of the bed of one woman is a board about 6 feet high, 2½ broad, and figured as shown at Fig. R, Plate 25. There the heavy shading indicates red paint. I am told that some others have theirs at the head of their beds, but have not seen them. They generally have some animal as their tamanamus, although these look very little like any. Most of the Indians, however, have no figure to represent their tamanamus. How it is chosen or when, I have not learned from them, but suppose it to be done as other Indians on this coast do. There is very much about the whole subject which I do not fully understand, though I am trying constantly to learn more.

B.—HOLY PLACES AND OBJECTS.

Sacred legends, litanies, or laws.—That God made the world; that He made man, but that there were different centers of creation for man, the ancestors of each tribe being created where that tribe now lives; that there was a flood, but that it was not very long ago, and that it did not overflow all their land, but that the summit of Mount Olympus, the highest mountain near here, was not submerged, and that a number of people remained there until the flood subsided; that before it subsided a number of the canoes broke from their fastenings, and carried the people who were in them far away, so that they never returned, which accounts for there being so few left here, and the mountain is called Fastener in their language, from the fact that they broke from their fastening; that none but good Indians were saved at all; that the pigeon or dove did not die, but went abroad to see who were dead; that there has been a great fire, which burned up everybody and everything except good Indians; that one person, very wicked, was turned into a rock, and hence that all wicked Indians will be turned into a rock or else into some beast; and that God at some time formerly came down to this world. (See III, 17, F. Incarnation.)

Bull. U. S. Geol. and Geogr. Survey, Vol. III.

Plate 25.

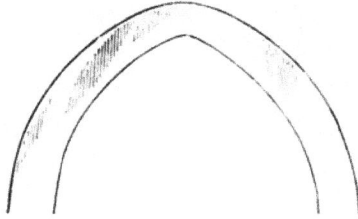

Fig. P.

Fig. Q.

Fig. R.

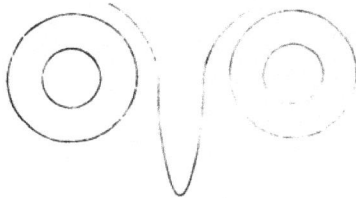

Fig. S.

Totems, &c., of the Twana Indians.

C.—ECCLESIASTICAL ORGANIZATION.

Medicine-men, rain-makers, sorcerers, devotees.—No sorcerers or devotees. There are medicine-men. No special class of rain-makers; but there is a certain rock in Hood's Canal, near the reservation, which they have thought if any one should strike in a certain way it would bring rain. But they have about lost faith in it now.

Part taken by the laiety in religious ceremonics.—At tamanamus they are present and help make the noise, while the medicine-man draws forth the evil spirit. (See III, 17, D, Exorcism.) In their old mode of worship, by dancing, they danced.

D.—SACRED RITES.

Installation of dignitaries.—At present, when a chief is chosen, he makes a short speech, and a few others congratulate him.

Exorcism, generally called tamanamus.—A wicked medicine-man is supposed to be able to send a woodpecker, squirrel, bear, or any treacherous animal, to the heart of his enemy, to eat his heart, plague him, make him sick, or kill him. The good medicine-man finds out, from his sickness, what kind of an animal it is, and then tries to draw it forth ; and while the common people make a noise, pounding on a rough drum, on sticks, hallooing, singing, &c., the medicine-man places his hands on some part of the body, where to him seems best, and draws forth with his hands, or says he does, the evil spirit ; and when he says he has it, he holds it between his hands, invisible, and blows it up, or takes it to another man, who throws a stone at it and kills it. When the sick person is not cured, they say there are several evil spirits, but sometimes the person dies before they are all drawn out, or else the opposing medicine-man is stronger than he, and so he cannot draw them all out. Sometimes the good spirit of the person is gone, and he is sick. Then the medicine-man tries, with his hands, to draw it back, and so cure him.

Choosing a totem.—See A of present section.

Sacrifice.—Formerly, when they went to a new land to live for any length of time, they would build a fire, and then burn some fish, good mats, or something valuable made with the hand, except clothes, which they said they gave to the land in order to gain its favor. Even now in some of their tamanamus ceremonies they do something similar.

Purification.—None as a religious rite. Formerly the women were considered unclean when changing to womanhood, and also at the birth of a child ; on account of which they were kept out of the house, and purified by washing with certain leaves. These customs are almost extinct.

Exorcism.—A wicked medicine-man can also, in an invisible manner, shoot a stone, ball, or poison into the heart of the sick person, and the animal spoken of, to eat the heart of the person, is also sent in an in visible manner. They believe in it so firmly, that they say when the heart of one who has died has been opened that often this stone, or bone, or the like, has been found. When the good medicine-man tamanamuses over the sick person, sometimes he gets well and sometimes he does not. When he does, often I think he would have recovered had there been no tamanamus, and sometimes I am inclined to think it might, perhaps, be attributed to mesmeric power on the part of the doctor, or to the powers of the imagination, as often spoken of in mental philosophy, on the part of the sick person. There are enough cures to make them firm believers in it, and enough deaths to make them believe that there is some other doctor stronger than the one who is trying to cure. They pay the doctor who is trying to cure whatever they wish, but generally considerable, so as to secure his services again if they need him, and if they can discover to their satisfaction the bad doctor who sends the sickness, they will extort considerable from him.

In addition to this, which might be called tamanamus for the sick, there are at least three other kinds which are called by the name of tamanamus—the black tamanamus—which is the most savage (see III, 15, A, Secret orders), that for the living and that for the dead.

I do not know all the order of ceremonies, but there is, in connection with the last two of them, very much feasting, pounding, singing, hallooing, dancing, &c., and some fasting.

In the tamanamus for the living, the candidate starves himself until he is about sick, when all his friends gather and make the noise, he singing a kind of solo at times and they responding; and this is kept up more or less for several days and nights, with intervals of rest more or less long. The object of it is to gain the favor of his tamanamus or guardian spirit.

Tamanamus for the dead:—Some time before a person dies, it may be months, it is supposed that a spirit comes from the spirit-world and carries away the spirit of the person, after which the person gradually wastes away or suddenly dies. If by any means it can be discovered that this has been done, and there are those who profess to do it, then they attempt to get the spirit back by a tamanamus, and, if it is done, the person will live.

There are three traditions about tamanamus which I have learned.

One is of a man, a long time ago, who formed an image of a man, into which he put his tamanamus, and over which he had considerable power, even to making it dance. Two young men did not believe it, and at one time, when many were gathered in the house where it was, were told that, if they did not believe it, to take hold of it and hold it still. But when they did so, the man made it dance, and soon, instead of the two men holding it still, it made them dance, one holding to an arm on each side of it, nor could they stop or let go, but after dancing a while in the house it took them outside, dancing toward the salt-water. All the people followed, trying to stop it, but could not. It took them into the water, and then all three became changed into something like the fish called a skate, went underneath the water like a fish, and were seen no more.

They also say that one woman, called Jane, now on the reservation, could, before the whites came, make certain blocks of wood which she had, and which were a foot or two long and about a foot in diameter, dance by means of her tamanamus without touching them, but cannot do it now, and since the whites came she has taken them off into the woods and buried them.

They also say that a long time ago a man who lived at Union City, and was very successful in catching porpoises, had a brother who was his enemy, who lived up the river, and who tried to injure him, but could not. He especially tried to injure him by seeking to prevent his catching porpoises, but could not. Failing in this, he made a wooden porpoise, put his tamanamus into it, and put it into the water, where he thought his brother would catch it. His brother at Union City found it, and thinking that surely it was a porpoise, caught it, but found really that it was too strong for him, and that he was caught by it, for it took him north under water to the unknown place where ducks live in summer, which is also inhabited by a race of pigmy men a foot or two high, between whom and the ducks there is war. He helped the pigmies, killed many ducks and ate some, whereupon the pigmies called him a cannibal, and became enraged at him. At last, a whale caught him, and brought him back nearly to Union City. He very much wished to be thrown out on dry land or in shallow water near the land. But his wish was not granted, for by some means the whale vomited him up in deep water, and he swam to land. This is the reason why the dentalia, the species of shell formerly used as money, are found in deep water, for they were vomited up with him. If his wish had been granted, and he thrown on dry land or in shallow water, they would have been found there.

Many of these things have caused some white people to believe that their religion was a kind of spiritualism.

For a long time it troubled me to know what was meant by the word "tamanamus", it being most generally used in connection with the work of the medicine-men over the sick. It, however, means more; anything supernatural, except, perhaps, the direct work of God and Satan.

The noun good tamanamus hence means any spirit between God and man, and an evil tamanamus any between Satan and man. It also means any stick, stone, or the like in which this spirit may dwell, and also the work of trying to influence this spirit. The verb means to work in such a way as to influence these spirits, and is done in sickness by medicine or tamanamus men, but in other cases, as described above, by individuals alone, or in companies; so that a tamanamus is often the work of people tamanamusing.

I have sometimes asked them why their tamanamus does not affect white men. In fact, the superintendent of Indian affairs offered their medicine-men a hundred dollars to make him sick or kill any of his horses, for they profess to have power to kill horses as well as persons, but they could do nothing, and say that the white man's heart is hard, so that the invisible stone cannot affect it, but the Indian's heart is soft like mud, and is easily affected.

The fifth, month, sta-ko-lit, was so named because it was the month for tamanamus formerly. The practice which gave it the name has now entirely ceased, and is hardly known to the younger ones, and indeed there are many who hardly know the old name, or indeed any of the names of the months. The ancient practice, it is said, in this month, was to go far off into the mountains, wash themselves very frequently, remain half-naked, build a very large fire a hundred feet long and twenty feet wide, and remain for seven days or thereabouts without sleep. I suppose that they tamanamused also in other ways. When they returned, they rested and slept very much.

E.—MYTHS.

Hades and heaven.—Their idea of heaven formerly was that it was be low, and a place for good hunting and fishing, for good Indians. They had no hell, as they supposed wicked persons would be turned into a rock or beast. Now most of them believe the heaven and hell of the Bible to be true, I think.

Omens.—When they see something very unusual, they think something bad will happen. For instance, if they find a fish very different from any they have ever seen, or a white squirrel, or find a frog cut open and laid on a rock, or anything very unusual, they think something bad will happen, as a great storm, or that some one will die, or something else bad, and if it does not occur till a year passes, but then occurs, they think the omen is fulfilled. To go near a dead person, especially if children should do so, is an omen that those doing so may die soon.

Inanimate objects.—There is a rock a few miles from Union City, which, if touched by any person, would cause the hand to dry up and wither. There is at Eneti, on the reservation, an irregular basaltic rock, about three feet by three feet and four inches and a foot and a half high. On one side there has been hammered a face, said to be the representation of the face of the thunder-bird, which could also cause storms. It is delineated in diagrammatic outline at Fig. S, Plate 25. The two eyes are about six inches in diameter and four inches apart, and the nose about nine inches long. It is said to have been made by some man a long time ago, who felt very badly, and went and sat on the rock, and with another stone hammered out the eyes and nose. For a long time, they believed that if the rock was shaken, it would cause rain, probably because the thunder-bird was angry. They have now about lost faith in it, so much so that about two years ago they formed a boom of logs around it, many of which often struck it. That season was stormy, and some of the older Indians said, however, " No wonder, as the rock is shaken all of the time." It is on the beach, facing the water, where it is flooded at high tide, but not at low tide, and the impression is being gradually worn away by the waves.

Eclipse.—An eclipse of the sun almost annular occurred about two weeks ago, which gave me an opportunity to learn some of their ideas about it. They formerly, as near as I can learn, supposed that a whale was eating up the sun. At the time of the eclipse, several of the women and old persons told me that they stopped work, went to their houses and prayed in their minds to God. Many wished to know what I thought was the cause of it.

Prodigies.—(1) Stick Siwash, a great man or giant, by some thought to be as large as a tree, who would carry off women and children when alone or nearly alone, does not attack men. He lives in the woods. (2) A great land animal which carried off a woman was pursued by a large number of people, who attacked it, cut it with knives, speared it, and did many things, enough to have killed very many common animals, but were unable to kill it, and left it. (3) A great water animal, which has overturned canoes and eaten up the people, but cannot be killed.

Prayer.—In connection with their worship of the Great Spirit, or literally the Chief Above, as given (see Great Spirit, III, 17, F), they pray to the Great Spirit, asking Him to take care of them, help them, and make them good.

F.—BELIEF.

Animism or the existence of the soul.—They firmly believe in this.

Transmigration.—They believe that some wicked people have been turned to animals, or did formerly believe it.

They have a tradition of a dog which was bad, which swam from Eneti to Union City, and back near to the graveyard, a distance of about five miles, and was turned into a long rock, now lying there; also that a certain kind of round flat shell about four inches in diameter was formerly their gambling-disks, but that these disks were changed to these shells.

Worship of a Great Spirit.—They believe in Him and worship Him, chiefly as the Americans do; the old way, which has now ceased, being by girding themselves, singing, and dancing before Him.

Incarnation.—They have a tradition that God once came down to earth, because of a certain impression in a rock on this canal (now washed away), which looked somewhat like a large footstep, and since they have been told that Christ came to this earth, they say they know it to be true.

In addition to the tradition given in connection with gambling (see III, 10, A) they also have a tradition that when the Son of God walked over this land, as He was walking on the beach, north of the mouth of the Skokomish River, He slipped, and because of it He cursed the ground, and it has been a salt-water marsh ever since,

8 BULL

as it is now; also that in crossing a stream down the canal, which was very full of fish, He slipped again, and then cursed the stream, and hence fish never go up this stream, though they inhabit all others.

Resurrection of the dead.—None according to their old ideas; the spirit went to the spirit-land; the body was not raised in this world, but gradually, as it decomposed, was taken there also.

Retribution.—That the wicked will be turned into a rock or animal, formerly. Now, most believe in future punishment as taught in the Bible.

Merit and demerit in sight of Deity.—All were good except the very bad, formerly. They had no dividing line. The Great Spirit divided the good from the bad at death.

Eternity of happiness and woe.—Happiness was eternal. The wicked were turned into a rock and always remained so, or into an animal, as long as it lived. At present most believe in the eternity of happiness and woe, as taught in the Bible.

Progress in religion.—It is but four years and a half since the first Protestant services were held among them. About twenty-three years ago, a Roman Catholic priest taught them a little and baptized some; but this instruction was given up a long time ago, and most of them have given up their belief in it. When the present Indian policy began, four and a half years ago, this reservation was turned over to the Congregationalists under the American Missionary Association. The attendance on the sabbath services has been increasing every summer, the Sabbath attendance averaging about eighty during the past summer (1875). In the winter there are not so many, as most of them live from one to three miles away, and the weather is often bad. One of their number has united with the church here, and there are others whom I believe to be Christians. Most of them say they believe the Bible is true, and that Christ came to this world; but still they cling strongly to their tamanamus, some of them I think as a religion, and some merely as a superstition. The ideas of many in regard to the Bible are dim yet, even respecting the most important truths, and this is not strange when we remember that they cannot read. They are in a transition state in this respect, as in many others.

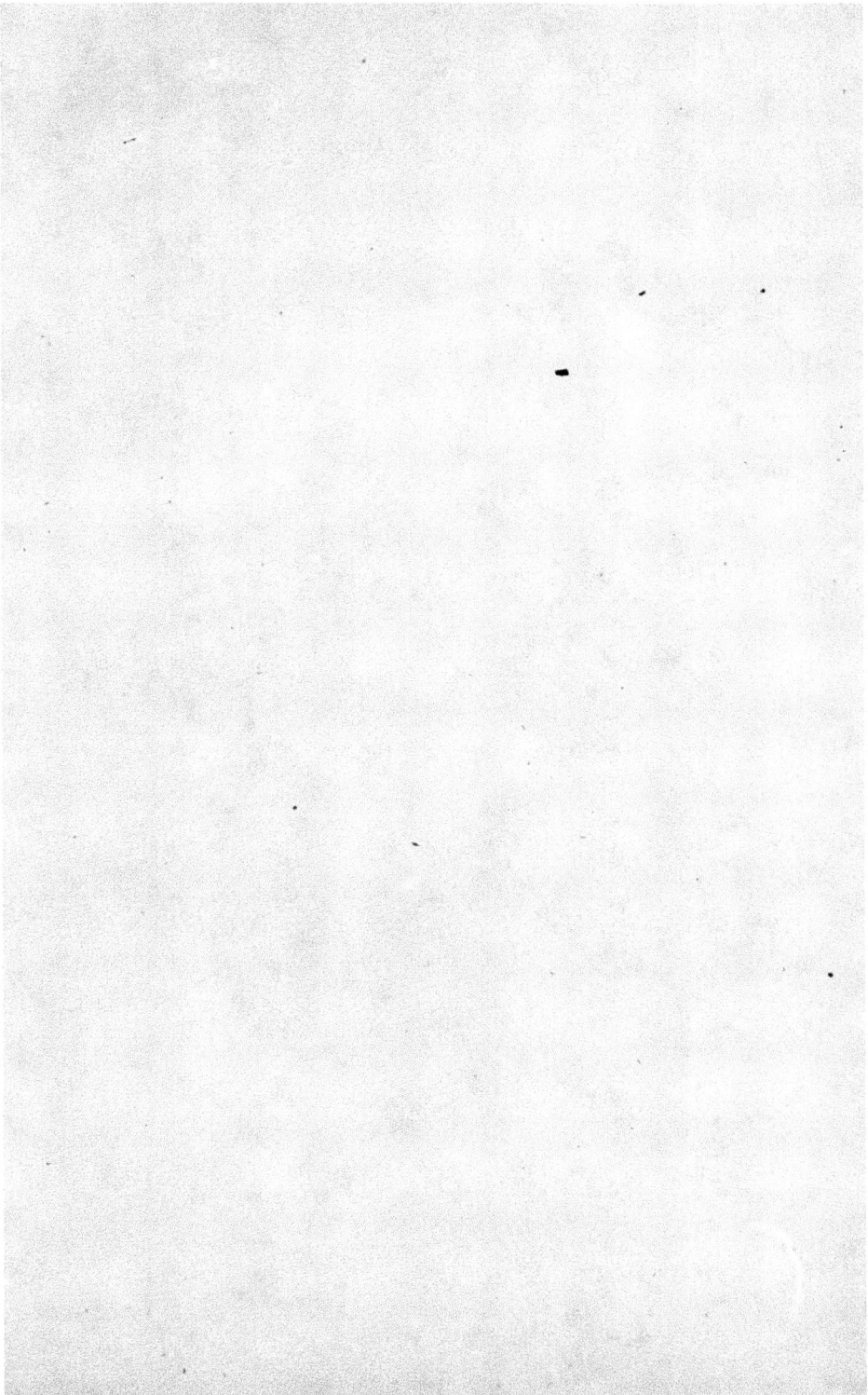

TEN YEARS

OF

MISSIONARY WORK

AMONG THE INDIANS

AT

SKOKOMISH, WASHINGTON TERRITORY.

1874–1884.

By Rev. M. EELLS,

Missionary of the American Missionary Association.

———◆———

BOSTON :

Congregational Sunday-School and Publishing Society,

CONGREGATIONAL HOUSE,

CORNER BEACON AND SOMERSET STREETS.

Electrotyped and printed by
Stanley & Usher, 171 Devonshire Street, Boston.

DEDICATION.

————

TO MY WIFE,

SARAH M. EELLS,

WHO has been my companion during these ten years of labor; who has cheered me, and made a Christian home for me to run into as into a safe hiding-place, and who has been an example to the Indians, — these pages are affectionately inscribed.

NOTE.

Much of the information contained in the following pages has been published, especially in *The American Missionary* of New York and *The Pacific* of San Francisco. Yet, in writing these pages, so much of it has been altered that it has been impracticable to give quotation-marks and acknowledgment for each item. I therefore take this general way of acknowledging my indebtedness to those publications.

PREFACE.

SAYS Mrs. J. McNair Wright: "If the church can only be plainly shown the need, amount, prospects, and methods of work in any given field, a vital interest will at once arise in that field, and money for it will not be lacking. The missionary columns in our religious papers do not supply the information needed fully to set our missions before the church. Our home-mission work needs to be 'written up.' The foreign field has found a large increase of interest in its labors from the numerous books that have been written, — *interestingly written*, — giving descriptions of the work, the countries where the missionaries toil, and the lives of the missionaries themselves. The Pueblo, the Mormon, and the American Indian work should be similarly brought before the church. A book gives a compact, united view of a subject; the same view given monthly or weekly in the columns of periodicals loses much of its force and, moreover, is much less likely to meet the notice of the young. A hearty missionary spirit will be had in our church only when we furnish our youth with more books on missionary themes." *

In accordance with these ideas the following pages have been written.

It is surprising to find how few books can be obtained on missionary work among the Indians. After ten years of effort the writer has only been able to secure twenty-six

* Among the Alaskans, pp. 271, 272.

books on such work in the United States, and five of these are 18mo. volumes of less than forty pages each. Only five of these have been published within the last fifteen years. Books on the adventurous, scientific, and political departments of Indian life are numerous and large; the reverse is true of the missionary department. Hence it is not strange that such singular ideas predominate among the American people in regard to the Indian problem. M. E.

Skokomish, Washington Territory, August, 1884.

CONTENTS.

INTRODUCTION.

THE Indians are in our midst. Different solutions of the problem have been proposed. It is evident that we must either kill them, move them away, or let them remain with us. The civilization and Christianity of the United States, with all that is uncivilized and un-Christian, is not yet ready to kill them. One writer has proposed to move them to some good country which Americans do not want, and leave it to them. We have been trying to find such a place for a century — have moved the Indians from one reservation to another and from one State or Territory to another; but have failed to find the desired haven of rest for them. It is more difficult to find it now than it ever has been, as Americans have settled in every part of the United States and built towns, railroads, and telegraph-lines all over the country. Hence no such place has been found, and it never will be.

Therefore the Indians are with us to remain. They are to be our neighbors. The remaining question is, Shall they be good or bad ones? If we are willing that they shall be bad, all that is necessary is for good people to neglect them; for were there no evil influences connected with civilization (!), they would not rise from their degradation, ignorance, and wickedness without help. When, however, we add to their native heathenism all the vices of intemperance, immorality, hate, and the like, which wicked men naturally carry to them, they will easily and quickly become very bad neighbors. Weeds will grow where nothing is cultivated.

If we wish them to become good neighbors, something must be done. Good seeds must be sown, watched, cultivated. People may call them savage, ignorant, treacherous, superstitious, and the like. I will not deny it. In the language of a popular writer of the day: "The remedy for ignorance is education;" likewise for heathenism, superstition, and treachery, it is the gospel. White people can not *keep* the civilization which they already have without the school and the church; and Indians are not so much abler and better that they can be raised to become good neighbors without the same.

Impressed with this belief, the writer has been engaged for the past ten years in missionary work

with a few of them in the region of Skokomish,
and here presents a record of some of the experiences. In the account he has recorded failures
as well as successes. In his earlier ministry,
both among whites and Indians, he read the
accounts of other similar workers, who often recorded only their success. It was good in its
place, for something was learned of the causes of
the success. But too much of this was discouraging. He was not always successful and sometimes wondered if these writers were ever disap-
pointed as much as he was. Sometimes when he
read the record of a failure it did him more good
than a record of a success. He took courage
because he felt that he was not the only one who
sometimes failed. The Bible records failures as
well as successes.

TEN YEARS AT SKOKOMISH.

I.

SKOKOMISH.

THE Skokomish Reservation is situated in the western part of Washington Territory, near the head of Hood's Canal, the western branch of Puget Sound. It is at the mouth of the Skokomish River. The name means "the river people," from *kaw*, a river, in the Twana language, which in the word has been changed to *ko*. It is the largest river which empties into Hood's Canal; hence, that band of the Twana tribe which originally lived here were called *the river people*. The Twana tribe was formerly composed of three bands: the Du-hlay-lips, who lived fourteen miles farther up the canal, at its extreme head; the Skokomish band, who lived about the mouth of the river, and the Kol-seeds, or Quilcenes, who lived thirty or forty miles farther down the canal. The dialects of these three bands vary slightly.

When the treaty was made by the United States in 1855, the land about the mouth of the Skokomish River was selected as the reservation ; the other bands in time moved to it, and the post-office was given the same name; hence, the tribe came to be known more as the Skokomish Indians than by their original name of Tu-án-hu, a name which has been changed by whites to Twana, and so appears in government reports.

The reservation is small, hardly three miles square, comprising about five thousand acres, nearly two thousand of which is excellent bottom land. As much more is hilly and gravelly, and the rest is swamp land. With the exception of the latter, it is covered with timber.

II.

PRELIMINARY HISTORY.

E VER since the Spanish traders and Vancouver in the latter part of the last century,
and the Northwest Fur Company and Hudson's
Bay Company in the early part of the present century, came to Puget Sound, these Indians have
had some intercourse with the whites, and learned
some things about the white man's ways, his Sabbath, his Bible, and his God. Fort Nisqually, one
of the posts of the Hudson's Bay Company, was
situated about fifty miles from Skokomish, so that
these Indians were comparatively near to it.

About 1850, Americans began to settle on Puget
Sound. In 1853 Washington was set off from Oregon and organized into a territory, and in 1855
the treaty was made with these Indians. Governor I. I. Stevens and Colonel M. C. Simmons
represented the government, and the three tribes
of the Twanas, Chemakums, and S'klallams were
the parties of the other part. The Chemakums
were a small tribe, lived near where Port Town-

send now is, and are now extinct. The S'klallams, or Clallams (as the name has since become),
lived on the south side of the Straits of Fuca,
from Port Townsend westward almost to Neah
Bay, and were by far the largest and strongest
tribe of the three. It was expected that all the
tribes would be removed to the reservation. The
government, however, was to furnish the means for
doing so, but it was never done, and as the Clallams and Twanas were never on very friendly
terms, there having been many murders between
them in early days, the Clallams have not come
voluntarily to it, but remain in different places in
the region of their old homes. The reservation,
about three miles square, also was too small for all
of the tribes, it having been said that twenty-eight
hundred Indians belonged to them when the treaty
was made. There were certainly no more.

The treaty has been known as that of Point-No-
Point, it having been made at that place, a few
miles north of the mouth of Hood's Canal on the
main sound, in 1855. It was, however, four years
later when it was ratified, and another year before
the machinery was put in motion, so that government employees were sent to the reservation to
teach the Indians. In the meantime the **Yakama**

War took place, the most wide-spread Indian war which ever occurred on this north-west coast, it having begun almost simultaneously in Southern Oregon, Eastern Oregon, and Washington, and on Puget Sound. The Indians on the eastern side of the sound were engaged in it, but the Clallams and Twanas as tribes did not do so, and never have been engaged in any war with the whites. They were related by marriage with some of the tribes who were hostile, and a few individuals from one or both of these tribes went to the eastern side of the sound and joined the hostiles, but as tribes they remained peaceable.

A WAR INCIDENT.

The Clallams were a strong tribe, and large numbers of them lived at an early day about Port Townsend. Here, too, was the Duke of York, who was for many years their head chief and a noted friend of the Americans. About 1850, he went to San Francisco on a sailing-vessel, and saw the numbers, and realized something of the power, of the whites. After his return the Indians became very much enraged at the residents of Port Townsend, who were few in numbers, and the savages were almost all ready to engage in war with them. Had they done so, they could easily have wiped out the place, and the white people knew it. The Indians were ready to do so, but the Duke of York stood between the Indians and the whites. For hours the savage mass surged to and fro, hungry for blood, the Duke of York's brother being among the number. For as many hours the Duke of York alone held them from going any farther, by his eloquence, telling them of the numbers and power of the whites; and that if the Indians should kill these whites, others would come and wipe them out. At last they yielded to him. He saved Port Townsend and saved his tribe from a war with the whites.

In 1860 the first government employees were sent to Skokomish, and civilizing influences of a kind were brought more closely to the Indians. With one or two exceptions, very little religious influence was brought to bear upon them. Of one of their agents, Mr. J. Knox, the Indians speak in terms of gratitude and praise. He set out a large orchard, and did considerable to improve them. In 1870, when all the Indians were put under the military, these Indians were put under Lieutenant Kelley. The Indians do not speak well of military rule. It was too tyrannical.

III.

EARLY RELIGIOUS TEACHING.

ABOUT 1850 Father E. C. Chirouse, a Catholic priest, came to Puget Sound, and for a time was on Hood's Canal. He had two missions among the Twanas, one among the Kolseed band, and the other among the Duhlaylips. He baptized a large number of them; made two Indian priests, and left an influence which was not soon forgotten. At a council held after a time by various tribes, the Skokomish and other neighboring tribes of the lower eastern sound were too strong for the Twanas and induced Father Chirouse to leave them. Not long afterward the Indians relapsed into their old style of religion, and on the surface it appeared as if all were forgotten : but when Protestant teachers came among them, and their old religion died, some of the Indians turned for a time to that Catholic religion which they had first learned, as one easier for the natural heart to follow than that of the Protestants.

From 1860 to 1871 but little religious instruction was given to these Indians. At different times Rev. W. C. Chattin, of the Methodist Episcopal Church, and Mr. D. B. Ward, of the Protestant Methodist Church, taught the school, and each endeavored to give some Christian teaching on the Sabbath, but they found it hard work, for Sabbath-breaking, house-building, trafficking, and gambling by the whites and the Indians were allowed in sight and hearing of the place where the services were held. "If it is wrong to break the Sabbath, why does the agent do so?" "If it is wrong to play cards and gamble, why do the whites do so?" These and similar questions were asked by the Indian children of their Christian teachers. It was somewhat difficult to answer them. It was more difficult to work against such influences. Still the seed sown then was not wholly lost. It remained buried a long time. I have seen that some of those children, however, although they forgot how to read, and almost forgot how to talk English, yet received influences which, fifteen or twenty years afterward, made them a valuable help to their people in their march upward.

In 1871, however, a decided change was made. In that year President Grant adopted what has been known as the peace policy, in which he as-

signed the different agencies to different missionary societies, asking them to nominate agents,
promising that these should be confirmed by the
Senate. While it was not expected that the government would directly engage in missionary work,
yet the President realized that Christianity was
necessary to the solution of the Indian problem,
and he hoped that the missionary societies who
should nominate these agents would become interested in the work, and encouraged them to send
missionaries to their several fields. These agents
were expected to coöperate with the missionaries
in their special work.

At that time the Skokomish Agency was assigned
to the American Missionary Association, a society
supported by the Congregationalists. In 1871
they nominated Mr. Edwin Eells as agent for this
place, who was confirmed by the Senate, and in
May of that year he took charge of these Indians.

Mr. Eells was the oldest son of Rev. C. Eells,
D.D., who came to the coast in 1838 as a missionary to the Spokane Indians, where he remained
about ten years, until the Whitman Massacre and
Cayuse War rendered it unsafe for him to remain
there any longer. The agent was born among
these Indians in July, 1841. Like most young

men on this coast, he had been engaged in various
callings. He had been a farmer, school-teacher,
clerk in a store, teamster, had served as enrolling
officer for government at Walla-Walla during the
war, and had studied law. At the age of fifteen
he had united with a Congregational church, and
had maintained a consistent Christian character.
All of these things proved to be of good service to
him in his new position, where education, farm-
work, purchase of goods, law business, intercourse
with government, the ideas which he had received
from his parents about the Indians and Christianity, were all needed.

In 1871, soon after he assumed his new duties,
he began a Sabbath-school and prayer-meeting.
He selected Christian men as employees. These
consisted of a physician, school-teacher, and matron,
carpenter, farmer, and blacksmith. He also selected men with families as being those who would
be likely to have the best influence on the Indians.
In 1872 Rev. J. Casto, M.D., was engaged as government physician, and Rev. C. Eells, the father
of the agent, went to live with his son, and both
during the winter preached at the agency and in
the camps of the Indians. During 1874 a council-
house was built, with the consent of government,

at a money-cost to the government of five hundred dollars — besides the work which was done by the government carpenter. This has since been used as a church, and sometimes as a school-house. During that spring it was thought best to organize a church, for although at first it would be composed chiefly of whites, yet it was hoped that it would have a salutary influence on the Indians, and be a nucleus around which some of the Indians would gather. This was done June 23, 1874, the day after the writer arrived at the place. It was organized with eleven members, ten of whom were whites, and one, John F. Palmer, was an Indian. He was at that time government interpreter. The sermon was by Rev. G. H. Atkinson, D.D., of Portland, superintendent of Home Missions for Oregon and Washington, and one of the vice-presidents of the American Missionary Association; the prayer of consecration by Rev. E. Walker, who had been the missionary associate of Rev. C. Eells during his work among the Spokane Indians; the right hand of fellowship by Rev. A. H. Bradford, a visitor on this coast from Montclair, New Jersey; and the charge to the church by the writer. Thus affairs existed when I came to the place.

IV.

SUBSEQUENT POLITICAL HISTORY.

AS far as the government was concerned, affairs remained much the same until 1880. Then the time agreed upon by the treaty for which appropriations were to be made — twenty years — expired. By special appropriation affairs were carried on for another year, however, as usual. In July, 1881, the government ordered that the carpenter, blacksmith, and farmer be discharged, and Indian employees be put in their places. Some of these were afterward discharged. The next year the three agencies on the sound, the Tulalip, Nisqually, and Skokomish, were consolidated enough to put them under one agent, without, however, moving the Indians in any way. The three agencies comprised ten reservations, which were under the missionary instruction of the Presbyterians, Congregationalists, and Catholics. By the consolidation there was to be no interference with the religious affairs of the Indians. Mr. E. Eells, the agent at Skokomish, was selected as the one who was to have charge of all, but his head-quarters were moved to the Tulalip Agency, which was under the religious control of the Catholics. Thus, after more than eleven years of residence at Skokomish, he departed from the place; after which he usually returned about once in three months on business. A year later this large agency was divided; the five Catholic reservations were set off into an agency, and the five Protestant reservations were continued under the control of Mr. Eells, whose head-quarters were moved to the Puyallup Reservation, near Tacoma.

V.

THE FIELD AND WORK.

THE work has been about as follows: At Skokomish there were about two hundred Indians, including a boarding-school of about twenty-five children. Services were held every Sabbath morning for them in Indian. The Sabbath-school was kept up, immediately following the morning service. English services were held once or twice a month, on Sabbath evening, for the white families resident at the agency and the school-children. On Thursday evening a prayer-meeting was held regularly. It was in English, as very few of the non-English-speaking Indians lived near enough to attend an evening service, had they been so inclined. Various other meetings were held, adapted to the capacities and localities of the people: as prayer-meetings for school-boys, those for school-girls, and those at the different logging-camps.

Thirty miles north of Skokomish is Seabeck, where about thirty Indians live, most of whom gain a living by working in the saw-mill there. For several years I preached to the whites at this place, about eight times a year, and when there, also held a service with the Indians.

Twenty miles farther north is Port Gamble, one of the largest saw-mill towns on the sound. Near it were about a hundred Clallam Indians, most of whom became Catholics, but who have generally received me cordially when I have visited them two or three times a year. They, however, have obtained whiskey very easily, and between this and the Catholic influence comparatively little has been accomplished.

Thirty-five miles farther on is Port Discovery, another saw-mill town, where thirty or forty Indians have lived, whom I have often called to see on my journeys ; but so much whiskey has been sold near them and to them, that it has been almost impossible to stop their drinking, and hence, very difficult to make much permanent religious impression on them. By death and removal for misconduct, their number has diminished so that at one time there were only one or two families left. But the opportunity for work at the mill has been so good that some of a fair class have returned and bought land and settled down.

Forty miles from Port Gamble, and seventeen from Port Discovery, is Jamestown, near Dunginess, on the Straits of Fuca. This is the center of an Indian settlement of about a hundred and forty. Previous to 1873 these Indians were very much addicted to drinking — so much so, that the white residents near them petitioned to have them removed to the agency, a punishment they dreaded nearly as much as any other that could be inflicted on them. The threat of doing this had such an influence that about fifteen of them combined and bought two hundred acres of land. It has been laid off into a village ; most of the Indians have reformed, and they have settled down as peaceable, industrious, moral persons. I have generally visited them once in six months, and they have become the most advanced of the Clallam tribe. A school has been kept among them, a church organized, and their progress has been quite interesting — so much so, that considerable space will be devoted to them in the following pages.

Once a year I have calculated to go farther : and twenty miles beyond is Port Angelos, with about thirty nominal Indian residents. But few of them are settlers, and they are diminishing, only a few families being left.

Seven miles further west is Elkwa, the home of about seventy Indians. It was, in years past, the residence of one of the most influential bands of the Clallam tribe, but they are diminishing, partly from the fact that there have been but few white families among them from whom they could obtain work, and, with a few exceptions, they themselves have done but little about cultivating the soil. As they could easily go across the straits to Victoria in British Columbia, about twenty miles distant, where there is little restraint in regard to their procuring whiskey, because they are American Indians, they have been steadily losing influence and numbers. Four or five families have homesteaded land, but as it was impossible for them to procure good land on the beach, they have gone back some distance and are scattered. Hence they lose the benefits of church and school. Still the old way of herding together is broken up, and they obtain more of their living from civilized pursuits.

Thirty-five miles farther is Clallam Bay, the home of about fifty more. This is the limit of the Indians connected with the Skokomish Agency. They are about a hundred and fifty miles from it, as we have to travel. In 1880

they bought a hundred and sixty acres of land
on the water-front, and are slowly following the
example of the Jamestown Indians. This is the
nearest station of the tribe to the seal-fisheries of
the north-west coast of the Territory; by far the
most lucrative business, in its season, which the
Indians follow.

VI.

DIFFICULTIES IN THE WAY OF
RELIGIOUS WORK.

(a) LANGUAGES.

ONE great difficulty in the missionary work is
the number of languages used by the people. The Clallams have one, the Twanas another;
about one sixth of the people on the reservation
had originally come from Squaxin, and spoke the
Nisqually; the Chinook jargon is an inter-tribal
language, which is spoken by nearly all the Indians, except the very old and very young, as far
south as Northern California, north into Alaska,
west to the Pacific Ocean, and east to Western
Idaho. It was made by the early traders, especially the Hudson's Bay Company, out of Chinook,
French, and English words, with a few from several other Indian languages, for use in trade. It
serves very well for this purpose, and is almost
universally used in intercourse between the whites
and Indians. Very few whites, even when married
to Indian women, have learned to talk any

Indian language except this. But it is not very good for conveying religious instruction. It is too meager. Yet so many different languages were spoken by the seven or eight hundred Indians connected with the agency that it seemed to be the only practicable one, and I learned it. I have learned to preach in it quite easily, and so that the Indians say they understand me quite well. The Twana language would have been quite useful, but it is said to be so difficult to learn that no intelligent Indian advised me to learn it. The Nisqually is said to be much easier, and one educated Indian advised me to learn it, but it did not seem to me to be wise, for while nearly all the Twana Indians understood it, as, in fact, nearly all the Indians on the upper sound do, yet it was spoken by very few on the reservation.

Hence I have often used an interpreter while preaching on the Sabbath at Skokomish, for then usually some whites, old Indians, and children were present who could not understand Chinook. At other times and places I constantly used the Chinook language. But a good interpreter is hard to obtain. "It takes a minister to interpret for a minister," was said when Mr. Hallenback, the evangelist, went to the Sandwich Islands, and there is much truth in it. The first interpreter I had was good at heart, but he used the Nisqually language. While most of them understood it, yet this person had learned it after he was grown, and spoke it, the Indians said, much like a Dutchman does our language. Another one, a Twana, cut the sentences short, so that one of the school-boys said he could have hardly understood all that I said had he not understood English. A third could do well when he tried, but too many times he felt out of sorts and lazy, and would speak very low and without much life. Hence sometimes I would feel like dismissing all interpreters, and talking in Chinook, but then I was afraid that it would drive away the whites, who could not understand it, but whose presence, for their examples' sake, I much desired. I feared also that it would drive away the very old ones, who sometimes made much effort to come to church, and also that the children, whose minds were the most susceptible to impressions, would lose all that was said. So there were difficulties every way.

The medley of services and babel of languages of one Sabbath are described as follows: The opening exercises were in English, after which was the sermon, which was delivered in English, but translated into the Nisqually language, and a prayer was offered in the same manner. At the close of the service two infants were baptized in English, when followed the communion service in the same language. At this there were present twelve white members of the Congregational church here, and one Indian; two white members of the Protestant Methodist church; one Cumberland Presbyterian, and one other Congregationalist. There were also present about seventy-five Indians as spectators. The Sabbath-school was held soon after, seventy-five persons being present. First, there were four songs in the Chinook jargon; then three in English, accompanied by an organ and violin. The prayer was in Nisqually, and the lesson was read by all in English, after which the lessons were recited by the scholars. Five classes of Indian children and two of white children were taught in English, and one class partly in English and partly in Chinook jargon. There was one Bible-class of Indian men who understood English, and were taught in that language, a part of whom could read and a part of whom could not, and another of about forty Indians of both sexes whose teacher talked

English, but an interpreter translated it into Nisqually ; and then they did not reach some Clallam Indians. Next followed a meeting of the Temperance Society, as six persons wished to join it. A white man who could do so, wrote his name, and five Indians who could not, touched the pen while the secretary made their mark. Three of these were sworn in English and two in Chinook. The whole services were interspersed with singing in English and Chinook jargon.

This was soon after I came here. During the past year we have often sung in English, Chinook jargon, Twana, and Nisqually, on the same Sabbath. Another medley Sabbath is given under the head of the Jamestown Church, in connection with its organization.

(*b*) THEIR RELIGION.

Another great difficulty in the way of their accepting Christianity is their religion. The practical part of it goes by the name of *ta-mah-no-us*, a Chinook word, and yet so much more expressive than any single English word, or even phrase, that it has almost become Anglicized. Like the *Wakan* of the Dakotas, it signifies the supernatural in a very broad sense. There are three kinds of it.

First. The Black Tamahnous. This is a secret
society. During the performance of the ceremonies connected with it, all the members black
their faces more or less, and go through a number
of rites more savage than any thing else they do.
They do not tell the meaning of these, but they
consist of starving, washing, cutting themselves,
violent dancing, and the like. It was introduced

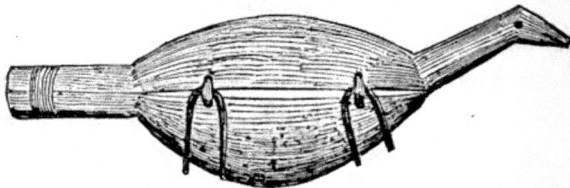

BLACK TAMAHNOUS RATTLE.

among the Twanas from the Clallams, who practised it with much more savage rites than the
former tribe. It is still more thoroughly practised by the Makahs of Cape Flattery, who join
the Clallams on the west. It was never as popular among the Twanas as among some other
Indians, and is now practically dead among them.
It still retains its hold among a portion of the
Clallams, being practised at their greatest gather-
ings. It is believed that it was intended to be
purifical, sacrificial, propitiatory.

Second. The Red, or Sing, Tamahnous. During the performance of its ceremonies, they generally painted their faces red. It was their main ceremonial religion. During the fall and winter they assembled, had feasts, and performed these rites, danced and sang their sacred songs; it might be for one night, or it might be for a week or so.

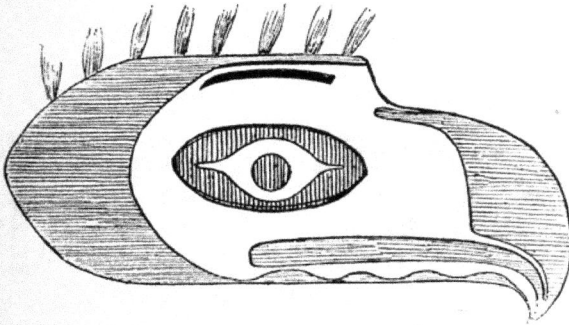

BIRD MASK USED IN THE BLACK TAMAHNOUS CEREMONIES BY THE CLALLAMS.

Sometimes this was done for the sake of purifying the soul from sin. Sometimes in a vision a person professed to have seen the spirits of living friends in the world of departed spirits, which was a sure sign that they would die in a year or two, unless those spirits could be brought back to this world. So they gathered together and with singing, feasting, and many ceremonies, went in spirit

to the other world and brought these spirits back.
This spirit-world is somewhere below, within the
earth. When they are ready to descend, with
much ceremony a little of the earth is broken, to
open the way, as it were, for the descent. Having
traveled some distance below, they come to a
stream which must be crossed on a plank. Two

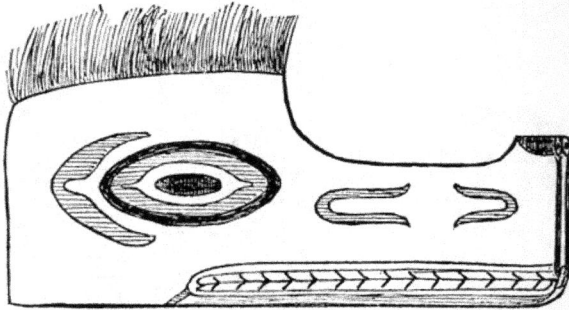

SWINE MASKS USED IN THE BLACK TAMAHNOUS CERE-
MONIES BY THE CLALLAMS.

planks are put up with one end on the ground and
the other on a beam in the house, about ten feet
above the ground, in a slanting direction, one on
one side of the beam, and the other on the other
side, so that they can go up on one side and down
on the other. To do this is the outward form of
crossing the spirit-river. If it is done successfully, all is well, and they proceed on their jour-

ney. If, however, a person should actually fall from one of these planks, it is a sure sign that he

MASK USED IN THE BLACK TAMAHNOUS CEREMONIES
BY THE CLALLAMS.

[The markings are of different colors. The wearer sees through the nostrils.]

will die in a year or so. They formerly believed this to be so, but about twelve years ago a man

did fall off, and did die within a year, so then they
were certain of it.   Having come to the place of
the departed spirits, they quietly hunt for the
spirits of their living friends, and when they find
what other spirits possess them, they begin battle

BLACK TAMAHNOUS MASK.

and attempt to take them and are generally successful.   Only a few men descend to the spirit-
world, but during the fight the rest of the people
present keep up a very great noise by singing,
pounding on sticks and drums, and in similar
ways encourage those engaged in battle.   Having

obtained the spirits which they wish, they wrap them up or pretend to do so, so that they look like a great doll, and bring them back to the world and deliver them to their proper owners, who receive them with great joy and sometimes with tears of gratitude.

At other times they go through other ceremonies somewhat different. This form has now mostly ceased among the Twanas, but retains its hold among a large share of the Clallams. The Christian Indians profess wholly to have given it up.

Third. The Tamahnous for the sick. When a person is very sick, they think that the spirit of some bad animal, as the crow, bluejay, wolf, bear, or similar treacherous creature, has entered the individual and is eating away the life. This has been sent by a bad medicine-man, and it is the business of the good medicine-man to draw this out, and he professes to do it with his incantations. With a few friends who sing and pound on sticks, he works over the patient in various ways.

This is the most difficult belief for the Indian to abandon, for, while there is a religious idea in it, there is also much of superstition connected with it. As the Indian Agent at Klamath, Oregon, once wrote: "It requires some thing more

than a mere resolution of the will to overcome
it." "I do not believe in it now," said a Spokane Indian, "but if I should become very sick, I
expect I should want an Indian doctor." It will
take time and education to eradicate this idea. It
is the only part of tamahnous, which I think an
Indian can hold and be a Christian, because it is
held partly as a superstition and not wholly as a
religion. Some white, ignorant persons are superstitious and, at the same time, are Christians.
The bad spirit which causes the sickness is called
a bad tamahnous. Soon after I first came here,
we spent several evenings in discussing the qualifications of church membership, the main difference of opinion centering on this subject of
tamahnous over the sick. I took the same position then that I do now, and facts seem to agree
thereto ; for, among the Yakamas, Spokanes, and
Dakotas, who have stood as Christians many
years through strong trials, have been some who
have not wholly abandoned it, it remaining apparently as a superstition and not a religion.

CHEHALIS JACK.

As an illustration of the reason why they still
believe in it, the following examples are given : —

Chehalis Jack is one of the most intelligent and civilized of the older uneducated Twana Indians. He has been one of those most ready to adopt the customs and beliefs of the whites ; has stood by the agent and missionary in their efforts to civilize and Christianize his people when very few other Indians have done so, and was one of the first of the older Indians to unite with the church. He was a sub-chief, and tried to induce his people to adopt civilized customs, setting them an example in building by far the best house erected by the Indians on the reservation, and in various other ways. He was told by some who opposed civilization that because of this some enemy would send a bad tamahnous into him and make him sick. In July, 1881, he was taken sick, evidently with the rheumatism, or some thing of the kind, and the threats which he had heard began to prey upon his mind, as he afterward said. Yet for six weeks he lived at his home a mile from the agency, and would have nothing to do with an Indian doctor. The agency physician attended him, and his rheumatism seemed to leave him, but he did not get well and strong. At last the physician said that he did not believe that any physician could find what was the matter with him. After

six weeks thus spent, by the advice of friends he
tried some Indian doctors on the reservation, but
some in whom he had little confidence. He grew
worse. He left the reservation for other Indian
doctors, twenty miles away, who said they could
cure him, but he did not recover. He came back
home, and imported another Indian doctor from
a hundred miles distant, but was not cured. We
were afraid that he would die, and it was plain to
several whites that he was simply being frightened
to death. I had long talks with him on the subject, and told him so, but could not convince him
of the truth of it. He said : "Tamahnous is true !
Tamahnous is true ! You have told us it is not,
but now I have experienced it, and it keeps me
sick." During the winter the agency physician
resigned, and another one took his place in March,
1882. Jack immediately sent for him, but failed
to recover. By the advice of white friends, who
thought they knew what was the matter with him,
he gave up his Indian doctor and tried patent
medicines for a time, but to no purpose. He left
his home, and moved directly to the agency, being
very near us, having no Indian doctor. Thus the
summer passed away and fall came. Intelligent
persons had sometimes said that if he could be

made to do some thing his strength would soon return to him, and he would find that he was not very sick. He had had fourteen cords of wood cut on the banks of the Skokomish River. There was no help that he could obtain to bring the wood to his house except a boy and an old man. He was much afraid that the rains would come, the river would rise, and carry off his wood. He left the agency and returned to his home, and had to help in getting his wood. About the same time he employed another Indian doctor in whom he seemed to have considerable confidence, and between the fact of his being obliged to work and his confidence in the Indian doctor, he recovered. It was the effect of the influence of the mind over the body. The principles of mental philosophy could account for it all, but he was not versed in those principles, and so thoroughly believes that a bad tamahnous was in him and that Old Cush, the Indian doctor, drew it out. Since that time he has worked nobly for civilization and Christianity — but his belief in tamahnous still remains in him. When the question of his joining the church came up, as nothing else stood in the way, I could not make up my mind that this superstition ought to do so, and after two and a half years of church membership the results have been such that I am satisfied that the decision was wise.

ELLEN GRAY.

She was a school-girl, about sixteen years of age, and had been in the boarding - school for several years, nearly ever since she had been old enough to attend, but her parents were quite superstitious. One Friday evening she went home to remain until the Sabbath, but on Saturday, the first of January, 1881, she was taken sick, and the nature of her sickness was such that in a few days she became delirious. Her parents and friends made her believe that a bad tamahnous had been put into her, and no one but an Indian doctor could cure her. They tamahnoused over her some. The agency physician, Dr. Givens, was not called until the sixth, when he left some medicine for her, but it is said that it was not given to her. Hence she got no better, and her friends declared that the white doctor was killing her. The agent and teacher did not like the way the affair was being manœuvered, took charge of her, moved her to a decent house near by, and placed white watchers with her, so that the proper medicine should be given, and no

Indian doctor brought in. The Indians were, however, determined, if possible, to tamahnous, and declared that if it were not allowed, she would die at three o'clock A.M. They kept talking to her about it and she apparently believed it, and said she would have tamahnous. But it was prevented, and before the time set for her death, she was cured of her real sickness. But she was not well. Still the next day she was in such a condition that it was thought safe to move her in a boat to the boarding-house, where she could be more easily cared for. The Indians were enraged and said that she would die before landing, but she did not. Watchers were kept by her constantly, but the Indians were allowed to see her. They talked, however, to her so much about her having a bad tamahnous, that all except her parents were forbidden to see her. They also were forbidden to talk on the subject, and evidently obeyed. But the effect on her imagination had been so great that, for a time, she often acted strangely. She seldom said any thing; she would often spurt out the medicine, when given her, as far as she could; said she saw the tamahnous; pulled her mother's hair, bit her mother's finger so that it bled, seemed peculiarly vexed at her; moaned most of the time, but sometimes screamed very loudly, and even bit a spoon off. Sometimes she talked rationally and sometimes she did not. But by the fifteenth she was considerably better, walked around with help, and sat up, when told to do so, but did not seem to take any interest in any thing. Every thing possible was done to interest her and occupy her attention, and she continued to grow better for three or four days more, so that the watchers were dispensed with, except that her parents slept in the room with her. But one night she threw off the clothes, took cold, and would not make any effort to cough and clear her throat ; and on the twenty-second, she died, actually choking to death. It was a tolerably clear case of death from imagination, easily accounted for on the principles of mental philosophy, but the Indians had never studied it, and still believe that a bad tamahnous killed her. I was afraid that this death would cause trouble, or, at least, that a strong influence against Christianity would result from it, but the certificates of allotment to their land came just at that time, which pleased them so much that the affair was smoothed over.

These and some other instances somewhat similar, though not quite so marked, have led me to make some allowances for the older Indians, which I would not make for whites. With small children, who were too young to have any such belief in tamahnous, I know of not a single instance like these mentioned. Indeed, the Indian doctors have been among the most unfortunate in losing their children, several of them having lost from five to ten infants each.

Some of the older uneducated Indians with the most advanced ideas have said lately that they were ready to give up all Indian doctors, and all tamahnous for the sick; still they would not acknowledge but that there was some spirit in the affair, but they said it was a bad spirit, of which the devil was the ruler, and they wished to have nothing to do with it.

One woman, as she joined the church, wished to let me have her tamahnous rattles, made of deer hoofs, for she said she was a Christian, had stopped her tamahnous, and would not want them any more. Still she thought that a spirit dwelt in them, only she thought it was a bad spirit. Hence she was afraid to have them remain in her house, for fear the spirit would injure her; for the same reason she was afraid to throw them away; she

was for the same reason afraid to give them to
any of her friends, even to those far away, and so
she thought that the best thing that could be
done with them was to let me take them, for she
thought I could manage them. I was willing, and
prize them highly because of the reason through
which I obtained them.

Other points in their religious belief did not
stand so much in the way of Christianity. They
believe in the existence of a Supreme Being,
though very different from that of the whites —
so much so, that the latter has not received the
name of the former; in a Deity called Do-ki-
batl by the Twanas, and Nu-ki-matl by the
Clallams, who became incarnate and did many
wonderful things; in man's sinfulness and immor-
tality; in the creation, renovation, and government
of the world by their great Beings; in a flood, or
deluge, the tradition of which has enough simi-
larity to that of the Bible to make me believe
that it refers to the same: while it has so much
nonsense in it as to show that they did not receive
it from the whites; in thanksgiving, prayer, sacrifices, and purification; in a place of happiness for
the soul after death, situated somewhere within
the earth, and in a place of future punishment,

also situated within the earth. The Clallams
believed that the Sun was the Supreme Deity,
or that he resided in the sun, but I have never
been able to discover any such belief among the
Twanas. They believe that the spirits dwell in
sticks and stones at times, and I have seen one
rough idol among the Twanas.

(c) BESETTING SINS.

The more prominent of these are gambling, betting, horse-racing, potlatches, and intemperance.

Gambling is conducted in three different native
ways, and many of the Indians have also learned
to play cards. The betting connected with horse-
racing belongs to the same sin. Horse-racing has
not been much of a temptation to the Clallams
because they own very few horses, their country
being such that they have had but little use for
them. Nearly all of their travel is by water. The
Twanas have had much more temptation in this
respect.

One of the native ways of gambling belongs to
the women, the other to the men : but there is far
less temptation for the women to gamble than
there is for the men, because summer and winter,
day-time and evening, there is always something

for them to do. But with the men it is different. The rainy season and the long winter evenings hang heavily on their hands, for they have very little indoor work. They can not read, and hence the temptation to gamble is great.

One mode of gambling by the men is with small round wooden disks about two inches in diameter. There are ten in a set, one of which is marked.

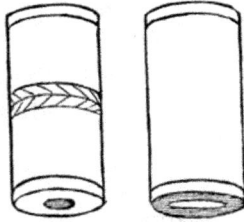

GAMBLING BONES.

Under cover they are divided, part of them under one hand and the rest under the other, are shuffled around, concealed under cedar-bark, which is beaten up fine, and the object of the other party is to guess under which hand the marked disk is.

The other game of the men is with small bones, two inches long and a half an inch in diameter, or sometimes they are two and a half inches long and an inch in diameter. Sometimes only one of the small ones is used, and sometimes two, one of which is marked. They are passed very quickly back and forth from one hand to the other, and the object is for the opposite party to guess in which hand the marked one is. An accompaniment is kept up by the side which is playing by singing and pounding on a large stick with smaller ones. With both of these games occasionally the large drum is brought in, and tamahnous songs are sung, so as to invoke the aid of their guardian spirits.

In the women's game usually four beaver's teeth are used, which have peculiar markings. They are rapidly thrown up, and the way in which they fall determines the number of counts belonging to the party playing. The principle is somewhat the same as with a game of dice.

BEAVER'S TEETH FOR GAMBLING OF WOMEN.

Formerly they bet large sums, sometimes every thing they owned, even to all the clothes they had, but it has not been the custom of late years. When Agent Eells first came to Skokomish, under orders from the Superintendent of Indian Affairs he tried to break up the gambling entirely, but there were hardly any Indians to sustain him in the effort. They would conceal themselves and gamble, do so by night, or go off from the reservation where he had no control, and carry on the game — so for a time he had to allow it, with some restrictions; that is, that the bets must be small, the games not often, but generally only on the Fourth of July, at great festivals, and the like. Occasionally they have had a grand time by gathering about all the Indians on the reservation together, both men and women, and perhaps for four days and nights, with very little sleep, have kept up the game.

On account of their want of employment in the winter and their inability to read, probably the sinfulness of this sin is not so great with them as with whites. Some good, prominent Indian workers have thought that it was hardly right to proscribe a Christian Indian from gambling. I learned of one Protestant church which admitted Indians without saying any thing on this subject, but which tried to stop it after they were in the church; but I could never bring myself to think that a church full of gambling Indians was right, and this became one of the test questions with the men in regard to admittance into the church.

When I first saw the infatuation the game possessed for them I felt that nothing but the gospel of Christ would ever stop it. Among the Clallams off of the reservation none except the Christians have given it up. On the reservation within the

Potlash House, Skokmish. — Page 57.

last few years so many of the Indians have become Christians that public opinion has frowned on it, and there is very little, if any, of it, though some of the Indians who do not profess to be Christians, when they visit other Indians, will gamble, although they do not when at home.

The *Potlatch* is the greatest festival that the Indian has. It is a Chinook word, and means "to give," and is bestowed as a name to the festival because the central idea of it is a distribution of gifts by a few persons to the many present whom they have invited. It is generally intertribal, from four hundred to two thousand persons being present, and from one to three, or even ten, thousand dollars in money, blankets, guns, canoes, cloth, and the like are given away. There is no regularity to the time when they are held. Three have been held at Skokomish within fifteen years, each one being given by different persons, and during the same time, as far as I know, a part or all of the tribe have been invited to nine others, eight of which some of them have attended.

The mere giving of a present by one person to another, or to several, is not in itself sinful, but this is carried to such an extreme at these times that the morality of that part of them becomes

exceedingly questionable. In order to obtain the
money to give they deny themselves so much for
years, live in old houses and in so poor a way, that
the self-denial becomes an enemy to health, comfort, civilization, and Christianity. If they would
take the same money, buy and improve land, build
good houses, furnish them, and live decently, it
would be far better.

But while two or three days of the time spent
at them is occupied in making presents, the rest
of the time, from three days to two and a half
weeks, is spent in gambling, red and black tamahnous, and other wicked practices, and the temptation to do wrong becomes so great that very
few Indians can resist it.

When some of the Alaska Indians, coveting the
prosperity which the Christian Indians of that
region had acquired, asked one of these Christians
what they must do in order to become Christians,
the reply was: "First give up your potlatches."
It was felt that there was so much evil connected
with them that they and Christianity could not
flourish together. Among the Twanas, while
they are not dead, they are largely on the wane.
Among a large part of the Clallams they still
flourish.

Intemperance is a besetting sin of Indians, and it is about as much a besetting sin of some whites to furnish intoxicating liquors to the Indians. The laws of the United States and of Washington Territory are stringent against any body's furnishing liquor to the Indians, but for a time previous to 1871 they had by no means been strictly enforced. As the intercourse of the Indians with the whites was often with a low class, who were willing to furnish liquor to them, they grew to love it, so that in 1871 the largest part of the Indians had learned to love liquor. Its natural consequences, fighting, cutting, shooting, and accidental deaths, were frequent.

VII.

TEMPERANCE.

IN 1871 the agent began to enforce the laws against the selling of liquor to the Indians, and, according to a rule of the Indian Department; he also punished the Indians for drinking. Missionary influence went hand in hand with his work, and good results have followed. For years very few Indians on the reservation have been known to be drunk. Punishment upon the liquor-drinker as well as the liquor-seller has had a good effect. Far more of the Clallams drink than of the Twanas. They live so far from the agent that he can not know of all their drinking, and, if he did, he could not go to arrest them all; and many of them live so close to large towns where liquor is very easily obtained, that it has been impossible to stop all of their drinking. Still his occasional visits, the aid of a few white men near them, and of the better Indians, together with what they see of the evil effects of intemperance on themselves, have greatly checked the evil. Very few complete reformations, however, have taken place among those away from the reservation, except those who have become Christians. In addition, a good share of the younger ones have grown up with so much less temptation than their parents had, and so much more influence in favor of temperance, that they have become teetotalers.

For a long time, beginning with 1874, a temperance society flourished, and nearly all the Indians of both tribes joined it. Each member signed the pledge under oath, and took that pledge home to keep, but in time it was found that the society had no penalty with which to punish offenders sufficient to make them fear much to do so again. The agent alone had that power — so the society died. But the law and gospel did not tire in the work and something has been accomplished.

The agent could tell many a story of prosecuting liquor-sellers; sometimes before a packed jury, who, when the proof was positive, declared the prisoner not guilty; of having Indian witnesses tampered with, and bought either by money or threats, so that they would not testify in court, although to him they had previously given direct testimony as to who had furnished them with the

liquor; of a time when some of the Clallam Indians became so independent of his authority that
they defied him when he went to arrest them,
and he was obliged to use the revenue-cutter in
order to take them, and when, in consequence, his
friends feared that his life was in danger from the
white liquor-sellers, because the latter feared the
result of their lawlessness; of a judge who,
although a Christian man, so allowed his sympathies to go out for the criminal that he would
strain the law to let him go; or, on the other
hand, of another judge who would strain the law
to catch a rascal; of convicting eight white men
at one time of selling liquor to Indians, only to
have some of them take their revenge by burning
the Indians' houses and all of their contents.
Still in a few years he made it very unsafe for
most permanent residents to sell intoxicating
liquors to the Indians, so that but few except
transient people, as sailors and travelers, dared to
do so.

"For ways that are dark and tricks that are
vain" the Indian and the liquor-seller can almost
rival the "heathen Chinee." A saloon is on the
beach, and so high that it is easy to go under it.
A small hole is in the floor under the counter.

A hand comes up with some money in it : after dark a bottle goes down, and some Indians are drunk, but nobody can prove any thing wrong.

An Indian takes a bucket of clams into a saloon and asks the bar-tender if he wishes them. " I will see what my wife says," is the reply, and he takes them to a back room. Soon he comes back and says : " Here, take your old clams, they are bad and rotten." The Indian takes them, and soon a company of Indians are " gloriously drunk," a bottle having been put in the bottom of the bucket. Sometimes a part of a sack of flour is made of a bottle of whiskey.

An Indian, having been taken up for drunkenness, was asked in court, in Port Townsend, where he obtained his liquor. " If I tell, I can not get any more," was the blunt reply. Others have found theirs floating in the river or lying by a tree, which may all have been true, yet some man who understood it was the gainer of some money, which perhaps he found. Many an Indian, when asked who let him have the liquor, has said : " I do not know ; " or, " I do not know his name."

Yet there are stories on the other side which make a brighter picture. In 1875 the Twana and Nisqually Indians met as they had often done during previous years for feasting, visiting, trading, and horse-racing. The first agreement was to meet on the Skokomish Reservation, but continued rains made the race-track on the reservation almost unfit for use, it being bottom land. There was another track on gravelly land about ten miles from Skokomish. On the Sabbath previous to the races the sermon had reference to the subject, because of the betting and danger of drunkenness connected with it. A Nisqually Indian came then and urged the Skokomish Indians to go to the other race-track at Shelton's Prairie, because the one at Skokomish was so muddy. The Skokomish Indians replied that they did not wish to go to the prairie for fear there would be whiskey there, but that they would go to work and fix their own track as well as they could. One sub-chief, the only one of the chiefs who had a race-horse, said he would not go there. This word was carried to the Nisqually Indians who were camped at the prairie, but they refused to come to Skokomish, and sent their messenger to tell the Skokomish Indians so. Several hours were occupied in discussing the question. In talking with the agent, the head-chief asked him if he would send one of the employees to guard them, should they decide to go to the prairie. The head-chief then went to the prairie and induced the Nisquallys to come to the reservation for the visit, trading, and marriage, which was to take place, and for the races if the track should be suitable. From Wednesday until Saturday was occupied by the Indians as agreed upon, but the weather continued rainy and the track was unfit for use. On Saturday the Nisqually Indians went back to the prairie and invited the Skokomish Indians to go there for the races. On Monday twenty-five or thirty of them went, but this number did not include a chief or many of the better class, the great fear being that they would be tempted to drink. According to the request of the chief, one white man from the reservation went, together with the regular Indian policemen. There were also present ten or twelve other white men from different places, one of whom carried considerable liquor. The Indian policemen on seeing this went to him and told him he must not sell or give any of it to any of the Indians, and he promised that he would not. He was afterward seen offering some to a Nisqually Indian, who refused. When night came it was found that, with three or four exceptions, all of the

white men present had drank some, and a few
were quite drunk, while it was not known that any
of the Indians present had taken any. That the
better class of Indians should not go to the races,
and that all should earnestly contend against
going to that place for fear of temptation ; that
they asked for a white man to guard them ; that
an Indian told a white man not to give liquor to
his fellow-Indians, and that, while most of the
white men drank some, it was not known that any
Indian drank at all, although it was not the
better class of Indians who were present, were
facts which were encouraging.

A sub-chief of the Clallam Indians, at Elkwa,
one hundred and twenty miles from the reservation, in 1878, found that an Indian from British
Columbia had brought a keg of liquor among his
people. He immediately complained before a
justice of the peace, who arrested the guilty man,
emptied his liquor on the ground, and fined him
sixty-four dollars.

The head-chief of the Clallams, Lord James
Balch, has for nine years so steadily opposed
drinking, and imprisoned and fined the offenders
so much, that he excited the enmity of the Indians, and even of their doctors, and also of some

white men, much as a good Indian agent does. Although he is not perfect, he still continues the good work. Fifteen years ago he was among the worst Indians about, drinking, cutting, and fighting.

In January, 1878, I was asked to go ninety miles, by both Clallams and Twanas, to a pot-latch, to protect them from worthless whites and Indians, who were ready to take liquor to the place. The potlatch was at Dunginess, given by some Clallams. I went, in company with about seventy-five Twanas, and it was not known that more than eight of them had tasted liquor within four years, although none of them professed to be Christians. During that festival, which continued nine days, and where more than five hundred Indians were present, only one Indian was drunk.

More than once a whiskey-bottle has been captured from an Indian, set out in view of all on a stump or box, a temperance speech made and a temperance hymn sung, the bottle broken into many pieces, and the contents spilled on the ground.

The Indians say that the Hudson's Bay Company first brought it to them, but dealt it out very sparingly, but when the Americans came they brought barrels of it. They seem to be proud that it is not the Indians who manufacture it, for if it were they would soon put a stop to it ; nor is it the believer in God, but wicked white men who wish to clear them away as trees are cleared from the ground.

Thus, when we take into consideration the condition of these Indians fifteen years ago, and the present condition of some other Indians in the region who lie beastly drunk in open sight, and compare it with the present status of those now here, there is reason for continued faith in the God of the law and gospel of temperance.

VIII.

INDUSTRIES.

L OGGING, farming in a small way, and work
as day-laborers, have been the chief means of
civilized labor among the men on the reservation.
A large share of their land is first-class, rich
bottom land, though all was covered originally
with timber. It had been surveyed, assigned to
the different heads of families, and certificates of
allotment from the government issued to them.
Nearly all of them have from one to ten acres
cleared, most of which is in hay.

Still when there has been a market for logs at
the neighboring saw-mills, they have preferred that
work, not because there is more money in it, for
actually there is less, but because they get the
money quicker. It comes when the logs are sold,
generally within three months after they begin
a boom. But in regard to their land, they must
work some time after they begin to clear it, before
it is done ; then a year or two longer, before they
can obtain much of a crop of hay from it. Hence

it has been up-hill work to induce most of them
to do much work at clearing land. For several
years before their annuities ceased, in 1881, the
government made a rule that no able-bodied man
should receive any annuities until he had performed labor on his land equal in value to the
amount he should receive. From the example of
the few adjoining settlers, some are beginning to
see that farming is more profitable than logging.
The largest share of good timber on the reservation has been taken off during the past twenty
years, so that now a number have bought timber
off the reservation for logging. They own their
own teams, keep their own time-books, and at
present attend to all their own business in connection with these camps. In one respect they
differ from white folks — in their mode of conducting the business. Instead of one or two men
owning every thing, hiring the men, paying all
expenses, and taking all the profits, they combine
together and unitedly share the profits or losses.
When the boom is sold, and all necessary
expenses which have been incurred are paid,
they divide the money among themselves according to the amount of work each has done. A few
have tried to carry on camps as white people do,
but have always failed.

Very few now pursue the old avocations of fishing and hunting, except the old ones. Nearly all the able-bodied men work at some civilized pursuit. Take a ride over the reservation on almost any pleasant day, and nearly all the men will be found to be busy at something.

In the winter, however, it is different. They have very little work for rainy days, and so there is more temptation to gamble and tamahnous. "Satan finds some mischief still for idle hands to do."

The women have less temptation than the men in winter. When they have no outdoor work, or it is stormy, they can sew, do housework, make mats and baskets, and all, even the very old ones, are commonly busy at some of these things. Some of them are good washerwomen and some are cooks in the logging-camps. They are by no means so near in a state of slavery as some Indian women in the interior, but are treated with considerable propriety by their husbands.

A few of the young men, after having been in school for a time, have been apprenticed to the trades of carpenter, blacksmith, and farmer, and have done so fairly, that they were employed by the government after the white employees were discharged.

The Clallams have done very little logging or farming. A number have obtained land at Port Discovery, Jamestown, Elkwa, and Clallam Bay, but only a little of it is first-class land, and they have used it for gardens and as a place for a permanent home, so that they should not be driven from one place to another, more than for farming. At Seabeck, Port Gamble, Port Townsend, and Port Discovery, they work quite constantly in the saw-mills; at Jamestown, for the surrounding farmers; at Port Angeles, Elkwa, and Clallam Bay, more of them hunt and fish than elsewhere. A number earn considerable money taking freight and passengers in their canoes. The obtaining of dog-fish oil is something of a business, as logging-camps use a large amount of it. In September there is employment at the Puyallup and surrounding region, about ninety miles from Skokomish, in picking hops. Hop-raising has grown to be a large business among the whites, and Indians have been preferred for picking the hops, thousands of whom flock there every year for the purpose, from every part of the Sound, and even from British Columbia and the Yakama country. Old people, women, and children do as well at this as able-bodied men. It has not, however, always been a healthy place for their morals, as on Sundays and evenings gambling, betting, and horse-racing have been largely carried on. At one time "The Devil's Playground," in the Puyallup Valley was noted as the place where Indians and low whites gathered on the Sabbath for horse-racing and gambling, but it became such a nuisance to the hop-growers, as well as to the agents, that they combined and closed it.

A part of the Clallams earn considerable money by sealing, off the north-west coast of the Territory, a very profitable business generally from January to May. In 1883 the taxes of those Clallams who live in Clallam County were $168.30.

IX.

TITLES TO THEIR LAND.

THE plow and the Bible go together in civilizing Indians," is the remark of Rev. J. H.
Wilbur, who for more than twenty years was one
of the most successful workers among them : but
neither Indians nor whites feel much like clearing
land and plowing it unless they feel sure that the
land is theirs.

When the treaty was made in 1855 it was the
understanding that whenever the Indians should
settle down on the reservation, adopt civilized
habits, and clear a few acres of land, good titles
would be given to them by the government. With
this understanding, not long after Agent Eells took
charge, he had the reservation surveyed and divided, so that each head of a family whose home
was on the reservation should have a fair portion.
He gave them papers, signed by himself, in 1874,
describing the land, with the expectation that the
government in a short time would give them good
titles, he having been thus assured by his supe-

riors in office. Other agents did the same. But new movements by the government with reference to the Indians are usually very slow, as they have no votes, and this was no exception. Agent Eells, as well as others, plead and plead time and again, to have this stipulation in the treaty fulfilled, but for a long time to no purpose. Often he had no reply to his letters. People of both political parties put this as a plank into their platform; those of all religions and no religion; those who opposed the peace policy as well as those who favored it, signed petitions to this effect, but in vain. This delay was the source of much uneasiness to the Indians, more, I think, than any other cause, for men were not wanting who told them that they would be moved away; there were plenty of people who coveted their land, and examples were not wanting of Indians who had been moved from place to place by the government. It has been the only thing which has ever caused them to talk about war. Some Indians left the reservation because they feared they would be moved away. "I am not going to clear land and fence it for the whites to use," was what one said and others felt.

When the treaty was made it was believed by

the Indians that they possessed all the land, and
that they sold all except the reservation, to which
they supposed they had a good title, at least as
good as the United States had, and white people
believed the same ; but a decision of the Supreme
Court of the United States in 1873 reversed this
idea, and they learned that they had sold all the
land, and that government graciously allowed
them to stay on the reservation according to its
will.   In the spring of 1875 they were forbidden
to cut a log and sell it off of the reservation, and
found that they had no rights to the land which
the government was bound to respect, but if she
wished to remove them at any time she could
do so.

The question came up early in missionary work.
The Indians said : " You profess to be Christians,
and you have promised us titles to our land. If
these titles come we will believe your religion to
be true, but if not it will be evidence that you are
deceiving us."

The agent worked nobly for the object, but
receiving no reply for a long time he grew almost
discouraged.   He could work in only one way, by
writing to his first superior officer, hoping that he
would successfully press the subject upon those
more influential.

About this time, in 1878, I determined to see what I could do through another channel : through the Board of Indian Commissioners, where missionaries would naturally look. Accordingly, in May, a long letter was written to the secretary of the American Missionary Association, and his influence was invoked to work upon the Board. He gladly did so. At the annual meeting of the Congregational Association of Oregon and Washington, in June of the same year, I plead strongly for the same object, whereupon a committee of five of the influential men of the denomination was appointed, who drafted strong resolutions, which were passed and sent to the Board of Commissioners. The fact that the Bannack Indians of Eastern Oregon were then engaged in a war with the whites, and that they had attempted to induce the Indians of Puget Sound to assist in it, was an argument used, and of no small weight. I intended to urge the passage of similar resolutions through the Presbytery of Puget Sound, and the Methodist Episcopal Conference of Oregon, both of whom had missions among the Indians, and were asking for similar favors from the government ; but before those bodies met I received a letter from Hon. D. H. Jerome, of the Board of

Commissioners, who had been appointed a committee by that Board in regard to titles of Indians to
their lands, promising to press the matter upon
the department until titles should be issued, or a
good reason given for not doing so, and requesting
a description of the lands for which titles were
asked.   I gave the letter to the agent, who had
the desired information, and who quickly gave it.
The Board nobly fulfilled its promise, and in
March, 1881, certificates of allotment were sent
to the Indians.   They were not wholly satisfac-
tory.   The title to the land still remained in the
United States.   They said that each Indian is
entitled to take possession of his land, "and the
United States guarantees such possession, and will
hold the title thereto in trust for the exclusive use
and benefit of himself and his heirs so long as
such occupancy shall continue."   It prohibited
them from selling the land to any one except
other members of the same tribe.

These certificates, however, proved to be better
than was at first feared.   It was decided that
under them the Indians had a right to sell the
timber from the land.   The Indians were satisfied
that they would not be removed, and were quieted.

Efforts are still being made to obtain the patents,

and with considerable hope of success, as they have been granted to Indians on three other reservations on Puget Sound through the efforts of Agent Eells, but owing to various causes they have not been obtained as yet for the Skokomish Indians.

The Clallam Indians have bought their land or taken it by homestead, and so have not had the same difficulty in regard to titles. One incident, however, occurred which was rather discouraging. Four of the Clallam Bay Indians, in 1879, determined to secure, if possible, the land on which their houses stood. They were sent to the clerk of the Probate Court, who knew nothing about the land, but told them that it belonged to the government, and offered to get it for the usual fee, nineteen dollars each. They paid him the seventy-six dollars, and he promised to send it to the land-office and have their papers for them in two weeks. They waited the two weeks but no papers came. In the meantime they learned that the man was not to be trusted, although he could lawfully attend to the business, and that the land had been owned by private individuals for fifteen years. He, too, on writing to the land-office, found the same to be true. But the difficulty was

to get the money back. This man was an invet-
erate gambler, and the evidence was quite plain
that he had gambled the money off very soon
after he received it. I saw him soon afterward,
and he told me that it had been stolen, that he
would soon get it, and the like. One Indian
spent three weeks, and two others two weeks
each, in trying to recover it, but failed to do so.
Then the agent took it into court, but through an
unjust ruling of the judge, or a catch in the law,
he was neither compelled to pay it nor punished
for his deed. The Indians received about the
amount they lost, as witness fees and mileage for
their attendance on court. Yet that man, at that
time, was also postmaster, United States commissioner, and deputy sheriff, and had offered fifty
dollars to the county treasurer, to be appointed
his deputy.

This was a strange contrast to the action of the
Indians. I felt very sorry for them. For four
years we had been advising them to obtain land,
and they were swindled in their first attempt.
When I saw them, before the case was taken
to the court, I was fearful lest they should
become discouraged, and offered them ten dollars,
saying, " If you never get your money, I will lose

this with you: but if you do obtain it, you can then repay me." One tenth of my income has long been given to the Lord, and I felt that thus much would do as much good here as anywhere. When I first mentioned this to them, they refused to take it, saying that they did not wish me to lose my money, if they did theirs; but two weeks later, when I left the last one of them, he reluctantly took it.

X.

MODE OF LIVING.

IN 1874 most of the Indians of both tribes lived on the ground, in the smoke, in their large houses, where several families resided. That year the agent induced those on the reservation to receive lumber as a part of their annuity goods, and the government carpenter erected small frame-houses for most of them, but left them to cover and batten the houses. They were slow to do so. At first they used them to live in during the summer, but during the winter they found these houses too open and cold and returned to their smoke-houses. It was two or three years before they made them warm enough to winter in them, but since that time nearly all, except a few of the very old ones, have lived off of the ground and out of the smoke. Although the government gave no aid to those living off of the reservation to build them homes, yet about three fourths of them have built for themselves similar or better houses. Many of them have lived near saw-mills where they could easily get lumber for their houses.

All of them dress in citizen's clothes, and they obtain about three quarters of their living from civilized labor, and the rest by fishing and hunting, supposing that hunting and fishing are not civilized pursuits. Many of them have sewing-machines, bureaus, and lace curtains, while clocks and watches, chairs, bedsteads, and dishes, tables, knives and forks are very common.

Neatness. — It is easier to induce them to have good houses, with board floors, than to keep them clean. Grease is spilled on the floor, and, mingling with the dirt, sometimes makes the air very impure. The men are careless, bring in dirt, and spit on the floor; the women are sometimes lazy, or else, after trying, become discouraged about keeping the house clean.

This impure air has been the cause of the death of many of their children. They breathe the poison, and at last waste away. The older ones are strong and can endure some of it, and, moreover, are in the pure air outdoors much of the time. But the little ones are kept in the house, are so weak that they can not endure such air, and they die. The old Indian houses on the ground had, at least, two advantages over the board floors, although they had more disadvantages. The

ground absorbed the grease, as boards can not ;
and, if the houses became too bad, they could
easily be torn down and moved a few yards away
to a better place.   But good houses are too costly
for this.

Time, teaching, and example have, however,
worked some changes for the better.   There are
many of the Indian women who wash, at least,
the floors of their front rooms every week.   Still
the bedrooms, which are not likely to be seen, are
often topsy-turvy, and the kitchens often have a
bad smell, and the back door needs lime and
ammonia.   Occasionally, however, a house is
found where there is a fair degree of neatness
all the way through.

XI.

NAMES.

WHITE people do not usually take kindly to the jaw-breaking Indian names, hence a "Boston" name has generally been given them. But the white men who lived around Skokomish were mostly loggers, who among themselves went by the name of Tom, Jack, Jim, and the like, and seldom put Mr. to any body's name. As the Indians mingled with them they received similar names, and as there soon came to be several of the same name, they were distinguished by some prefix, usually derived from some characteristic — their size, or the place from which they came. So we had Squaxon Bill, Chehalis Jack, Dr. Bob, Big John, Little Billy, and the like. These were bad enough, but when their children came to take these as their surnames, they sometimes became comical, for we had Sally Bob, Dick Charley, and Sam Pete. Therefore, we soon found that it was best to give every school-child a decent name, and Bill's son George became George Williams,

and John's boy became Henry Johnson, and
Billy's daughter was Minnie Williamson, and so
on.   At first, when the older ones were married,
it was done with the old Indian nickname, but I
soon thought that if in time they were to become
Americans they might as well have decent names.
So, at their first legal recognition, as at their
marriage, baptism, or on entering school, they
received names of which they had no need to be
ashamed in after years.

EDUCATION.

THIS has been conducted entirely by the government, but generally in such a way as to be a handmaid to religion. On the reservation a boarding-school has been kept up during the ten years of missionary labor, as well as many years before, for about ten months in the year. About half of the time, including the winter, the school has been kept six hours in the day, and during the rest of the time for three hours ; the scholars being required to work the other half of the day — the boys in the garden getting wood and the like, and the girls in the house sewing, cooking, housekeeping, and doing similar things.

The position of the one in charge has been a difficult one to fill, for it has been necessary that the man be a teacher, disciplinarian, handy at various kinds of work, a Christian, and, during the last year and a half after the agent left, he had charge of the reservation ; while it was almost as necessary that his wife be matron, with all the

qualifications of taking care of a family of from
twenty to forty. It has been difficult to find all
these qualifications in one man and his wife, who
were willing to take the position for the pay which
the government was willing to give, for during the
later years the pay was cut down to the minimum.
It has not been strange that with all the burdens
frequent changes have taken place. There have
been seven teachers in the ten years, but most of
them were faithful, some of them serving until
their health failed. Yet the school has been carried on generally in as Christian a way as if the
Missionary Society had had charge of it. All of
the teachers and their wives have been Christians
— not all Congregationalists; for it has been
often impossible to obtain such; in fact, only three
have been; but there has been a plain understanding with the others that they should teach
nothing in regard to religion which conflicted with
the teachings from the pulpit — an understanding
which has been faithfully kept, with one exception.
In 1874 the school numbered about twenty-four
scholars, but it gradually increased until it numbered about forty, which was more than all the
children of school age on the reservation, though
it did not include many of the Clallams. They

were so far away that it was not thought wise to compel them to remain so steadily so far away from their parents year after year.

The school has been a boarding-school, for nearly all the children lived from one to three miles away, and it has been impossible to secure any thing like regular attendance if they lived at home, while some have come from ten to seventy miles distant.

Attendance on school has been compulsory — the proper way among Indians. While the parents speak well about the school, and say that they wish to have their children educated, yet, when the children beg hard to stay at home, parental government is not strong enough to enforce attendance, especially as long as the parents do not *realize* the value of education. The children have not all liked to go to school, and at first some of them ran away. The agent and his subordinates could tell some stories of getting runaway children, by pulling them out of their beds, taking them home in the middle of the night, and the like. In this respect the government had the advantage of a missionary society, which could not have compelled the children to attend school.

There was no provision in the treaty for more than one school, and that on the reservation. But after the Clallams at Jamestown had bought their land, laid out their village, built their church, and become somewhat civilized, they plead so hard for a school, offering the use of the church-building for the purpose, that the government listened to them, and in 1878 sent them a teacher. This was a day-school, because funds enough were furnished to pay only a teacher, and nearly all the children lived in the village within less than a half-mile from the school. A very few of the children walked daily five or six miles to school, and some of the better families of the village did nobly in making sacrifices to board their relations, when the parents would not furnish even the food for their children. This school has varied in numbers from fifteen to thirty children, and has been conducted in other respects mainly on the same principles as the one on the reservation. It has been of great advantage to the settlement.

A few of the rest of the Clallam children, whose parents were Catholics, have sent their children to a boarding-school at Tulalip, a Catholic agency, and others have not gone to school, there being difficulties in the way which it has been almost or quite impossible to overcome.

The schools have been conducted entirely in English. This is the only practicable plan, for the tribes connected with the school speak three different languages, and it is impossible to have books and newspapers in their languages, while teachers can not be found who are willing to acquire any one of these languages sufficiently well to teach it. It is also the only wise plan. If the Indian in time is to become an American citizen, — and that is the goal to be reached, — he must speak the English language, and it is best to teach it to him while young. In large tribes like the Sioux, where the children will speak their native language almost wholly after they leave school, and where there are enough of them to make it pay to publish books and papers in their own tongue, it is probably best to have the schools in their native language, as a transition from one language to the other. This transition will necessarily take a long time among so large a number of Indians, and needs the stepping-stone of native schools and a native literature to aid it. But where the Indian tribes are small, as is the case on Puget Sound, and surrounded by whites with whom they mingle almost daily, who are constantly speaking English to them, this stepping-

stone is not needed. It is possible for the next
generation to be mainly English-speaking in this
region ; in fact, most of them will understand it
whether they go to school or not, and it is not
wise, were it possible, to retard it by schools in
the native language.

CORRECTING THOMSON'S PRACTICAL ARITHMETIC.

An incident occurred in the school, in 1878,
worthy of note. One of the scholars in arithmetic found four examples which he could not do,
and after a time took them to his teacher, Mr.
G. F. Boynton, for assistance. After the teacher
(who was a good scholar) had tried them to his
satisfaction, he found that there was a mistake
about the answers in the book and told the boy
so, and then, in a half-joking way, said to him :
"You had better write Dr. Thomson and tell him
about it." The boy did so, telling also who he
was. In due time he received a reply from Dr.
Thomson, who said that two of the mistakes had
been discovered and corrected in later editions,
but that the other two had not before been found ;
and then he wondered how an Indian boy out in
Washington Territory should be able to correct
his arithmetic. He invited the boy to continue
the correspondence, but I believe he never did.

XIII.

THE FOURTH OF JULY.

THIS day has always been celebrated in some way, at least by a dinner. During the first few years the agent furnished the beef and most of the provisions at government expense. On the Fourth of July, 1874, among other exercises, I married seven couples ; on the next Fourth, three couples, and in 1878 four more. Speech-making by some of the whites, explaining the day, and music were interspersed. Long tables have usually been made, on which were dishes, knives, and forks, while beef, bread, tea, coffee, sugar, cake, pie, rice, beans, doughnuts, and such things were the principal food.

It was not until 1878 that they took upon themselves the main burden of the day, both of expense and labor, and since that time they have furnished both. The following, from the *Tacoma Herald* of July, 1879, will answer for

THE FOURTH OF JULY ON SKOKOMISH RESERVATION.

"Among the Indians, from all appearances, the Fourth of July will probably in time take the place of the potlatch. The latter is spoken of by their white neighbors as being so foolish, while the former is held in such high esteem ; and as Indians, like others, enjoy holidays and festivals, it now seems as if the potlatch would be merged into the Fourth, changed a little to suit circumstances and civilization. The potlatch has always been given by a few individuals to invited guests and tribes, presents of money and other things being made to those who came, while in return a great name and honorable character was received, It lasts several days or weeks and is accompanied by gambling, feasting, tamahnous, and the like.

"The Fourth of July on the Skokomish Reservation began about a week beforehand and so lasted as long as a short potlatch. The Nisqually and Puyallup Indians, having resolved to have celebrations of their own, the attendance was smaller than it otherwise would have been. The Chehalis Indians came a full week before the Fourth in wagons and on horseback, while those from Squaxon, Mud Bay, and Seabeck came between that time and the Fourth. A few of the Skokomish Indians were at the head of the celebration, bore most of the' expense, and received most of the honor. Other Indians besides these few, however, occasionally invited all the visitors to a feast.   The guests, on arriving at Skokomish, brought more or less food with them, — much as at a potlatch, only on a smaller scale, — and they were received with less ceremony.   A table a hundred feet long was made in a pleasant shady grove, and here for more than a week — when the guests were not invited to the house of some friend to a meal — they feasted on beef, beans, rice, sugar, tea, coffee, and the like : sitting on benches, eating with knives, forks, and dishes, and cooking the food on two large stoves brought to the grounds for the purpose ; visiting, horse-racing, and other sports filled up the rest of the time.

"The Fourth was the central day of the festival and was celebrated in much the same style with the other days, only on a larger scale, there being more Indians present, more flags flying, more firing of guns, and more whites on the grounds. By invitation the whites on the reservation were present and were assigned to a very pleasant place on the grounds, where they might have had tables if they had done as the Indians did : made them for themselves ; but, as it was, they picnicked on the ground, while their colored brethren sat at the tables.   A few white men, rather the worse for

liquor, visited the horse-races after the dinner;
but not an Indian is known to have tasted liquor
during the week."

The Clallam Indians seldom have celebrations
of their own. They usually attend those of the
whites near them, often being invited to take part
in canoe-races. There has always been much
drunkenness among the whites at these times;
the Indians have often been sorely tempted to do
the same, and many of them have fallen then who
seldom have done so at other times.

The Fourth of July, 1884, in many respects has
the best record at the reservation. It was indeed
not the greatest, most expensive, or most numer-
ously attended. As the leading ones had decided
not to have any horse-racing or betting, the
younger ones thought that they could have no celebration, and it was only the day before that they
decided to have one. It consisted of a feast, after
which they went to the race-track. I felt fearful
that some professing Christians would fall, but
thought it not best for me to go near that place,
but leave them and await the result. When the
report came, it was that, while they had some fun
with their horses, hardly any of which was regular
racing, not a cent had been bet by any one.

XIV.

CHRISTMAS.

THIS day has been celebrated with as much
regularity as the Fourth of July, but the
former remains yet as our affair, while the latter
has passed into their hands. They have no building large enough to contain much of a celebration
of the day. The church is at the agency, and is
the most suitable building for the purpose, and
the exercises naturally center around the school,
so the older Indians come to us on Christmas, and
we go to them on the Fourth.

Usually there have been some speeches made,
and presents from the government, school-supplies
to the Indian school-children. Private presents
have been made among the whites, but it has
only been during the last two or three years that
the outside Indians have taken much interest in
this custom of ours. Indeed, during the first few
years generally but few of them were present.
It was far from their homes, the nights were
dark, the roads muddy, so that they did not take

much interest in it, but as the first school-children have grown up they have kept up the idea they received in school, and imparted it to others, and of late years a good share of them have been present.   On Christmas 1882 and 1883 they made quite a number of private presents; more on the last one than ever before.   Usually nuts and candy have been provided from contributions by the whites, and apples which are raised at the agency for the older Indians.   A Santa Claus Christmas-tree, or something of the kind, has been the usual way for distributing the presents.   The report of the Sabbath-school for the year has been a central item in the exercises, showing the attendance, the number of times each has been on the roll of honor, with the distribution of some extra present to those who have been highest on this roll.

In 1878 quite an exhibition was made by the school, consisting of pieces spoken, dialogues, compositions, tableaux, and the like.   In 1879 I arranged so that about twenty of the aged Indians, who had neither land nor good houses, came to the agency and had a dinner of rice, beans, bread, and tea.   This was new to them, they generally being the neglected ones, but I thought it to be according to the principles of the New Testament.

The celebration for 1883 suited me better than any previous one in many respects. The first part of the exercises were more of a religious service than usual — more of a celebration of Christ's birth. This idea suited also the minds of the Indians better than to have it mainly consist of sport. The Indian girls did nearly all the singing and playing, six of them playing each one piece on the organ. The year before three of them had done so, but this year it was still better. Then five of the older Indians made speeches, including two of the chiefs and two of the young men who had been in school. This was new for them on this day. More of the Indians also made private presents than ever before. Thus they took up the work, as the whites who previously had done it had been discharged, and it is better for them to do so.

The people at Jamestown for several years have had a celebration of their own, consisting often of a Christmas-tree, and they have borne the whole expense. I have never been present, but they have always been spoken of as enjoyable affairs, a good number of the surrounding whites feeling that it was a pleasant place for them to spend the evening.

XV.

VARIETY.

"JACK-AT-ALL-TRADES and good at some"
was the pleasant way in which Dr. Philip
Schaff put it, when some of the students in the
Theological Seminary at Hartford, Connecticut,
had done up some furniture for him, to send to
New Haven. I have often been reminded of this,
as I have had, at times, to take up a variety of
work. Missionaries among the Indians have to be
the first part of the sentence and console themselves with the hope that the latter part may
sometimes prove true.

On one tour among the Clallams, I find the
following: When three miles from home, the first
duty was to stop and attend the funeral of a white
man. Forty-five miles on, the evening of the
next day until late at night, was spent in assisting
one of the government employees in holding
court over four Indians, who had been drunk; a
fifth had escaped to British Columbia and was
safe from trial. This kind of business occasion-

ally comes in as an aid to the agent. I seldom
have any thing to do with it on the reservation,
as the agent can attend to it ; but when off from
the reservation, where neither of us can be more
than once in six months or thereabouts it sometimes saves him much trouble and expense, and
seems to do as much good as a sermon. It is
of but little use to preach to drunken Indians,
and a little law sometimes helps the gospel.
The agent reciprocates by talking gospel to them
on the Sabbath on his trips.

On reaching Jamestown, the afternoon was
spent in introducing an Indian from British
Columbia, who had taken me there in his canoe,
to the Clallam Indians and the school ; and in
comforting two parents, Christian Indians, whose
youngest child lay at the point of death. The
next day she died, and, as no minister had ever
been among these Indians at any previous funeral,
they needed some instruction. So it was my duty
to assist in digging the grave and making the
coffin, comfort them, and attend the funeral in a
snow-storm.

The Sabbath was spent in holding two services
with them, one of them being mainly a service of
song ; and, as there was a part of the day unoc-

cupied, at the request of the whites near by I
gave them a sermon. The next day I found that
"Blue Monday" must be adjourned. Years ago
the Indians purchased their land, but owing to a
mistake of the surveyor, it was necessary that the
deeds should be made out again. So, in order to
get all the Indians together who were needed,
with the proper officer, I walked fourteen miles,
rode six in a canoe, and then, after half-past three
o'clock, saw that nineteen deeds were properly
signed, which required sixty - two signatures,
besides the witnessing, acknowledging, and filing
of them, which required seventy-six more signatures. The plat of their town — Jamestown — was
also filed and recorded. When this was done, I
assisted the Indians to obtain two marriage-
licenses, after which we went to the church,
where I addressed them on two different subjects,
and then the two weddings took place, and by
nine o'clock we were done.

The monotony of the next day was varied by a
visit to the school ; helping the chief to select a
burying-ground (for their dead had been buried in
various places) ; a walk of ten miles and a wedding of a white couple, who have been very kind
to me in my work there, one of them being a
member of the Jamestown church.

On my way home, while waiting for the steamers to connect at Port Gamble, I took a trip of about fifty miles, to Port Madison and back, to help in finishing the Indian census of 1880 for General F. A. Walker and Major J. W. Powell; and then on my way home, by the kindness of the captain of the steamer, who waited half an hour for me, I was able to assist the chief in capturing and taking to the reservation the fifth Indian at Port Gamble who had been drunk, and had, by that time, returned from the British side.

The variety of another trip in 1878 is thus recorded : As to food, I have done my own cooking, eaten dry crackers only for meals, been boarded several days for nothing, and bought meals. As to sleeping, I have stayed in as good a bed as could be given me for nothing, and slept in my own blankets in an Indian canoe, because the houses of the whites were too far away and the fleas were too thick in the Indian houses. They were bad enough in the canoe, but the Indians would not allow me to go farther away, for fear that the panthers would catch me. As to work, I have preached, held prayer-meetings, done pastoral work, helped clean up the streets of

Jamestown, been carpenter and painter, dedicated
a church, performing all the parts, been church
organist, studied science, acted for the agent, and
taken hold of law in a case where whiskey had
been sold to an Indian, and also in making a will.
As to traveling, I have been carried ninety miles
in a canoe by Indians, free, paid an Indian four
dollars for carrying me twenty miles, have been
carried twenty more by a steamer at half-fare, and
twenty more on another for nothing, have rode on
horseback, walked fifty miles, and "paddled my
own canoe" for forty-five more.

I have never had a vacation since I have been
here, unless such things as these may be called
vacation. They are recreation, work, and vacation, all at once. They are variety, and that is
rest, the vacation a person needs, with the satisfaction that a person is doing something at the
same time.

XVI.

MARRIAGE AND DIVORCE.

THE Indian idea of the marriage bond is that
it is not very strong. They have been accustomed to get married young, often at fourteen
or sixteen years of age, to pay for their wives in
money and articles to the value of several hundred
dollars, and the men have had, oftentimes, two
or three wives.

When they married young, in order that two
young fools should not be married together, often
a boy was married to an elderly woman, and a
young girl to an elderly man, so that the older
one could take care of the younger, with the expectation that when the younger one should grow
older if they did not like each other they should
be divorced.

Such ideas naturally did not suit the government, the agent, or the Bible. The agent has had
about all the children of school age in school, and
thus had control of them, so that they could not
get married as young as formerly. In 1883 the

government sent word to prevent the purchase of any more wives, and this has been generally acquiesced in by the Skokomish Indians. Some of the Clallam Indians, however, are so far from the agent, and are so backward in civilization, that it has not been possible to enforce these two points among them as thoroughly as among the Twanas.

The Commissioner of Indian Affairs, in his report for 1878, recommended the passage of a law compelling all Indians who were living together as man and wife to be married. The law has not been made, but the agent worked on the same principles long before 1878 — indeed ever after he first took charge in 1871. He urged them to be married, making for a time special presents from government annuities to those who should consent, as a shawl or ladies' hat, and some consented. Only two couples had been thus married when I went there. It seemed rather comical on the Fourth of July, 1874, when I had been on the reservation only about two weeks, to be asked to join in marriage seven couples, some of whom had children. One Sabbath in 1883 a couple stood up to be married, the bride having a baby in her arms, and she would probably have held it during the ceremony had not my wife whispered to a sister of the bride to go and get it. During the ten years I have married twenty-six couples among the Twanas, and twenty-nine couples among the Clallams, and a number of other Clallams have been married by other persons. Some very comical incidents have occurred in connection with some of these ceremonies. In 1876 I was called upon to marry eleven couples at Jamestown. All went well with the first ten, the head chief being married first, so that the others might see how it was done, and then nine couples stood up and were married with the same set of words. But the wife of the other man was sick with the measles. She had taken cold and they had been driven in, but had come out again, so that she was as red as a beet. Still they were afraid that she would die, and as I was not to be there again for several months they were very anxious to be married so as to legalize the children. She was so near death that they had moved her from their good house to a mat-house, which was filled with smoke. The fire was thrown out, and soon it became less smoky. She was too sick to stand, and only barely able to sit up. This, however, she managed to do in her bed, which was on the ground. Her husband sat beside her and took her hand, and I married them, measles and all. She afterward recovered.

At another time I married a couple who had homesteaded some land, and who had been married in Indian style long before. As they had never seen such a ceremony I took the man aside and explained it to him as well as I was able. After I had begun the ceremony proper, and had said the words : "You promise to take this woman to be your wife," and was ready to say : "You promise to love and take care of her," he broke out, saying, "Of course I do! You do not suppose that I have been living with her for the last fifteen years and am going to put her away now, do you? See, there is my boy, fourteen years old. Of course I do!" As it was no use to try to stop him, I did not try, but waited until he was through, when I said: "All right," and went on with the ceremony, but laughed very hard in my sleeve all the time.

A girl in the boarding-school was to be married, and her schoolmates thought that it ought to be done in extra style. Thanks to the teacher and matron, the supper and their share of the duties passed off in an excellent manner. But five of the girls thought that they would act as bridesmaids, and they were left to manage that part among themselves. Each one chose a young man who had previously been in school to act as her escort. Thinking that they would hardly know how to act with so much ceremony, I invited them to my house fifteen minutes before the marriage was to take place in church, so that I could instruct them. They came on time, but what was my surprise to see the bride and groom and the five girls march into my house, but not a single groomsman, and they thought that it was all right, even if their partners did not come. Those whom they had expected were off in the woods, or at home, or if near by, were far from being dressed for the occasion, while the bridesmaids had spent a long time in getting themselves ready, and were in full dress. What a time I had hunting up partners for them! I had to borrow clothes for those who were on the ground, others whom I wished felt that they had been slighted so long that they did not care to to step into such a place then, and the ceremony was delayed some before it could all be arranged. But how I was surprised to see five bridesmaids march in without a single partner!

At another time, as a sub-chief, well dressed, came forward to be married, he began to pull off his coat as if ready for a fight, although his intentions were most peaceable. I told him that it was just as well to let his coat remain on, and he obeyed.

The following is from *The Port Townsend Argus* of December 2, 1881 : —

"*Married.* — Clallam Bay is alive! One of the sensations of the season occurred at that place on the sixteenth of November, and is news, though not published till this late day. Five of the citizens having complied with the laws of the Territory in regard to licenses were married by Rev. M. Eells to their respective partners. Nearly all the inhabitants of the place assembled, without regard to race or color, some of whom had come from miles distant. First came a short address by Mr. Eells on the history of marriage, beginning with the days of Adam and Eve, and setting forth some of the reasons against polygamy and divorce, after which Mr. Charles Hock-a-too and Mrs. Tau-a-yi stood up. Mr. H. has been the only Mormon of the place, having had two whom he called wives, but being more progressive than the Mormons, he boldly resolved to choose only one of them, and cleave only to her so long as they both should live. When the marriage ceremony was over, and he

was asked if thus he promised to do, he replied in
a neat little speech, fully as long as the marriage
ceremony, very different from the consent of some
persons whom the public presume to have said yes,
simply because silence gives consent. It is impossible to reproduce the speech. It will live in
the memories of those who heard it, however, as
coming from an earnest heart and being all that
could be desired. The bride did not blush or
faint, but also made her speech, showing that she
knew what was said to her. After this the four
other couples stood up, Mr. Long John Smittain
and Kwash-tun, alias E-ni-so-ut; Mr. Tom Jim-
myak and Wal-lis-mo; Captain Jack Chats-oo-uk
and Nancy Hwa-tsoo-ut; also Mr. Old Jack Klo-
tasy, father of the Captain, and Mary Cheenith.
In regard to the ages of the last two, from what
we learn, the familiar lines would apply : —

> ' How old is she, Billy boy, Billy boy,
>   How old is she, charming Billy ? '
> ' She 's three times six, four times seven,
>   Twenty-eight and eleven.
> She 's a young thing and can not leave her mother.'

While she probably is not eighty-five, yet she was
old enough to obtain a license and leave her

mother.   He was about seventy years old.   These
were all married with one set of words, when con-
gratulations followed — regular hand-shaking, none
of those present so far forgetting themselves as to
indulge in the (im)propriety of kissing the brides.
The ceremony having been concluded, a part of
those present, the invited guests (but here there
was a distinction as to race and color) sat down
to the marriage-feast.   It was none of your light,
frosted, airy cake (in fact, there was not any cake
in sight), but substantial *solid* bread and the like.
[Here the line went down, and the meager accounts
we could gather about the elegant and varied cos-
tumes worn by the charming brides, the number
and appearance of the bridesmaids, etc., had better
be supplied from the vivid imaginations of the
readers.]   All of the high contracting parties, we
may say, however, are tax-payers of Clallam County
and land-owners.   *Kloshe hahkwa* ("good so").

Not much of a direct war was waged on plural
marriages.   They were simply fenced in and
allowed to die out.   In 1874 there were only five
Twana men who had more than one wife, and
there were about as many more among the Clallams.   Those who had one wife were never allowed
to obtain another as long as they were living with

the first. When one of the wives died of those who had more than one, or was willingly put away, they were not allowed to take another in her place. On some reservations where plural marriages have been numerous, the plan has been adopted of having the man choose one of his wives as the one to whom he should be legally married; and then, in order to save the others and their children from suffering, they have been told to provide for them until the women should be married to some other man. Among these Indians it has now come to be practically the same. One is the real wife, and the others are so old that they are simply taken care of by their husbands, except when they take care of themselves, until they shall get married again; only they do not get married to any one else, being willing to be thus cared for.

They soon learned that a legal marriage meant more than an old-fashioned Indian one and that a divorce was difficult to obtain. The agent took the position that he had no legal right to grant a divorce even on the reservation, and that if the parties obtained one they must apply to the courts. This involved too much expense, and so not a divorce has been obtained by those legally married. But it has taken a long, strong, firm hand to compel some of the parties to live together, and this made others of them somewhat slow to be legally married. One day I asked a man who had then recently obtained a wife, Indian fashion, if he wished to be married in white style. "I am a little afraid," he said, "that we shall not get along well together. I think we will live together six months; and then, if we like each other well enough, we will have you perform the ceremony." It was never done, for, they soon separated.

The most severe contest the agent ever had with the Indians on the reservation was to prevent divorce. In 1876 one man, whose name was Billy Clams, had considerable trouble with his wife and wanted a divorce, but the agent would not allow it. He tried every plan he could think of to make them live peaceably together, and consulted with the chiefs and the relations of the parties; but they would still quarrel. At one time he put him in charge of his brother-in-law, a policeman, with handcuffs on; but with a stone he knocked them off and went to the house of his uncle, a quarter of a mile from the agency. To this place the agent went with two Indians and

told him to go with him. With an oath Billy
Clams said he would not. The agent then struck
him with a stick quite severely. Billy got a larger
stick, which the agent wrenched from him. Then
Billy grabbed the agent around the waist, and,
with the help of his uncle, threw him down. The
other Indians who went with the agent took them
off. Then the agent locked the door and sent the
friendly Indians to the agency for two white men,
the carpenter and the blacksmith, for help. Twice
Billy and his uncle tried to take the key away
from the agent, but failed ; three times Billy tried
to get out of the window, but the agent stopped
him. Then they made an excuse that a very old
man must go out ; and while the agent was letting
him go, Billy ran across the room, struck the middle of the window with his head, and went through
it ; and the agent went so quickly out in the same
way, that he lit on Billy's neck with one foot, after
which the window fell on him, and, as he was
knocking that off, Billy got away and ran through
the woods. Being swift of foot, he escaped ; but
there had been a fresh fall of snow, and the agent
and two white men, with a number of Indians,
followed him all day. They, however, could not
take him. The agent at night offered a reward of
thirty dollars if any of the Indians would bring

him in ; but their sympathies were too much with him, and at night one sub-chief and his son, with a cousin of Billy Clams, helped him off, and he went to some relations of his at Port Madison, sixty or seventy miles away. The next day Billy's uncle was put in irons in the jail, and not long after those who had furnished Billy with a canoe, blankets, and provisions also went into the jail, while the sub-chief was deposed. The Indians worked in every way possible to have them released, but the agent said that he would only do so on condition that Billy Clams should be brought in. They had said that they did not know where he was ; but in a short time after the agent said this, he came in and delivered himself up and was confined in the jail for six months. But a number of the Indians, including the head chief and a sub-chief, encouraged by some white men near by, had been to a justice of the peace and made out several charges against the agent for various things done during all his residence among them, and had them sent to the Commissioner of Indian Affairs at Washington. The principal charges were for shooting at an Indian (or ordering an employee to do so), burning ten Indian houses, selling annuity goods, collecting large fines for small offences, and having the employees work for him. The real cause of their sending these was the trouble with Billy Clams and his friends. The commissioner sent to General O. O. Howard, in charge of the military department of the Columbia, and requested him to investigate the charges. The commissioner said that on the face of the letter, it bore evidence of being untrue; but still he desired General Howard's opinion. Accordingly Major W. H. Boyle was detailed for this purpose. He examined six Indians and three white men, as witnesses against the agent, and one white employee in his favor, — giving the agent an opportunity to defend himself, — and found that the charges amounted to so nearly nothing that he went no further.

After Billy Clams had served out his term of six months in jail, he secretly abandoned his wife and took another, and then they ran away to Port Madison. The agent quietly bided his time, found out the whereabouts of the offending party, and, with a little help from the military, had him arrested and conveyed to Fort Townsend, where he worked six months more, with a soldier and musket to watch him. This showed the Indians that they could not easily run away from the agent, or break the laws against divorce, and greatly strengthened his authority among them.

XVII.

SICKNESS.

THE department of the physician has always been a discouraging one. The government, for twenty-five years, has furnished a physician free, and yet it is difficult to induce the Indians to rely on him. There are three reasons for this: (1) The natural superstition an Indian has about sickness. This has been quite fully discussed under the head of native religion. (2) The Indian doctor does not like to have his business interfered with by any one. It is a source of money and influence to him, and he often uses his influence, which is great among the Indians, to prevent the use of medical remedies. (3) If a medicine given by the physician does not cure in a few doses, or, at least, in two or three days, they think it is not strong, or it is good for nothing — so often when medicine is given, with directions how to use it, it is left untouched or thrown away. When using medicine they often employ an Indian doctor, and his practices often kill all the good effects of medicine, so that sometimes the physicians have felt that, when Indian doctors were employed, it was almost useless for them to do any thing.

At the same time there have been some things which have aided our methods very materially. Under the head of native religion, two cases have been given, where it seemed to the Indians as if their mode was true. This has occasionally been the effect with older people. But with young children, too young to go to school, the opposite has been true. Infants have continually died. Their mortality has been very great, when they lived at home, where they could have all the Indian doctors they wanted with no one to interfere. The medicine-men have been especially unfortunate in losing their own children. One Indian doctor has buried twelve and has only three left. Another has buried four and has one left. And others have lost theirs in like proportion. On the other hand, in the school, where we could have more control over them, both as to observing the laws of health and the use of medicine, when they were sick there have been very few deaths. Only five children in ten years have died in school, or been taken fatally sick while there, while the attendance has been from twenty-five to forty.

During November and December, 1881, we passed through a terrible sickness. It seemed to be a combination of scarlet fever, diphtheria, measles, and chicken-pox, about which the physician knew almost nothing. It was a new hybrid disease, as we afterward learned. The cases were mostly in the school and in the white families, there being comparatively few among the outside Indians. There were sixty cases in five weeks, an average of two new ones every day. At one time every responsible person in the school was down with it. A number of the children, while all the physician's family, himself included, had it, and one of them lay dead. Five persons died with it, but not one of them was a scholar. There were then twenty-four scholars, and all but three had it. Nineteen outside Indians had it, of whom three died. The rest, who were sick and died, belonged to the white families and the Indian apprentices and employees. The favor which was shown to the school in saving their lives was of great value to it.

And now the older Indians are gaining more and more confidence in the physician, slowly but steadily, some within a year having said that they will never have an Indian doctor again. In the winter of 1883–84, four Indian children died, and not an Indian doctor was called. In one case the parents had just buried one, and another was fatally sick. The parents came to me and said : " If you can tell us what medicine will cure the child, we will go to Olympia and get it (thirty miles distant). We do not care for the expense, we do not care if it shall cost fifty dollars, if you will only tell us what will cure it." The child died, but they had no Indian doctor, although its grandfather strongly urged the calling of one. After the death of these two children, the family went to live with an aunt of the mother's, where they remained about five months. At that time a child of this aunt was sick, and an Indian doctor was called, whereupon the bereaved family left the house, because they did not wish to remain in a house where such practices were countenanced, even if those doing so were kind relations.

XVIII.

FUNERALS.

THE oldest style of burial was to wrap the body in mats, place it in one canoe, cover it with another, elevate it in a tree or on a frame erected for the purpose, and leave it there, burying with it valuable things, as bows, arrows, canoes, haiqua shells (their money), stone implements, clothes, and the like. After the whites came to this region, the dead were placed in trunks, and cloth, dishes, money, and the like were added to the valuables which were buried with them.

But one such burial has taken place within ten years, and that was the daughter of an old man. The next step toward civilization was to bury all the dead in one place, instead of leaving them scattered anywhere they might chance to die, make a long box instead of using a trunk and canoe, and elevate it on a frame made for the purpose only a few feet high, or, perhaps, simply lay it on the ground, erecting a small house over it. This was frequently done during the first few years after I was here.

On the opening of a new burying-ground, in August, 1878, the head chief of the Twanas said to me : "To-day we become white people. At this burying-ground all will be buried in the ground, and no cloth or other articles will be left around,

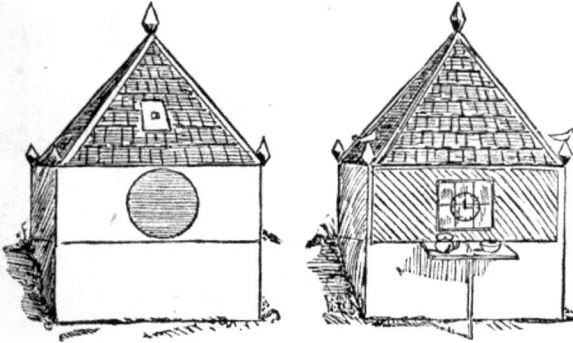

CLALLAM GRAVES AT PORT GAMBLE.

These are painted, with no cloth on them. (*a*) Looking-glass.
(*b*) A shelf, on which is a bowl, teapot, etc., with rubber toys floating in them, such as ducks, fish, etc.

at least, above ground." At that place this promise has been faithfully kept, as far as I know, though since that time, at other places, they have left some cloth above ground. They often yet fill the coffin, now generally made like those of white people, with much cloth and some other things.

A grave-stone, which cost thirty dollars, marks the last resting-place of one man, put there by his wife.

Most of them had a superstitious fear of going near a dead body, for they were afraid that the evil spirit, which killed the deceased was still around.

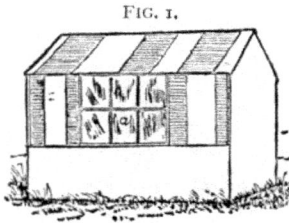

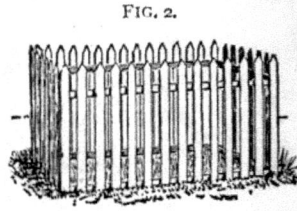

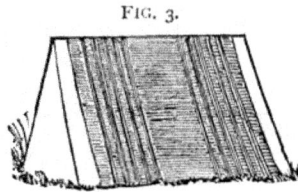

FIG. 1.   FIG. 2.

FIG. 3.

These are grave-enclosures at the burying-ground at the Skokomish Reservation. In Figures 1 and 3 they are covered altogether with cloth, and that which is not colored is white. Figure 3 is chiefly covered with a red blanket; *a* in Figure 1 is a glass window, through which a red shawl covers the coffin, which is placed a foot or so above the ground. In all grave-enclosures which I have seen where glass windows are placed the coffin is above ground. Sometimes more than one is placed in an enclosure. Figure 2 is almost entirely after the American fashion, and was made last year. — (December, 1877.)

and would kill others who might be near. This, together with the fact that they cared but little for Christianity, made them have no desire to have Christian services at their funerals at first. Before I came, only one such service had been held. And, for the first few years after I came, notwithstanding the efforts of both agent and missionary, there were but few such services. Sometimes they would hurry off a deceased person to the grave, and I would not hear of the death until after the burial, much less have a chance to ask whether they wished for such services.

But steady effort, together with the example of the surrounding whites, who, previous to my arrival, had had no minister to hold such services, in time produced a change, so that they wished for them at the funerals of all persons whom they considered of much importance. At the funeral of one poor vagabond, who had almost no friends, I had my own way, and many thought it very strange that I should hold such a service. It was well enough, they said, with persons of consequence, but with such a person they thought it useless.

Not long after they opened their new burying-ground, already spoken of, I was absent from home when one person died. When I returned, a sub-chief said to me: "We felt badly when we buried a person and no white man was present to say a Christian word. We wish that when you are away, you would make arrangements with some of the whites at the agency to attend our funerals, for we want such services." Since then, I have almost constantly held them, except when they preferred to have the Indian Catholic priest to attend them.

But now a new error arose at the other extreme. This was that such services helped the soul of the deceased to reach heaven. It came from Catholic teaching. I have had to combat it constantly, but some believe it still.

Most of the Clallams now put their dead in the ground. Those who are Catholics have a funeral service by their own priest. In February, 1881, I was at Jamestown, when a child of Cook House Billy died. I went through with the services — the first Christian ones that had ever been held there. They soon asked how they should do if I were absent, and I instructed them as best I could. Since then the Christian part of the community have obtained a minister of any Protestant denomination, if there was one to be obtained, to hold services at their funerals.

THE DEATH OF SKAGIT BILL.

Skagit Bill was in early days an Indian Catholic priest, but afterward went back to his gambling, drinking, and tamahnous. He died in August, 1875, of consumption. When he was sick, he came to the agency, where he remained for five weeks for Christian instruction. He seemed to think the old Indian religion of no value, and wished for something better. Sometimes I thought that he leaned on his Catholic baptism for salvation, and sometimes I thought not. His dying request was for a Christian funeral and burial, with nothing but a plain fence around his grave. The following, from the pen of Mrs. J. M. Walker, and taken from the *Pacific Christian Advocate*, gives the opinions of one other than myself : —

"Yesterday came to us fraught with solemn interest. Our flag hung at half-mast, reminding us that death had been in our midst and chosen another victim. This time he has not selected one rich in the treasures of this world, of high birth or noble blood, or boasting much culture or refinement. The lowly mien and dusky complexion of the deceased might not have attracted much attention from me or you, kind reader. But

such are they whom our blessed Lord delights to
honor; and, while we turn wearily from one to
another, looking vainly for suitable soil in which
to plant the seeds of true righteousness and true
holiness, the Holy Spirit descends on some lonely,
barren spot, and lo! before our astonished gaze
springs into luxuriant growth a plant of rare
holiness, meet even to be transplanted into the
garden of paradise.

"I think it is not a common thing for a dying
Indian to request a strictly Christian burial;[1]
brought up as they are in the midst of superstition, with no religion but misty traditions and
mysterious necromancy, the very fabulousness of
which seems strangely adapted to their nomadic
existence — surely no influence less potent than
that of God's Holy Spirit could induce one of
them, while surrounded by friends who cling
tenaciously to their heathenism and bitterly
resent any innovations of Christian faith, to
renounce the whole system with its weird ceremonies, and demand for himself the simple
burial service used ordinarily by Christians.

"At eleven o'clock A.M. the coffin was brought
into the church, and the funeral discourse

[1] It was not at that time, at this place.

preached; and we all felt that the occasion was one of deep solemnity. Probably every one present had seen dear friends lying, as this man now lay, in the icy embrace of death, and the keen pain in our own hearts, at the remembrance of our unhealed wounds, made us sympathize deeply with the afflicted mourners in their present bereavement. What is so potent to bind human hearts together in purest sympathy and kindest charity as common woe!

"A beautiful wreath lay upon the coffin, formed and given, I suspect, by the agent's wife, a lady possessing rare nobility of mind and heart, and eminently fitted for the position she occupies. This delicate token I deemed emblematic; for as each bud, blossom, and sprig fitted its respective place, giving beauty and symmetry to the whole, so all of God's creatures fit their respective places, and the absence of one would leave a void: and so also in heaven's economy the diadem of the Prince of Light is set with redeemed souls of nationalities varied and diverse, each so essential to its perfection, that the highest ransom of which even Omniscience could conceive has been paid for it.

"Quite a number of Indians were present, and

as the deceased had been with them and they had seen him die happy in his faith in Christ and his atonement, a rare opportunity offered for bringing the truth home to their hearts.

"The Indians here are, for the most part, shrewd and intelligent, capable of reasoning on any subject, where their judgment is not darkened by superstition ; but, alas ! most of them are in the gall of bitterness and bond of iniquity. . . . The body was taken for interment to a grave-yard some three miles from here. Our esteemed pastor, Rev. M. Eells, preached the funeral discourse, and also officiated at the grave, aided on each occasion by the usual interpreter [Mr. John F. Palmer], a man of considerable intellectual culture, of gentlemanly bearing, and pleasant address. This man, though greatly superior to any of his race whom I have met, is yet humble and strives to do his fellows good in a quiet, unostentatious manner, worthy the true disciple of the meek and lowly Jesus, which can not fail of great results, whether he live to enjoy them or not.

"What is so refining in its influences as true religion ? It expands the mind, ennobles the thought, corrects the taste, refines the manners by the application of the golden rule, and works marvelous transformations in character. May a glorious revival of this pure religion sweep over our land, carrying away the bulwarks of Satan and leaving in their stead the 'peaceable fruits of righteousness,' until every creature shall exclaim : 'Behold, what hath God wrought! Sing, O ye heavens, for the Lord hath done it!'   A."

XIX.

THE CENSUS OF 1880.

IN the fall of 1880 the government sent orders
to the agent to take the census of all the
Indians under him for the United States decennial
census. To do so among the Clallams was the
most difficult task, as they were scattered for a
hundred and fifty miles, and the season of the
year made it disagreeable, with a probability of its
being dangerous on the waters of the lower sound
in a canoe. I was then almost ready to start on a
tour amongst a part of them and the agent offered
to pay my expenses if I would combine this with
my missionary work. He said that it was almost
impossible for him to go; that none of the employees were acquainted either with the country
or the large share of the Indians; that he should
have to pay the expenses of some one; and that
it would be a favor if I could do it. I consented,
for it was a favor to me to have my expenses paid,
while I should have an opportunity to visit all of
the Indians; but it was December before I was

fairly able to begin the work and it required four weeks.

In early life I had read a story about taking the census among some of the ignorant people of the Southern States and the superstitious fear that they had of it, and I thought that it would not be strange if the Indians should have the same fear. My previous acquaintance with them and especially the intimacy I had had with a few from nearly every settlement who had been brought to the reservation for drinking and had been with us some time and whose confidence I seemed to have gained, I found to be of great advantage in the work. Had it not been for these, I would have found it a very difficult task.

The questions to be asked were many—forty-eight in number, including their Indian as well as "Boston" names, the meaning of these, the age, and occupation; whether or not a full blood of the tribe; how long since they had habitually worn citizen's dress; whether they had been vaccinated or not; whether or not they could read and write; the number of horses, cattle, sheep, swine, dogs, and fire-arms owned; the amount of land owned or occupied; the number of years they had been self-supporting, and the per cent. of support obtained from civilized industries and in other ways.

I began the work at Port Gamble one evening, and after much talk secured nineteen names, but the next forenoon I only obtained six. The men were at work in the mill, and the women, afraid, were not to be found. I then hired an interpreter, a boy who had been in school, and after talking a while had no more difficulty there. The best argument I could use why it was required was that some people said they were nothing but worthless Indians, and that it was useless to try to civilize them ; that some of us thought differently and wished for facts to prove it, and when found, that they would be published to the world. And this I did in the *Port Townsend Argus* and *American Antiquarian.* One man refused to give me any information because that, years before, a census had been taken and soon after there had been much sickness, and he was afraid that if his name were written down he would die. But I easily obtained the information most needed from others. I was almost through, and was at Seabeck, the last town before reaching home, when I found the only one who was at all saucy. He gave me false names and false information generally, as I soon learned from another Indian present and it was afterward corrected. The ages of the older ones were all unknown, but the treaty with the tribe was made twenty-five years previous, and every man, woman, and child was present who possibly could be, and I could generally find out about how large they were then. When I asked the age of one man he said two years, but he said he had two hundred guns. He was about forty-three years old and had only one gun. To obtain the information about vaccination was the most difficult, as the instructions were that they should show me the scars on the arm if they had been vaccinated, and many of them were ashamed to do this. As far as I knew, none of them made a false statement. When about half-way through I met Mr. H. W. Henshaw, who had been sent from Washington to give general information about the work, and he absolved them from the requirement of showing the scar. He said that all that was needed was to satisfy myself on the point. On this coast, a dime is called a bit, although in reality a bit is half a quarter, and the Indians so understand it. In finding how nearly a pure Clallam one man was, I was informed that he was partly Clallam and partly of another tribe. But when I tried to find out how much of the other tribe I was told: "Not much ; *a bit,* I guess."

I was instructed to take the names of not only those who were at home, but of a number who were across the straits on the British side, whose residence might properly be said to be on this side. In asking about one man I was told that he had moved away a long time ago, very long, *two thousand years*, probably, and so was not a member of the tribe.

It struck me that some pictures of myself, with descriptions of them would have adorned *Harper's Monthly* as well as any of Porte Crayon's sketches. With an old Indian man and his wife I sat on the beach in Port Discovery Bay all day waiting for the wind to die down, because it was unsafe to proceed in a canoe with the snow coming down constantly on one of the coldest days of the year, with a mat up on one side to keep a little of the wind off, and a small fire on the other side ; and, at last, we had to give up and return to Port Discovery, as the wind would not die. I waked up one morning on the steamer *Dispatch* to have a drop of water come directly into my eye, for there was a hard rain, and the steamer overhead (not

underneath) was leaky. I got up to find my shirt
so wet that I dared not put it on, while the water
in the state-room above me was half an inch deep
and was shoveled out with a dust-pan. I walked
from the west to the east end of Clallam Bay,
only two miles, but while trying to find a log
across the Clallam River I wandered about a long
time in the woods and brush, wet with a heavy
rain, and when I did find it it reached just *not*
across the river, but within a few feet of the bank,
and I stood deliberating whether it was safe or
not to make the jump ; trying to jump and not
quite daring to run the risk of falling into the
river, sticking my toes and fingers into the bank,
and the like, but at last made the crossing safely.
It took half a day to travel those two miles. I
ate a Sunday dinner at Elkwa, between church-
services, of some crumbs of sweet cake out of a
fifty-pound flour-sack, so fine that I had to squeeze
them up in my hands in order to get them into
my mouth. An apple and a little jelly finished
the repast — the last food I had. At Port Angeles I rode along the beach on horseback at high
tide, and at one time in trying to ford a slough I
found we were swimming in the water. I partly
dried out at an Indian house near by, taking the

census at the same time. Again, the steamer *Dispatch* rolled in a gale, while the water came over the gunwales, the food and plates slid off the tables, the milk spilt into gum boots, the wash-dish of water upset into a bed, and ten minutes after I left her at Dunginess the wind blew her ashore, dragging her anchors. But there were also some *special providences* on the trip. "He who will notice providences will have providences to notice," some one has said, and I was reminded of this several times. I came in a canoe from Clallam Bay to Elkwa, the most dangerous part of the route, with the water so smooth that a small skiff would have safely rode the whole distance, thirty-five miles, to have a heavy storm come the next day, and a heavy gale, when I again went on the water, but then a steamer was ready to carry me. The last week, on coming from Jamestown home, in a canoe, I had pleasant weather and a fair north wind to blow me home the whole time, only to have it begin to rain an hour after I reached home, the commencement of a storm which lasted a week. Strange that a week's north wind should bring a week's rain. I have never noticed the fact at any other time.

But the most noticeable providence of all was

as follows : On my way down, the good, kind people of Seabeck, where I occasionally preached,
made me a present of forty dollars, and it was
very acceptable, for my finances were low.   At
Port Gamble I spent it all and more, too, for our
winter supplies, as I did not wish to carry the
money all around with me, and, also, so that I
might get at Port Townsend those things which
I could not find at Port Gamble.   I often did so,
and ordered them to be kept there until my return.
About three days later I heard that the store at
Port Gamble was burned with about every thing in
it, the loss being estimated at seventy-five thousand dollars.   The thought came into my mind,
Why was that money given to me to be lost so
quickly ?. On my return I went to Port Gamble to
see about the things and to my great surprise I
found that only about two wheelbarrow loads of
goods had been saved, and that mine were among
them.   They had been packed and placed at the
back door.   The fire began in the front part, so
they broke open the back door, and took the first
things of which they could lay hold, and they
were mine, and but little else was saved.

When I arrived at Seabeck the kind ladies of
the place presented my wife with a box containing

over thirty dollars' worth of things as a **Christmas** present. *Among these was a cloak.* **During my** absence she had been trying to make herself one, supposing that she had cloth enough, but **when** she began to cut it out to her dismay she **found** that with all the twisting, turning, and **piecing** that she could do, there was not cloth enough, **so** she had given it up and made a cloak for **our little** boy out of it. She naturally felt badly, as **she did** not know how she should then get one. "**All** these things are against me," said Jacob, but **he** found that they were all for him. Others **besides** Jacob have found the same to be true.

The statistical information obtained in this census is as follows : —

In the Clallam tribe there were then 158 **men,** 172 women, 86 boys, and 69 girls ; a total of **485** persons. Six were on or near the reservation, 10 near Seabeck, 96 at Port Gamble, 6 at **Port Lud-** low, 22 at Port Discovery, 12 at Port **Townsend,** 18 at Sequim, 86 at Jamestown, 36 at or **near** Dunginess. (Those at Sequim and near **Dunginess** were all within six miles of Jamestown.) **Fifty-** seven at Port Angeles (but a large share of **them** were across the straits on the British side), **67 at** Elkwa, 24 at Pyscht, and 49 at or near **Clallam**

Bay. There were 290 full-blooded Clallams among them, and the rest were intermingled with 18 other tribes. Fifteen were part white. During the year previous to October 1, 1880, there had been 11 births and 9 deaths. Forty-one had been in school during the previous year, 49 could read and 42 write; 135 could talk English so as to be understood, of whom 69 were adults; 65 had no Indian name; 33 out of 123 couples had been legally married.

They owned 10 horses, 31 cattle, 5 sheep, 97 swine, 584 domestic fowls, and 137 guns and pistols, most of them being shot-guns. Thirty-four were laborers in saw-mills; 22 were farmers. There were 80 fishermen, 23 laborers, 17 sealers, 15 canoe-men, 6 canoe-makers, 6 hunters, 3 policemen, 11 medicine-men, 4 medicine-women, 1 carpenter, 2 wood-choppers, 1 blacksmith, and 40 of the women were mat and basket makers. Twenty-eight persons owned 576 acres of land with a patented title, four more owned 475 acres by homestead, and twenty-two persons, representing 104 persons in their families, cultivated 46 acres.

During the year they raised 2,036 bushels of potatoes, 14 tons of hay, 26 bushels of oats, 258 bushels of turnips, 148 bushels of wheat, 20

bushels of apples, 5 of plums, and 4 of small fruit.
They had 113 frame-houses, valued by estimate at
$5,650, four log-houses, worth $100, twenty-nine
out-houses, as barns, chicken-houses, and canoe-
houses, two jails, and two churches. They cut
250 cords of wood; received $1,994 for sealing,
$646 for salmon, and $1,000 for work in the Port
Discovery mill. I was not able to learn what they
had earned at the Seabeck and Port Gamble saw-
mills. Two hundred and eleven of them were out
of the smoke when at home. I estimated that on
an average they obtained seventy-two per cent. of
their living from civilized food, the extremes being
fifty and one hundred per cent.

Twana Indians. — This census was taken by
government employees mainly, and some of the
estimates differed considerably from what I should
have made. Probably hardly two persons could
be found who would estimate alike on some points.
They numbered 245 persons, of whom there were
70 men, 84 women, 41 boys, and 47 girls. The
residence of 49 was in the region of Seabeck,
and of the rest on the Skokomish Reservation.
There were only 20 full-blooded Twanas, the rest
being intermingled with 15 other tribes; 24 were
partly white. During the year there were 8 births

and 3 deaths. Twenty-nine had been in school during the previous year; 35 could read, and 30 could write; 68 could talk English; 37 had no Indian name. Out of 67 couples 23 had been legally married. They owned 80 horses, 88 cattle, 44 domestic fowls, and 36 guns. There were 42 farmers, 4 carpenters, 2 blacksmiths, 4 laborers, 7 hunters, 20 fishermen, 21 lumbermen and loggers, 1 interpreter, 1 policeman, 6 medicine-men, 7 washer-women, 6 mat and basket makers, and 1 assistant matron. Forty-seven of them, representing all except about 40 of the tribe, held 2,599 acres of unpatented land, all but 40 of which was on the reservation. They raised 80 tons of hay and 450 bushels of potatoes during the year. They owned 60 frame-houses valued at $3,000. All but 25 were off of the ground and out of the smoke. It was estimated that on an average they obtained 78 per cent. of their subsistence from civilized food, the extremes being 25 and 100 per cent., but these estimates were made by two different persons who differed widely in their calculations.

XX.

THE INFLUENCE OF THE WHITES.

SOME of this has been good and some very bad. Wherever there is whiskey a bad influence goes forth, and there is whiskey not far from nearly all the Indian settlements. Still it must be acknowledged that the influence of all classes of whites has been in favor of industry, Christian services at funerals, and the like, and against tamahnous and potlatches. Around Skokomish — with a few exceptions of those whose influence has been very good — there are not many who keep the Sabbath and do not swear, drink whiskey, and gamble; but this influence has been partially counteracted by the employees on the reservation. It has not been possible to secure Christian men who could fill the places, but moral men have at least generally been obtained. It has been one of the happy items of this missionary work, that a good share of those who have come to the reservation as government employees, who have not at the time of their

coming been Christians, have joined the church
on profession of their faith before they have left.
The Christian atmosphere at the agency has been
very different from that of a large share of the
outside world. The church is within a few hundred yards of the houses of all the employees, and
thus it is very convenient to attend church, prayer-
meetings, and Sabbath-school. Thus those persons who were not Christians when they came,
found themselves in a different place from what
they had ever been. There are many persons
who often think of the subject of religion ; wish
at heart that they were Christians, and intend at
some time to become such, but the cares of this
world, and the deceitfulness of riches, and the
people with whom they associate, choke the good
thoughts. But let such people be placed in a
Christian community, where these influences are
small, and breathe a Christian atmosphere, and
the good seed comes up. So it has been among
the happy incidents of these ten years to receive
into the church some of these individuals.

Two brothers, neither of whom were Christians,
but whose mother was one, were talking together
on the subject of religion, at Seattle, when one of
them said that he believed it to be the best way.

Not long after that the other brother came to the reservation, where he became a Christian. He then wrote to his brother, saying, "I have now found by experience that it is the best way."

Another man and his wife had for years been skeptical, but were like "the troubled sea which can not rest," and were sincere inquirers after truth. In the course of time, after thorough investigation, they became satisfied of the truth of the Bible, as most people do who sincerely seek for light, and became Christians. A year afterward the gentleman said: "This has been by far the happiest year of my life;" and many times in prayer-meetings and conversation did they speak in pity of their old companions who were still in darkness and had not the means of obtaining the light which they had found.

Several of the children of the employees also came into the church; one of them, eleven years old, being the youngest person whom I ever received into church membership. Such events as these had a silent but strong influence upon the Indians, as strong I think as if these persons had been Christians before they came to the reservation. Thirteen white persons in all united with the Skokomish church, on profession of faith, and twenty-three by letter.

At Jamestown it was different. There was only a school-teacher as a government employee, and he was not sent there until 1878. There are only a few church privileges or Christians in the county, but fortunately a good share of the Christians have lived near to the Indian village, the Indians have worked largely for them, and I have sometimes thought that their influence has had as much to do in elevating the Jamestown people as that of the missionary and agent.

· "Hungry for preaching" was the way I felt about one old lady in 1880, who was seventy-six years old. With her son she walked two and a half miles to Jamestown to church to the Indian service in the morning, then a mile further to a school-house where I preached to the whites in the afternoon, and then home again — seven miles in all; and she has done it several times since, although now nearly eighty. She often walks to the Indian services when there is no white person to take charge of it.

On one communion Sabbath a lady too weak from ill-health to walk the three quarters of a mile between her house and the Indian church was taken by her husband on a wheelbarrow a good share of the way. In 1883 an old gentleman

seventy-three years of age stood up with four
Indians to unite with the church — the oldest
person I ever saw join a church on profession
of faith. As we went home he said: "This is
what I ought to have done forty years ago."
Such influences as these have done much to
encourage these Indians.

XXI.

THE CHURCH AT SKOKOMISH.

THE church was organized June 23, 1874, the day after I arrived, with eleven members, only one of whom was an Indian, John F. Palmer, who was government interpreter. I did not come with the expectation of remaining, but only for a visit. I had just come from Boise City, Idaho, and more than half-expected to go to Mexico, but that and some other plans failed, when the agent said that he thought I might do as much good here as anywhere, and the sentiment was confirmed by others. Rev. C. Eells had been here nearly two years, had been with the church through all its preliminary plans, and it was proper that he should be its pastor, and he was so chosen at the first church meeting after the organization. He almost immediately left for a two months' tour in Eastern Washington, and wished me to fill his place while I was visiting. The next summer he spent in the same way, only wintering with us. His heart was mainly set on work in that region, where he had spent a good share of his previous life. He felt too old, at the age of sixty-four, to learn a new Indian language, and so from the first the work fell into my hands, but he remained as pastor. When it was decided that I should remain, the American Missionary Association gave me a commission as its missionary, and I served as assistant pastor for nearly two years. In the spring of 1876 the pastor left for several months' work in the region of Fort Colville, hardly expecting to make this his residence any longer; hence he resigned, and in April, 1876, I was chosen as his successor.

During most of this time the congregations continued good, though once in a while the Indians would get very angry at some actions about the agency, and almost all would stay away from church, but the average attendance until the spring of 1876 was ninety. At that time the disaffection resulting from the trouble with Billy Clams, as spoken of under the subject of Marriage and Divorce, caused a considerable falling off, so that the average attendance for the next two years was only seventy. Although the people got over that disaffection in a measure, yet one thing or another came up, so that while in 1879 and 1880 the average attendance was better, the congregation never wholly returned until the fall of 1883. A Catholic service sprang up in 1881, which took away a number, and which will hereafter be more fully described among the Dark Days.

From the first there were a few additions to the church, but more of them during the first few years were from among the whites, several of them being children of the employees, than from among the Indians. When the Indians began to join, all the accessions, with one exception, were from among the school-children, and others connected with the work at the agency until 1883. Gambling, horse-racing, betting, and tamahnous had too strong a hold on them for them to easily give up these practices.

The following is from *The American Missionary* for April, 1877 : —

"Our hearts were .gladdened last Sabbath by receiving into our church three of the Indian school-boys, each of them supposed to be about thirteen years old. We had kept them on virtual probation for nearly a year, until I began to feel that to do so any longer would be an injury both to themselves and others. Their conduct, especially toward their school-teacher, although not perfect, has been so uniformly Christian that those who were best acquainted with them felt the best satisfied in regard to their change of heart. Said a member of our church of about fifty years' Christian experience : ' I wish that some of the white children whom we have received into the church had given half as good evidence of being Christians as these boys give.' On religious subjects they have been most free in communicating both to their teacher and myself by letter. I have thought that you might be interested in extracts from some of them, and hence send you the following.

" I am going to write to you this day. Please help me to get my father to become a Christian " (his father is an Indian doctor) "and I think I will get Andrew and Henry " (the other Christian boys) " to say a word for my father. I want you to read it to my father."

He wrote to his father the following, which I read to him : —

"AUGUST 3, 1877.

" MY DEAR BELOVED FATHER, — Your son is a Christian. I am going off another road. I am going a road where it leadeth to heaven, and you are going to a big road where it leadeth to hell. But now please return back from hell. I was long time thinking what I shall do, then my father would be saved from hell. I prayed to God. I asked God to help my father to become a Christian."

The letter of another to his Indian friends : —

" You have not read the Bible, for you can not read, but you have heard the minister read it to you. You seem not to pay good attention, but you know how Jesus was crucified ; how he was put on the cross ; how he was mocked and whipped, and they put a crown of thorns, and he was put to death."

The letter of the other to me : —

" Oh, how I love all the Indians ! I wish they should all become Christians. If you please, tell them about Jesus' coming. It makes me feel bad because the Indians are not ready."

To his Indian friends : —

" The first time I became a Christian, I found it a very hard thing to do, but I kept asking Jesus to help me, and so he did, for I grew stronger and stronger. So, my friends, if you will just accept Jesus as your King, he will help you to the end of your journey. You must trust wholly in Jesus' strength, and yield your will, your time, your talents, your reputation, your strength, your property, your all, to be henceforth and forever subject to his divine control — your hearts to love him ; your tongues to speak for him ; your hands and feet to work for him, and your lives to serve him when and where and as his Spirit may direct. Don't be proud, but be very good Christians ; be brave and do what is right.

" Your young friend,

" ——— ———."

It is but just to say now that the first two of these have been suspended from the church for misconduct, and still stand so on our record. The other one has done a good work, and has been one of the leaders of religion with the older people, sometimes holding one and two meetings a week with them and teaching the Bible class of fifty on the Sabbath.

The Twanas and the Clallams were formerly at war with each other, and even now the old hostile feeling, dwindled down to jealousy, will show itself at times. A like unpleasant feeling has often been shown between the whites and Indians, yet, on the first Sabbath in April, 1880, three persons united with the church and received baptism, who belonged one to each of these three classes. Another noticeable fact was the reason which induced them to become Christians. In reply to my question on this point, each one, unknown to the other, said that it was because they had noticed that Christians were so much happier than other people. Two of them had tried the wrong road with all their heart, and had found to their sorrow that "the way of transgressors is hard."

The following table will show the state of the church during the ten years : —

	Added by Letter.	Added on Profession of Faith.	Of those Joining on Profession, these were Indians.	Dismissed by Letter.	Died.	Excommunicated.	Membership on Last Day of Fiscal Year.	Absentees.
Organized with	9	2	1				11	
June, 1874–75	2						13	
June, 1875–76	4	4	1				21	
June, 1876–77	2	2	2	9			16	2
June, 1877–78		3	3				19	2
June, 1878–79		6	4		2	1	22	4
June, 1879–80	4	11	7	1			36	5
June, 1880–81	2	5	3		3		40	10
June, 1881–82	2	5	4* 5	16			31	13
June, 1882–83	1	5	5 5	6			31	13
June, 1883–July, 1884	1	18	7 17	5	1	1	43	10
Total	27	61	64	37	6	2		

*Added to the Jamestown Church, and inserted here to give a view of the whole work.

The large diminution in 1876–77 was caused by the removal of employees. The same cause operated in 1881–82, for then the Indians were believed to be so far advanced in civilization that the government thought it wise to discharge all of the employees except the physician and those at work in the school. During that year the church also granted letters to seven of its members who lived at Jamestown, to assist in organizing a church there. Thus when the reasons for the reduced membership of that year were considered there was no particular cause for discouragement, but rather for encouragement. One white man and one Indian have been ex-communicated.

The next year the agent moved away, and while he still retained his membership in the church, and aided it financially almost as much as when he resided here, still his absence has been felt, as from the beginning he had been its clerk and treasurer, for a part of the time its deacon, and his councils had always been of great value.

The absentees grew in number mainly because white employees moved away, and did not always unite with another church.

On July 4, 1880, the first Indian infant was baptized. Some cases of discipline have been necessary, four being now suspended. Most cases of discipline have resulted favorably.

XXII.

BIG BILL.

A MONG those who about thirty years previous
had received Catholic instruction and baptism was Big Bill. He was one of the better Indians. When in 1875 I went to their logging-
camps to hold meetings, as related under the head
of Prayer-meetings, he seemed to be a leading one
in favor of Christianity. When I offered to teach
them how to pray, sentence by sentence, the other
Indians selected him, as one of the most suitable, in
their opinion, thus to pray. I never knew him to
do any thing which was especially objectionable,
even in a Christian, except that he clung to his
tamahnous, and at times he seemed to be even trying to throw that off. Quite often he would have
nothing to do with an Indian doctor when he was
sick, although he was related to some of them —
then again he would call on them for their assistance. In time consumption took hold of him, together with some other disease, and he wasted
away. He wanted to join the church and be bap-

tized. One reason given was that he had heard
of another Indian far away who had been sick
somewhat as he was, who was baptized and
recovered. Of course this reason was good for
nothing, and he was told so, yet because of his
previous life and his Christian profession this
point was overlooked as one of the things for
which we should have to make allowance, and he
was received into the church May 9, 1880. I
had made up my mind not to ask him to unite
with the church, notwithstanding his apparent
fitness in some respects, because of doubts which
I had on other points, but when he made the
request it seemed to me as if a new aspect were
put on the affair, and I was hardly ready to refuse.

He came to church as long as he was able,
though he lived two miles away, and always
seemed glad to see me. But his sickness was
long and wore on his mind. His nervous system
was affected. Before he died he saw some strange
visions when he was not asleep. His visions
combined some Protestant teaching, some of the
Catholic, and some of their old native superstitions, and had reference especially to heaven.
He sent for me to tell me about them, but I was
not at home. When I returned three or four

days afterward I went to see him. I found that
Billy Clams, the leader of the Catholic set, was
there, and I suspected that his weak mind was
turning to that religion of which he had been
taught in his younger days. It was so. I often
went to see him, and he always received me well,
yet he kept up his intimacy with Billy Clams.
He told me much of his visions, and seemed hurt
that I did not believe them to be as valid as the
Bible. Amongst other things in his visions he
saw an old friend of his who had died many years
previous, and this friend taught him four songs.
They were mainly about heaven, and there was
not much objection to them, except that they said
that Sandyalla, the name of this friend, told him
some things. This was a species of spiritualism
perpetuated in song. He taught these songs to
his friends. When he could no longer come to
church he instituted church services at his house,
twice on each Sabbath and on Thursday evening,
to correspond with ours. Hence I could not
attend them, and his brothers, who leaned toward
the Catholic religion, and Billy Clams had every
thing their own way. When I went to see him he
was glad to have me sing and hold services in my
way. The whole affair became mixed. He died

June, 1881, and his relations asked me to attend the funeral. I did so. They also prepared a long service of his own and Catholic song and prayers, of lighted candles and ceremonies which they went through with after I was done. (It was the first and last funeral in which they and I had a partnership.)

He had two brothers and a brother-in-law, the head chief, who inclined to the Catholic religion. They had always given as an excuse for not coming to church that as Big Bill could not come they went to his house for his benefit and held services. But after his death their services did not cease. They kept them up as an opposition, partly professing that they were Catholics, and partly saying that their brother's last words and songs were very precious to them, and they must get together, talk about what he had said and sing his songs. In course of time this proved a source of great trouble — one of the most severe trials which we had. More will be told of this under the head of Dark Days.

About the only good thing, as far as I knew, in connection with these visions, was that they induced him to give up his tamahnous, or Indian doctors, and he advised his relations to do the

same. He said that in his visions he had learned
that God did not wish such things.

After his death his brother told me that Big
Bill had foretold events which actually took place,
as the sickness and death of several persons, and
so they believed his visions to have come from
God. It may have been so. I could not prove
the contrary, but it was very hard for me to believe it. Big Bill never told me those prophecies,
nor did his brother tell me of them until after
each event occurred. Singly after each death or
sickness took place I was informed that he had
foretold it.

XXIII.

DARK DAYS.

FEBRUARY, 1883, covered about the darkest period I have seen during the ten years. It was due to several causes.

(1) *The Half-Catholic Movement.* — Ever since I have been here some of the Indians leaned toward the Catholic Church, when they leaned toward any white man's church, because of their instruction thirty years ago. In 1875 some of them spoke to me quite earnestly about inviting Father Chirouse, a prominent Catholic missionary, to come here and help me, a partnership about which I cared nothing. The matter slumbered, only slightly showing itself, until the time of the sickness and death of Big Bill. For two or three years previous to this Billy Clams professed to have reformed and become a Christian, but it was Catholic Christianity he had embraced, and he often held some kind of service at his house, occasionally coming to our church; but very few, if any, were attracted to it. After Big Bill's death the

affair took definite shape, there being a combination of Big Bill's songs and prayers and those of Billy Clams. The head chief was brother-in-law to Big Bill, and threw his influence in favor of the opposition church, and a considerable number were attracted to it. Religious affairs thus became divided and a number lost interest in the subject and went nowhere to church.

(2) *John Slocum.* — Affairs went on this way from June, 1881, until November, 1882; their efforts apparently losing interest for want of life. At that time John Slocum, an Indian who had many years before lived on the reservation, but who had for six or seven years lived twelve or fourteen miles away, apparently died, or else pretended to die, I can not determine which, though there is considerable evidence to me and other whites that the latter was true. The Indians believed that he really died. He remained in that state about six hours, when he returned to life, and said that he had been to heaven and seen wonderful visions of God and the future world. He said that he could not get into heaven, because that God had work for him to do here, and had sent him back to preach to the Indians. According to his order a church was built for him, and he held

services which attracted Indians from all around. At first his teaching agreed partly with what he had learned from me, partly with the Catholic religion, and partly with neither, but he was soon captured by the Catholics, baptized, and made a priest. There was much intercourse between him and Billy Clams and friends. Their waning church was greatly revived and ours decreased.

(3) *Mowitch Man.* — Mainly through the influence of John Slocum, another Indian on the reservation, Mowitch Man, who had two wives, but had some influence, was roused to adopt some religion. His consisted partly in following John Slocum, but largely in his own dreams. For a time he affiliated somewhat with Billy Clams and his set, but not always, being rather too dreamy for them, and at last there came a complete separation and we had a third church.

(4) *White Members.* — Owing to orders from the government, the agent and all of the white employees, except the school-teacher, the physician, and an industrial teacher, were removed. The school-teacher and wife were excellent people, and willing to do all that they could, but he had taken charge about the first of February and every thing was new to him. The government had promised

an industrial teacher to aid him, but the one procured had been drowned while coming on the
steamer *Gem*, that had been burned, and an old
gentleman had to be taken in his place for a time,
who was good and willing, but unable to do what
was required.   This threw additional work on the
school-teacher, which almost crushed him, and I
dared not call on him for much help, but rather
had to assist him.   He and his wife were the only
white resident members the church had except
the pastor and his wife.

(5) *The Government Physician.* — Unfortunately
the physician proved to be the wrong man in the
wrong place, but was retained for a time because
it was impossible to obtain any one else who
was better.   When the agent left the previous
fall, by orders from Washington, he was in charge
of the reservation until February.   His moral
and religious influence in many points was at zero.
The less said about him the better, but we had to
contend against his influence.

(6) *Indian Church Members.* — Previous to this
time nineteen Indians had been received into the
church on the reservation.   Of these four had
died, two had been suspended, and another ought
to have been, but for good reasons was suffered to

remain for a time ; two more were sisters of Billy Clams, and had gone with his church, but were not suspended because the church thought it best to be lenient with them for a time on account of their ignorance and the strong influence brought to bear on them ; three had moved away, and there were seven left, three of whom were school-girls.

The previous summer there were two young men who had assisted considerably in church work, and I was hoping much from them, but one of them in getting married had done very badly, had been locked up in jail and suspended from the church, and thus far, although I had kindly urged him, and it had been kindly received as a general thing, yet he had refused to make the public acknowledgment which the church required of him. The other, with so many adverse influences to contend against as there then were on the reservation, found it hard work to stand as a Christian without doing much as a teacher.

During the previous spring there had been considerable religious interest, and four men with their families had taken a firm stand for the right, but in August one of them for wrong-doing had been put in jail, and in the fall two others had fallen into betting and gambling at a great Indian wedding, and the remaining one, a sub-chief, whom I thought a suitable candidate for church membership, had declined to unite with the church when I suggested the subject to him.

(7) *An Indian Inspector.* — About the last of January, 1883, an inspector visited the reservation. I would not speak evil of our rulers, and personally he treated me with respect, and gave me all the privileges for which I could ask : but he was a rough, profane man. I have been much in the company of rough loggers and miners, but never, I think, met a man who was so rough and impolite in the presence of ladies as he was, nor have I ever had so many oaths repeated in my house, nor have my children heard so many from dirty, despised, heathen Indians for a long time, if ever. His intercourse with the Indians was more rough and profane than with me, and any thing but a help to their morality. He so offended Chehalis Jack, the only chief who remained on our side, that he did not come to church for a month. The influence he left with the school-children was also largely against religion. Through his influence my interpreter either refused to interpret, or did the work in so poor a manner that all were disgusted with him.

This seemed to cap the climax, and during February hardly an Indian who could not understand English came to church. There were present only the school-children, a very few whites, and occasionally a very few of the older Indians, nearly all of whom had previously been in school, so that I did not have occasion to preach in Indian during the whole of that month.

I felt somewhat discouraged, and then thought more seriously of leaving than at any other time during the ten years. I however determined to wait until July, during which time I expected to have opportunities to consult with several whose advice I valued, and in the meantime await further developments.

XXIV.

LIGHT BREAKING.

THERE was one good result from the whole excitement : it kept the subject of religion prominently before the people. It did not die of stagnation, as it had almost seemed to do during some previous years. In my visits I was well treated and was asked many questions on the subject. I was welcomed at two or three of the logging-camps during the winter for an evening service, where I talked Bible to them as plainly as I could. They at least asked me to go to them, although they would not come to our church. A constant call, too, came for large Bible pictures. In March a barrel came from the Pearl-street Church in Hartford, Connecticut, full of clothes and substantial good things, the value of which I estimated at about a hundred and twenty dollars. This came when the whites were mostly gone, salary failing, and seemed to be a voice from above, saying, "You go on with the work and I will take care of the support."

During the month of March some of the older

Indians came back again to church, so that I could hold the service in Indian. There had been three whom I had been willing to receive into the church for some time, and during the latter part of the month I found two more. The sub-chief who had declined joining in January was one of them and a policeman was another — both men of influence. So, on the first Sabbath in April, the five were received into the church, and we rejoiced with trembling. These had seen the whole opposition; they had mingled with its followers and had refused to join them, and hence were not likely to wander off into those errors. This was more of the older Twana Indians who had never been in school than had united with the church since its organization. These gave up horse-racing, betting, gambling, and all of tamahnous except that which had reference to the sick, to which they held as a superstition but not a religion. I felt that on this point they were as children, or persons with their heads and hearts in the right direction but with their eyes only half-open. In July two Indian women and a school-girl were added to the number and in October another school-girl and a woman. These drew with them so many that we had a respectable congregation.

XXV.

THE FIRST BATTLE.

AFFAIRS went on about the same until August. The report then was that Billy Clams had been to John Slocum's and that they had arranged to have a great time. He came back and an invitation was extended to the whole reservation to go to John Slocum's, where it was said that four women were to be turned into angels; they would receive revelations directly from heaven, and many wonderful things would be done. Two logging-camps out of four were induced to shut down completely for the time, and some people went from one other. They were told that they would be lost if they did not go; that the baptism of those whom I had baptized was good for nothing, being done with common water, and that they must go and be baptized again, and that the world was coming to an end in a few days. About thirty-five Indians went from here and many others from other places, and there was great excitement. Some Catholic ceremonies

172

were held, something similar to the old black tam-ahnous ceremonies being added to them. These put the patient into a state somewhat like that of mesmerism, baptizing it with the name of religion. Visions were abundant; four people, it was said, died and were raised to life again; women, professing to be angels, tried to fly around. People went around brushing and striking others until some were made black for a week, the professed intent being to brush off their sins. A shaking took hold of some of them, on the same principle, I thought, that fifty years ago nervous jerks took hold of some people at the South and West at their exciting camp-meetings; and this continued with them afterward until they gained the name of the shaking set. Some acted very much like crazy people, and some indecent things were done. It was reported that they saw myself, Mowitch Man, and others in hell; that I was kept on the reservation to get the lands of the Indians away from them, and that I told lies in church. Such reports came to the reservation after a few days that the teacher here, who was in charge of the reservation, thought that he had better go and see it and perhaps try to stop it. He took two policemen and the interpreter with him and went there. He stayed one night and talked to them so plainly that they returned a day or two afterward; but their nervous excitement was not over. Some of them, as they returned, went to their homes, and a little cooling off, together with the talk of their friends, brought them to their senses; but about half of the number kept on. They mainly consisted of those who had been at work in the logging-camp of David, Dick & Co. Dick was head chief, and David was a brother of Big Bill and, next to Billy Clams, was the leader in the excitement. Their camp was eight miles from the reservation; but for about two weeks they stayed on the reservation, singing, brushing off sins, shaking, and professing to worship God in their own way. The excitement and other things, however, made Ellen, the wife of David, sick; in a few days her infant child died, and they thought she was about to die. Chief Dick was sick for more than a week. One of David's oxen, worth about a hundred and fifty dollars, mired, and for want of care died; and it seemed as if God were taking things into his own hands. The shaking set now said that all tamahnous was bad and that they would have no Indian doctor for their sick. Ellen had a sister who lived at the

Chehalis, a day and a half's ride distant, and she was sent for. When she came she was determined to have an Indian doctor, and with considerable of a war of words she conquered Ellen's husband and the whole set, and took Ellen off to an Indian doctor. There were two or three in the logging-camp who were tired of the affair, for they had lost three weeks of the best of weather for work, so they reorganized their shattered forces and moved to their camp. Ellen's husband and son, who also belonged to the set, now neglected her. They furnished her almost nothing, neither food, clothes, nor bedding, and when she wished to have her little boy, they would not allow it. If they could have had control of her they would have taken her to their camp, taken care of her, and held their ceremonies over her; they came twice to see her, but the Indian doctors would not be partners with their shakings, and drove them off. On the eighth of September she died, and her sister had possession of the body. All of the members of our church, Indian doctors, and all who were opposed to the shaking set, now joined company with her sister. They asked me if the body might be brought to our church and kept there until the coffin should be

made, and if I would hold the funeral services.
This had often been done in previous funerals,
and I could not well have said no if I had wished
so to do.   I consented, but saw plainly that it was
more than an ordinary request.   They feared that
her husband would come and claim the body.
Before her death she had requested her sister not
to give her body to her husband because he had
neglected her so.   The contest was to be over
this, and they thought that if the body was in my
possession her husband would probably not obtain
it.   A strange contest.   But the body was brought
to the church and left there.   About noon the
next day I met her husband and several friends
about three miles from the agency, apparently
coming to it.   They asked about the body, and
I told them all about it.   They said that they
were coming to the agency, and wanted to take
the body, have their services over it, and bury it.
I was being drawn into the contest, but with my
eyes open.   As a general thing, a man certainly
had a right to the body of his wife.   But they left,
as I thought, a place of escape, by saying that
they should go and see her sister.   If she gave
them the body, they would take it and bury it in
their way, but if not, they wished me to hold

funeral services over it and bury it in the best manner possible. I was satisfied with that remark, for I wished, if possible, to let them fight it out. I came home immediately, and told our side these things, most of whom where gathered at the agency. After this the coffin was finished; she was placed in it, a few words were said, and I was requested to keep the body until the next day, when the funeral was to take place. Three hours had now passed since I came home, but David and company had not arrived. They had turned aside and held their services during that time. All of our side started for their homes. But they had not gone far, and I had only been at my house a few minutes, when I was called to the door to meet Ellen's husband and son, Chief Dick, Billy Clams, and others. They asked me where the body was, and I told them. They said that her son wished to see his mother. I had no objections. Her son then said that he should take the body to his house, keep it for three days with lights burning at her head and feet, and then bury her with their ceremonies. He did not ask me for her, but said he should take her. Had her husband said so, I should have been in an awkward position. I asked if they had seen her sister and

obtained her consent, as they had said they would
do.   They replied that they had not seen her.   I
told them that the body had been placed in my
charge for the night, and I should not give it up
until her sister had consented; that when any
thing, be it a horse or a trunk, was left in my
possession, I expected to care for it until the one
who placed it with me called for it; that I had
waited three hours for them to come, and they
had not done so, and that they had not been to
see her sister, as they had promised to do; that
if they would go and see her sister, and gain her
consent, I would willingly give it up.   I appealed
to the physician, then present, and temporarily in
charge of the agency, for protection.   He had
been here only about six weeks, and was at first
a little afraid that they would take it out during
the night.   But I was not afraid of that.   Such
an act would kill their religion, and Billy Clams
had been in jail too much to dare to advise such
an act.   I told them I should not unlock the
church to let them see her unless they promised
to let her remain.   They at last consented to all
my propositions.   Had I yielded then I would
have gained great enmity from all of our side,
who had been at much expense to put her prop-

perly in the coffin, and would have made no friends on the other side. They promised to bring her sister down the next morning and settle it. The next morning Billy Clams came alone, and when I asked if all were soon coming, he replied that it was all settled; that they had talked with her sister some the previous night, and also on that morning; that her sister's words had been very fierce, and that they had concluded, since the body was in the church, it was not best to take it out, and that I should have complete control of the funeral; that they would not come to the church if I did not wish them to do so, but that they would wait on the road to the grave until the services were done, for they would like to go to the grave, if I had no objections. I replied that I was glad of their decision, and that I would be very glad to have them all attend the services in the church. They all came; were very cordial to our side. Some of them took especial pains to cross themselves and shake hands with my children and myself. We all went to the grave together; her son made presents to all there: and the first battle was fought and won by our Great Captain.

XXVI.

THE VICTORY.

BUT although cast down, they were not destroyed. I was a little surprised to see how strongly they still clung to their religion. They returned to their camp, held their services often from six o'clock until twelve at night, shook by the hour, lit candles and placed them on their heads and danced around with them thus, sang loud enough to be heard for miles away, acted much like Indian doctors, only they professed to try to get rid of sins instead of sickness, and so acted that in the physician's opinion it was likely to make some of them crazy. When Ellen was first taken sick I had more than half-expected that she would die, for I believed that Providence would take away one of their number before their eyes would be open enough to see the foolishness of it ——but I hoped that one death would be enough. In the meantime the agent made us a flying visit, and made some threats of what he might do if the foolishness was not stopped. As long as it was

purely a Catholic church he felt that he had no
right to interfere, but now the Catholic ceremonies were a very small part, merely like a thin
spreading of butter over something else, and he
knew that if a Catholic priest had charge he would
have locked them up very quickly. He proposed
to visit us again about the middle of October, and
spread a report that if they did not stop he might
depose the chiefs and banish Billy Clams. He
had the right to do the latter, because, when
Billy Clams had returned to the reservation a few
years previous, after having resided at Port Madison for quite a time, he was allowed to come only
on promise of good behavior. His misdeeds
were not to be forgotten, but only laid on a shelf
for future reference, if required. But this threat
apparently did not frighten them. The chiefs
did not care if they were deposed, were about
ready to resign, and did not wish to have any thing
more to do with the "Boston" religion or the
agent. Billy Clams was ready, if need be, to suffer
as Christ did : he was willing to be a martyr.

The agent came, as he had promised to do, and
spent eight days with us. He first took time to
look over affairs quite thoroughly, and felt a little
afraid to begin the contest, fearing that it would
do more injury to fight them than to let them

severely alone. But at last he decided that when
so many of the Indians who were trying to do
right were calling for help in the battle, and that
since he would thus have quite a strong Indian influence to support him, it was not right or wise for
him to refuse their appeal. He first sent for the
two chiefs. They came, putting on quite a show
of courage. He talked to them quite strongly, and
they resigned. It was better for the agent that
they should do so, than that he should depose
them, and they preferred to do so, in order that
they could say to the rest of the Indians that they
did not care. But the tide was turning. As soon
as they had resigned the other Indians did not
spare them, but ridiculed them until they became
very crestfallen. On the Sabbath the agent told
all the Indians that he wished them to come to
church. They did so, and he talked to them on
the religious aspect of the affair as far as was
proper on that day. The next day he held a
council. He did not threaten Billy Clams, but
told him how there had always been trouble where
Indians had tried to have two religions at the
same place ; how in order to prevent this trouble
the government, eleven years previous, assigned
different agencies to different denominations, and
he advised him to return to Port Madison, from

which he had come, where the Indians were all
Catholics, if he wished to be one. He made a
long speech, as strong as he could, on the subject,
told them that the shaking part of the religion
must be stopped on the reservation, and appointed
new chiefs, on whom he could depend, to see that
this order was enforced. They were conquered,
and consulted what was best to do. They all
agreed to abandon the shaking part of the so-
called religion. A part were in favor of keeping
up the purely Catholic religion, but the tide had
turned too much for this. Other Indians had
overcome their fears and talked strongly, and at
last they decided to abandon every thing in connection with their services. The first that I knew
of this decision was that Billy Clams came to me
and told me of this decision, and said that his set
were now without any religion, and that if I would
go and teach them they would be glad to have me
do so, but if not, they should go without any services. I replied that I would gladly teach them,
and went that evening to hold a service with them.
There were two young men in the band who had
long been in school. These now took hold well,
read to their friends from the Bible, made and
taught them new songs, and the victory was
gained.

XXVII.

RECONSTRUCTION.

STILL the process of reconstruction was slow. The wounds which had been made were deep, and distrust reigned between the two parties for a time. Although conquered, all were not converted, and some of them at times longed for the flesh-pots of Egypt. Two things gave much opportunity for gossip during the following winter. The business of logging had gone down and the Indians had little to do. Also, during the previous summer, the chiefs had not attended to their proper business, and had let a number of crimes go unpunished, especially drunkenness, and the new board of chiefs had so many to punish that it created considerable feeling. At first the shakers took hold well in our meetings, as well as if they were one with us. But a child of one of them was taken fatally sick, and while nothing could be proved, yet there was evidence enough to convince most of the Indians and whites that there was a little shaking among them, and then the other Indians lost confidence in their sincerity and did not longer want them as leaders of religion, and so they dropped into the common ranks.

A slightly new element also kept affairs disturbed. It was Big John. At the time of the big meeting in August he was present and was attacked with the shaking as badly as any one. His wife belonged in that region, and so he did not return to the reservation with the other Indians, and was not here when the victory over them was obtained. He went to Mud Bay and set up a party of his own, and he carried the shaking farther than the originators had done. He even out-Heroded Herod. He claimed to be Christ, a claim which was allowed him by his followers, and at the head of about seventy-five of them he rode through the streets of Olympia with his hands outstretched as Christ was when crucified. After the conquest had been made at Skokomish, he was ordered by the agent to return home, as he was creating so much trouble among other Indians under Agent Eells. But he was slow to obey. He came once in November, when he was so attacked in regard to his claims of being Christ by the school-teacher and the Indians, that he gave up this claim and said he was only a prophet. As he had not brought his wife with him, he returned to her, and it was not until several orders had been given for him to come home, and policemen had gone for him more than once, that he came. His orders then were to remain on the reservation, and stop shaking. He remained here for a time, but kept up a quiet kind of shaking more or less of the time. At last he left the reservation and went back without permission. He was again brought home and locked up for about four weeks. This conquered him, and he made but little further trouble, and this pretty effectually killed the return of any on the reservation to shaking.

Three of the shaking set have now been admitted to the church, after six and nine months' probation.

Off of the reservation this shaking spread. It took almost entire possession of the Indians on the Chehalis Reservation, and entered the school in such a way that the agent and school-teacher there felt obliged to stop it by force, or allow the school to be broken up.

At Squaxon there were no government employees and it was not possible to put a complete stop to it there, so it was allowed to have its own way more. Their great prophecy has been that the world would come to an end on the Fourth of July, 1884, but, although they assembled and held a big meeting, and waited for the expected result, it did not come, and so their faith has been somewhat shaken, although now they have extended the time one year. Going to various places to obtain work has also broken them into very small parties, and also occupied them, so that at present it seems to be dying.

XXVIII.

JOHN FOSTER PALMER.

HE was born near Port Townsend, about 1847,
and belonged to the now extinct tribe of
the Chemakums. His father died when he was
very young, through the effects of intemperance,
and also many others of his relations, and this
made him a bitter opponent of drinking.

When ten years old he went to live with the
family of Mr. James Seavey, of Port Townsend,
and went with them in 1859 to San Francisco,
where he remained for a year or two. He then
embarked on a sailing-vessel, and spent most of
the time until 1863 or 1864 near the mouth of the
Amoor River, in Asiatic Russia. Returning then
to Puget Sound, he served under the government
at the Neah Bay Reservation for a time, but about
1868 he came to the Skokomish Reservation, where
he ever afterward made his home, serving as interpreter a large share of the time, eight years under
Agent Eells.

He understood four Indian languages: the

John F. Palmer.

Ten Years at Skokmish.

Twana, Nisqually, Clallam, and Chinook jargon, also the Russian and English, and could read and write English quite well. He had a library worth fifty dollars, and took several newspapers and magazines, both Eastern and Western, although he only went to school two or three weeks in his life. To Mr. Seavey's family, and the captain's wife on the vessel when in Russian waters, he always felt grateful for his education.

When the church was organized at Skokomish, 1874, he united with it, being the first Indian to do so. He lived to see twenty others unite with it. On two points he was very firm : against intemperance and the heathen superstitions : being far in advance of any member of the tribe on the latter point, with the exception of M. F., soon to be mentioned — in fact, it was truly said of him, that he was more of a white man than an Indian.

He loved the prayer-meeting, and while temporarily living at Seabeck, a short time before his death, where he was at work, thirty miles from home, he returned to Skokomish to spend the holidays, and remained an additional week so that he might be present at the daily meetings of the Week of Prayer. He constantly took part in the prayer-meetings, and with the other older male members of the church took his turn in leading them.

He had no children of his own, but brought up his wife's two sisters. When he united with the church, he said : " Now I want my wife to become a Christian," and he lived to see her and her two sisters unite with the church. The elder of them married, and her child, Leila Spar, was the first Indian child who received the rite of infant baptism, July 4, 1880. He was killed instantly at Seabeck, February 2, 1881, while at work at the saw-mill, having been accidentally knocked off from a platform, and striking on his head among short sharp-cornered refuse lumber and slabs about ten feet below. The side of his head was crushed in, and after he was picked up he never spoke, and only breathed a few times. He was far in advance of his tribe, and has left an influence which will be felt for many years to come. It was a pleasure once for me to hear a rough, swearing white man, in speaking of him, say: " John Palmer is a gentleman!"

Milton Fisher.

Ten Years at Skokmish.

XXIX.

M—— F——.

HE was a full-blooded Twana Indian, but from
his earliest infancy lived with his step-
father, who was a white man. A part of the time
he lived very near to the reservation, and afterward about thirty miles from it. The region
where he lived was entirely destitute of schools
and church privileges. His step-father, however,
when he realized that the responsibility of the
moral and Christian training of his children rested
wholly upon himself, took up the work quite well.
His own early religious training, which had been
as seed long buried, now came back to him, and
he gave his children some good instruction which
had excellent effect on M. Still when he was
twenty-two years of age he had never been to
church, school, Sabbath-school, or a prayer-meeting. He was a steady, industrious young man,
had learned to farm, log, build boats, — being of
a mechanical turn of mind, — and had built for
himself a good sloop. When he was twenty-one

he had learned something of the value of an education from his lack of it, for he could barely read and write in a very slow way, and was tired of counting his fingers when he traded and attended to business. Therefore he saved his money until he had about two hundred dollars, and when he was twenty-two he requested the privilege of coming to the reservation and going to school. It was granted, not like other Indian children, for they were boarded and clothed at government expense, but because his step-father was a white man he was required to board and clothe himself, his tuition being free. He willingly did his part. This was a little after New Year's, 1877. He improved his time better than any person who has ever been in school, oftentimes studying very late. Thus he spent three winters at school, working at his home during the summers.

A few days before he left for home at the close of his first winter was our communion season. On the Thursday evening previous was our preparatory lecture and church-meeting, and the man and his wife where he was boarding presented themselves as candidates for admission. Nothing, however, was said to him about it. Indeed it is doubtful whether much had ever been said to him personally on the subject, for he was of a quiet disposition. But a day or two afterward he spoke to the family where he was boarding and said that he would like to join the church, but had been almost afraid to ask. The word was soon passed to my father, and the first I knew about it was that he came to me and said : " See, here is water, what doth hinder me from being baptized ? " I said : " What do you mean by that ? " His reply was : " I do not know but that we have just such a case among us." And then he explained about M. Another church-meeting was held and he was received into the church on the following Sabbath. Previous to this he had never witnessed a baptism or the administration of the Lord's Supper.

When he had finished going to school, he received in 1879 the appointment of government carpenter on the reservation, the first Indian ever in that place, and the first Indian employee on the reservation except the interpreter receiving the same wages as a white man. He remained in this position a few years, when his health failed and he resigned. No fault was found with his work, for he was very faithful and steady, and could be depended on to work alone, or to be in charge of apprentices and others with no fear that the work would be slighted. He afterward, for a time, lived mainly with the whites, as the government cut down the pay for all Indians so low that he could earn much better wages elsewhere. He often lived with a very rough class of whites at saw-mills and among loggers, but he held fast to his profession. In his quiet way he spoke many an effectual word for Christ, and gained the respect of those with whom he mingled by his consistent Christian life. Lately, however, he has gone to the Puyallup Reservation, where he has secured a good piece of land and has taken a leading part among those Indians.

XXX.

DISCOURAGING CASES AND DIS-
APPOINTMENTS.

F. A. was a Clallam, and one of the earlier school-boys. He had left the reservation previous to 1874 and lived and worked with his friends at Port Discovery. In April, 1875, he returned with three of his Port Discovery friends on a visit in good style. He said that he had worked steadily, earned hundreds of dollars, and he gave a brother of his in school quite a sum; that he had taught a small Indian school; that he was trying to have church services on the Sabbath; that the Indians at Port Discovery were about to buy some land for one hundred and fifty dollars, and that he had now come for advice, religious instruction, school-books, and the like. The agent furnished him with school-books and papers, and I gave him four written prayers, two Chinook-jargon songs, and a Testament. This was only a week after Balch and some of the Indians at Jamestown had visited us, who were making good progress. One of the employees on seeing F. A. come, just after the other (Clallam) Indians had visited us, said : " The agent is making his influence felt far and wide for good." But before F. A. left he wanted to be made head chief of the tribe. The agent said that the present chief was doing well, that he had no good reason for removing him, and that he would not do so unless a majority of the tribe desired it, but that he would make F. A. a policeman if he wished so to be. But he did not want this. He said that after what he had told his friends before leaving home, he would be ashamed to go back without his being made chief. His three friends said also that they wished him to be chief. This showed that something was wrong, and by the time all was ferreted out, it was found that he had procured the horses for his party at Olympia at a high price, which he had said the agent would pay, that his style was all put on, and that in reality he was very worthless. It cost his friends more than twenty dollars to pay for the use of the horses, which he had afterward to work out, as he had no money. He tried to run away with one of the girls not long afterward, and never said any thing more about his school, church, and land.

In 1883 he returned to the reservation to live, but does not help the Indians much in regard to Christianity.

L. was from Port Ludlow, fifty-five miles away, a half-breed, and was in school for a year or two. In the fall of 1879 he took hold well in prayer-meetings, and wished to join the church; but he was too desirous for this, it seemed to me, and answered questions too readily. The church deliberated long about him, for several were not fully satisfied, yet, on the whole, it was thought best to receive him, and it was done in January, 1880. The next summer he went home to remain, but while in most respects he has been steady and industrious, having a good reputation about not drinking or gambling, yet he does not honor a Christian profession.

M. was a half-breed school-boy, and was brought up in school. After the first three school-boys began to think that they were Christians, he joined them. After having been a year on probation, he was received into the church in July, 1878, when he was thirteen or fourteen years old. He did fairly until he left the reservation, three or four years afterward, when he went to a white logging-camp where his brother and brother-in-law were at work. Logging-camps are not noted for their morals, and their influence on a young man can not be good in this respect. He remained steadier than most whites around him, and his instruction is not lost, but his Christian life is sadly dwarfed, if it can be seen at all.

W. was among the first three of the school-boys to join the church, after a full year's probation, at the age of about thirteen. He stood well for about two years, while in school, as a Christian, endured considerable persecution, and was especially conscientious. But as he grew older he went the wrong way. His father was a medicine-man, and this probably had something to do with his life, for when he went out into the outer Indian world he seemed to grow peculiarly hardened, so that he seldom came to church or Sabbath-school, and did not treat religion with the respect which the older Indians did who made no pretensions to Christianity. For immoral conduct we were at last obliged to suspend him.

As I look over the church-roll I find that nearly all the first Indian members were from the school; then came the earlier uneducated Indians, and then the later ones. It makes me sad when I see how many of the first ones who have been educated have been suspended before they were settled in life. Yet it must be said that those school children prepared the way for the earlier uneducated Indians, and these likewise prepared the way for the later ones. This second class watching the failures of the first learned wisdom and stood firmer, and the last class learning more wisdom by further observation have stood still firmer.

Simon Peter was one of the better Indian boys of the Twanas, and was in school about as soon as he was old enough. A younger brother, Andrew, was one of the first three of the school-boys to join us in January, 1877, and, like the brothers in the Bible, where Andrew first found Christ and then led his brother Simon to him, so now Andrew evidently led Simon along until, in January, 1878, he joined the church. He belonged to a good family and was well respected and I hoped much from him in the future, but in this I was doomed to disappointment, for consumption had marked him as its own, and in June, 1879, he died. Just before he died he took his brother's hand, said he hoped this brother would not turn back from Christianity as some boys had done, and thus held him till he died. A young man of the Puyallup tribe, who is now an Indian preacher, told me that he owed his conversion to a letter he received from Simon Peter. Thus, " being dead, he yet speaketh."

XXXI.

THE CHURCH AT JAMESTOWN.

IN the section about the Field and Work some account has been given of the beginning of civilization at this place. The Indians there had at first no help from the government, because they were not on a reservation. They had, however, some worthy aspirations, and realized that if they should rise at all they must do so largely through their own efforts. This has been an advantage to them, for they have become more self-reliant than those on the reservation, who have been too willing to be carried.

The agent, on some of his first visits to them, gave them some religious instruction, and at times they gathered together on the Sabbath for some kind of religious worship, which then consisted mainly in singing a song or two and talking together.

In March, 1875, their chief, Lord James Balch, while on a business visit to the reservation, was very anxious to obtain religious instruction. All was given to him that I could furnish, which consisted of instruction, a Chinook song or two, and a few Bible pictures. He returned with more earnestness to hold meetings at home.

My first visit to them was the next fall, in a tour with the agent, and then their village was named Jamestown, after their chief. Since then I have generally been able to spend two Sabbaths, twice a year, with them.

They continued their meetings, and usually met in one of their best houses for church on the Sabbath. After a time they selected one of their number, called Cook House Billy, to pray in their church services, as he had lived for some time in a white family, could talk English, and knew at least more about the external forms of worship than the rest.

In 1877 the Indians began to think about erecting a church-building for themselves. They originated the idea, but it was heartily seconded by the agent and missionary. About the time of its dedication Balch said it was no white man who suggested the idea of building it to him, but he thought it must have been Jesus. It was so far completed by April, 1878, as to be dedicated on the eighth of that month.

About a hundred and twenty-five persons were seated in the house: ninety Clallams, ten Makah Indians, and twenty-five whites. The house is small, sixteen by twenty-four feet. It was made of upright boards, battened and whitewashed. It was ceiled and painted overhead. It was not quite done, for it was afterward clothed and papered and a belfry built in front, but was so far finished as to be used. Although not large or quite finished, yet there were three good things about it: it was built according to their means, was paid for as far as it was finished, and was the first church-building in the county. Its total cost at that time, including their work, was about a hundred and sixty-six dollars. Of this, thirty-seven dollars and fifty cents were given by white persons, mostly on the reservation, four dollars were given by Twana Indians, and some articles, as paint, lime, nails, windows, and door, came from their government annuities, it being their desire that these things should be given for this purpose rather than to themselves personally. It was the first white building in the village, and had the effect of making them whitewash other houses afterward.

The evening before the dedication the first

prayer - meeting ever among them was held. Five Indians took part, most or all of whom were accustomed to ask a blessing at their meals. This prayer-meeting has never since been suffered to die.

It was not, however, until the next December that any of them became members of the church. Then two men joined. They really united with the church at Skokomish, although they were received at Jamestown. For a time this became a branch of the Skokomish church. The first communion service was then held among them. Only five persons in all participated in the communion.

No more of those Indians joined until April, 1880, when four more became members, two of whom were Indians, and the next December two more joined.

A rather singular incident happened a year later. Some of the older Indians, including the chief, were not satisfied with the slow growth of the church; but instead of remedying affairs by coming out boldly for Christ, they chose three young men, who were believed to be moral at least, and asked them to join and help the cause along. These consented, although they had never taken any part in religious services or been known as Christians. As I was not informed of the wish until Sabbath morning, I did not think it wise to receive them then, but replied that if they held out well until my next visit, in five months, I should have no objection. They were hardly willing at first to wait so long, but at last submitted. Before the five months had passed, one of them, the least intelligent, had gone back to his old ways, where he still remains, and the other two were received into the church, one of whom has done especially well and has been superintendent of the Sabbath-school. Yet it always seemed a singular way of becoming Christians, more as if made so by others than of their own free will, they simply consenting to the wishes of others. God works in various ways.

During the winter of 1880–81 a medicine-man made a feast on Sabbath evening and invited all the Indians to it. It was to be, however, a bait for a large amount of tamahnous, which was to take place. The Indians went, the members of the church as well as the rest, leaving the evening service in order to attend it. The school-teacher felt very badly and wrote me immediately about it ; but a little later he learned that on that same evening the Christian Indians, feeling that they were doing wrong, left the place before the feast was over, went to one of their houses, where they held a prayer-meeting and confessed their sin, and on the following Thursday evening, at the general prayer-meeting made a public confession. We could ask for nothing more, but could thank the Holy Spirit for inclining them thus to do before any white person had spoken to them about it.

Knowing of four new ones who wished to join the church in April, 1882, I thought that the time had come to organize them into a church by themselves. So letters were granted by the Skokomish church to seven who lived at Jamestown, and the church was organized April 30, 1882, with eleven members, nine of whom were Indians. The services were in such a babel of languages that their order is here given: Singing in Clallam and then in English; reading of the Scriptures in English; prayer by Rev. H. C. Minckler, of the Methodist-Episcopal church, the school-teacher; singing in Clallam; preaching in Chinook, translated into Clallam; singing in Chinook; baptism of an infant son of a white church member in English; prayer in English; singing in English; propounding the articles of faith and covenant in English, translated into Clallam, together with the baptism

of four adults; giving of the right hand of fellowship, in English, translated into Clallam; prayer
in Chinook; singing in Chinook; talk previous to
the distribution of the bread, in Chinook, translated into Clallam; prayer in English; distribution of the bread; talk in English; prayer in
Chinook, followed by the distribution of the
cup; singing in English a hymn in which nearly
all the Indians could join; benediction in Chinook. A number of their white neighbors gathered in, to the encouragement of the Indians, six
of whom communed with us.

The next fall three more joined, and seven
more in 1883, one of whom was a venerable
white-haired white man, over seventy years old.
In the fall of that year five infants were baptized,
the first belonging to the Indians in the history of
the church.

In the fall of 1883 three of them accompanied
me on a missionary tour to Clallam Bay. They
gave their time, a week, and the American Missionary Association paid their expenses. It was
the first work of the kind which they had done,
and I was pleased with their earnestness and zeal.
The previous spring I had been there, and there
were some things which made me feel as if such a

trip might do good. Still it is a hard field because a majority of the men are over fifty, and, being in the majority, practise and sing tamahnous, and go to potlatches a good share of the time during the winter. There is very little white religious influence near them.

When the day-school first began, in 1878, the teacher, Mr. J. W. Blakeslee, began also a Sabbath-school. His successor, Rev. H. C. Minckler, carried it on until he resigned in April, 1883, and no other teacher was procured until early in 1884; but then they chose one of their own church members, Mr. George D. Howell, who had been to school some, and still carried on the school. He served until November, when he temporarily left to obtain work, and Mr. Howard Chubbs was chosen as his successor.

In 1880 they procured a small church-bell, the first in the county, and added a belfry to the church.

Not all, however, of the people in the village can be called adherents to Christianity. There is a plain division among them. Some are members of the church, a few who are not attend church, and some hardly ever go, but profess to belong to the anti-Christian party.

It is worthy of note that while Clallam County had so many people in it as to be organized into a county in 1854, and had in 1880 nearly six hundred white people, yet these Indians have the only church building in the county, the only church-bell, hold the only regular prayer-meeting, and at their church and on the Neah Bay Indian Reservation are the only Sabbath-schools which are kept up steadily summer and winter. One white person, who lives not far from Jamestown, said to me on one Sabbath, in 1880, as we came away from the church : " It is a shame, *it is a shame!* that the Indians here are going ahead of the whites in religious affairs. It is a wonder how they are advancing, considering the example around them."

XXXII.

COOK HOUSE BILLY.

HE will always be known by this name, probably, though on the church roll his name
is written as William House Cook. He is a Clallam Indian, of Jamestown. His early life was
wild and dissipated, he being, like all the rest of
his tribe, addicted to drunkenness. At one time,
when he was living at Port Discovery, he became
quite drunk. He was on the opposite side of the
bay from the mill, and, wishing for more whiskey,
he started across in a canoe for it; but he was so
drunk that he had not gone far before he upset his
canoe, and had it not been for his wife, who was
on shore and went to his rescue, he would have
been drowned.

In his early life he mingled much with the
whites. He lived with a good white family some of
the time; worked in a cook-house at a saw-mill for
a time, where he gained his name; and once went
to San Francisco in a ship. Thus he learned to
speak English quite well, and he knew more about

civilized ways, and even of religion, than any of the older Indians at Jamestown. He entered willingly into the plan to buy land, and soon after the people there first began to hold some kind of services on the Sabbath, they selected him as the one to pray, hardly because he was better than all the rest, though he was better than all with two or three exceptions, but because he had been more with the whites, and knew better how to pray. Soon after this, and long before he joined the church, a report, which was probably true, was in circulation that he had once or twice secretly drank some. Thereupon the chief took him and talked strongly to him about it. The chief did not wish him to be minister to his people if he was likely to do in that way, and at last asked him if he thought he had a strong enough mind to be a Christian for one year. The reply was, Yes. Then the questions were successively asked if he was strong enough to last two years, five years, ten years, all his life, and when he said Yes, he was allowed to resume his duties as leader of religion.

After this he remained so consistent that he was one of the first two in Jamestown to unite with the church, in December, 1878, when he was supposed to be about thirty-three years old. The road supervisor in his district sent his receipt for road taxes to him one year, addressing it to Rev. Cook House Billy.

When the church was organized at Jamestown in 1882, he was unanimously elected as deacon, and he has ever since filled that position.

Once, five or six years ago, when in Seattle, he was asked by a Catholic Indian of his own tribe, belonging to Port Gamble, to drink some whiskey, but he declined. When urged time and again to do so he still refused, giving as his excuse that he belonged to the church. "So do I," said his tempter; "but we drink, and then we can easily get the priest to pardon us by paying him a little money." "That is not the way we do in our church," said Billy.

But afterward, two years ago, he was very strongly tempted, and yielded, while at Seattle. It was known, and soon after his return home he made his acknowledgement to the church. On my next visit to them in the fall he was reprimanded, and suspended as deacon for five weeks. He often spoke of this fall of his, and seemed to be very sincere in his repentance. In 1883, just before he and nearly all the Indians of his village were going to Seattle again, either to fish or on their way to pick hops, he sent me a letter in which was written: "One day I was talking in meeting to them and said I hoped they would none of them follow my example last summer about drinking, for I had never got over it. I feel ashamed and feel bad every time I think about it, and hoped none of them would have occasion to feel as I did."

He is of a bright, sunny disposition, always cheerful, and has done more for school and church than any of the rest of his tribe, unless it may be the head chief, Balch. Sometimes he has boarded three children free of cost, so that they might go to school, whose parents, if alive, lived far away.

In 1881 two of his children died, a fact of which the opponents of religion made use against Christianity, and he was severely tried, but he stood firm. In 1883, with two others, he went to Clallam Bay with me to preach the gospel to those Indians, the first actual missionary work done by either Indian church. When he left his wife was sick; but, as he had promised to go, she would not keep him back, and he was willing to trust her with God. When we returned she was well.

His wife is a true helpmeet to him. She did

not join the church for a year and a half after he did; but he afterward said that she was really ahead of him, and urged him to begin and to stand fast. When I examined her for reception into the church, I noticed one expression of hers which I shall always remember. In speaking of her sorrow for her sins, she said that her "heart cried" about them. An expression was in use, which I also often used, that our hearts should be sick because of our sins; but I had never used her expression, which was deeper. She is the foremost among the women to take part in meeting, often beseeching them with tears to turn into the Christian path.

XXXIII.

LORD JAMES BALCH.

A FEW years previous to the appointment of Agent Eells, in 1871, this person was made head chief of the Clallams, although, until about 1873, he could get drunk and fight as well as any Indian. At that time he took the lead in the progress for civilization near Dunginess, as related in Chapter V.; and, although once after that, on a Fourth of July, he was drunk, yet he has steadily worked for the good of his tribe. He has had a noted name, for an Indian, as an enemy to drunkenness, and his fines and other punishments on his offending people have been heavy. He gave more than any other one in the purchase of their land, and, in 1875, it was named Jamestown in honor of him. He has taken a stand against potlatches, not even going six miles to attend one when given by those under him. For a long time he was firm against Indian doctors, though a few times within about three years he has employed them when he has been sick, and no white man's remedies which he could obtain seemed to do him any good. He was among the first three Indians to begin prayer, a practice which he kept up several years. But when in 1878 the other two united with the church, Balch declined to do so, although I had expected him as much as I had the others. He gave as his excuse that as he was chief, he would probably do something which would be used as an argument against religion — an idea I have found quite common among the Indian officers. In fact, a policeman once asked me if he could be a policeman and a Christian at the same time. Balch said that whenever he should cease being chief, he would "jump" into the church. He has continued as chief until the present time, and his interest in religion has diminished. At one time he seemed, in the opinion of the school-teacher, to trust to his morality for salvation. Then he turned to the Indian doctors, gave up prayer in his house, and now by no means attends church regularly. Still he takes a kind of fatherly interest in seeing that the church members walk straight; and the way in which he started and has upheld civilization, morality, education, and temperance will long be remembered both by whites and Indians, and its influence will continue long after he shall die.

XXXIV.

TOURING.

WHITE people have almost universally been very kind to me, the Indians generally so, but the elements have often been adverse. These have given variety to my life — not always pleasant, but sufficient to form an item here and there ; and there is nearly always a comical side to most of these experiences, if we can but see it.

One day in February, 1878, I started from Port Gamble for home with eight canoes, but a strong head-wind arose. The Indians worked hard for five hours, but traveled only ten miles and nearly all gave out, and we camped on the beach. It rained also, and the wind blew still stronger so that the trees were constantly falling near us. I had only a pair of blankets, an overcoat, and a mat with me, but having obtained another mat of the Indians, I made a slight roof over me with it and went to sleep. About two o'clock in the morning I was aroused by the Indians, when I learned that a very high tide had come and drowned them out. My bed was on higher ground than theirs, but in fifteen minutes that ground was three or four inches under water. We waded around, wet and cold, put our things in the canoes and soon started. There was still some rain and wind, and it was only by taking turns in rowing that we could keep from suffering. In four hours we were at Seabeck, where we were made comfortable, but that was a cold, long, dark, wintry morning ride.

I started from Jamestown for Elkwa, a distance of twenty-five miles, on horseback, but, after going ten miles, the horse became so lame that he could go no farther. I could not well procure another, so I proceeded on foot. Soon I reached Morse Creek, but could find no way of crossing. The stream was quite swift, having been swollen by recent rains. The best way seemed to be to ford it. So, after taking off some of my clothes, I started in. It was only about three feet deep, but so swift that it was difficult to stand, and cold as a mountain stream in December naturally is. But with a stick to feel my way, I crossed, and it only remained for me to get warm, which I soon did by climbing a high hill.

Coming from Elkwa on another trip on horse-

back, with a friend, we were obliged to travel on
the beach for eight miles, as there was no other
road.   The tide was quite high, the wind blowing,
and the waves came in very roughly.   There were
many trees lying on the beach, around which we
were compelled to canter as fast as we could when
the waves were out.   But one time my friend, who
was just ahead, passed safely, while I was caught
by the wave which came up to my side, and a part
of which went over my head.   It was very fortu-
nate that my horse was not carried off his feet.

Once I was obliged to stay in one of their
houses in the winter, a thing I have seldom done,
unless there is no white man's house near, even
in the summer, when I have preferred to take my
blankets and sleep outside.   The Indians have said
that they are afraid the panthers will eat me ; but
between the fleas, rats, and smoke (for they often
keep their old-fashioned houses full of smoke all
night), sleep is not refreshing, and the next morning I feel more like a piece of bacon than a
minister.

Traveling in February with about seventy-five
Indians, it was necessary that I should stay all
night in an Indian house to protect them from
unprincipled white men.   The Indians at the vil-

lage where we stayed were as kind as could be, assigning me to their best house, where there was no smoke; giving me a feather-bed, white sheets, and all very good except the fleas. Before I went to sleep I killed four, in two or three hours I waked up and killed fourteen, at three o'clock eleven more, and in the morning I left without looking to see how many there were remaining.

But Indian houses are not the only unpleasant ones. Here we are at a hotel, the best in a saw-mill town of four or five hundred people; but the bar-room is filled with tobacco-smoke, almost as thick as the smoke from the fires which often fills an Indian house. Here about fifty men spend a great portion of the night, and some of them all night, in drinking, gambling, and smoking. The house is accustomed to it, for the rooms directly over the bar-room are saturated with smoke, and I am assigned to one of these rooms. Before I get to sleep the smoke has so filled my nostrils that I can not breathe through them, and at midnight I wake up with a headache so severe that I can scarcely hold up my head for the next twenty-four hours. It is not so bad, however, but that I can do a little thinking on this wise : Who are the lowest — the Indians, or these whites? The smoke is of equal thickness : that of the Indians, how-

ever, is clean smoke from wood; that of the
whites, filthy from tobacco. The Indian has sense
enough to make holes in the roof where some of
it may escape; the white man does not even do
that much. The Indian sits or lies near the
ground, underneath a great portion of it; the
white man puts a portion of his guests and his
ladies' parlor directly over it. Sleeping in the
Indian smoke I come out well, although feeling
like smoked bacon, and a thorough wash cures it;
but sleeping in that of the white man I come out
sick, and the brain has to be washed.

In August, 1879, with my wife and three babies,
and three Indians, I was coming home from a
month's tour among the Clallams, in a canoe. One
evening from five o'clock until nine the rain
poured down, as it sometimes does on Puget
Sound. With all that we could do it was impossible to keep dry. Oilcloth, umbrellas, and blankets would not keep the rain out of the bottom of
the canoe, or from reaching some of our bedding.
At nine o'clock we reached an old deserted house
with half the roof off, and we crawled into it.
The roof was off where the fire-place was situated,
so we tried to dry ourselves, keep warm, and dry
some bedding, while holding umbrellas over us, in
order that every thing should not get wet as fast

as it was dried. As soon as a few clothes got dry, we rolled up a baby and he was soon asleep; and so on for three hours we packed one after another away, until I was the only one left. But the rest had all of the dry bedding. There was one pair of blankets left, and they were soaked through. I knew that if I attempted to dry them I might as well calculate to sit up until morning. So I warmed them a little, got close to the warm places, pulled on two or three more wet things, pulled up a box on one side to help keep warm, leaned up my head slantingwise against a perpendicular wall for a pillow, and went to sleep. Some writers say that a person must not sleep in one position all night; if he does he will die. I did not suffer from that danger during that night. The next morning we had to start about five o'clock because of the tide, without any breakfast. When about eight o'clock we reached a farm-house, and warmed up, where the people spent most of the forenoon getting a good warm breakfast for us, free of all charges, we did wish that they could receive the blessing forty times over mentioned in the verse about the cup of cold water, for it was worth a hundred cups of *cold* water that morning. No one of us, however, took cold on that night.

Only once have I ever felt that there was much danger in traveling in a canoe. I was coming from Clallam Bay to Jamestown in November, 1883, with five Indians. We left Port Angeles on the afternoon of the last day with a good wind, but when we had been out a short time and it was almost dark, a low, black snow-squall struck us. There was no safe place to land, and we went along safely until we reached the Dunginess Spit, which is six miles long. There is a good harbor on the east side of it ; but we were on the west side, and the Indians said that it was not safe to attempt to go around it, for those snow-squalls are the worst storms there are, and the heavy waves at the point would upset us. It was better to run the risk of breaking our canoe while landing than to run the risk of capsizing in those boiling waters. So we made the attempt, but could not see how the waves were coming in the darkness, and after our canoe touched the beach, but before we could draw it up to a place of safety, another wave struck it, and split it for nearly its whole length. But we were all safe. Fortunately we were only seven miles from Jamestown ; so we took our things on our backs and walked the rest of the way, all of us very thankful that we were not at the bottom of the sea.

XXXV.

THE BIBLE AND OTHER BOOKS.

NATURALLY most of the Indians did not care to buy Bibles at first. They were furnished free to the school-children, and, like many other things that cost nothing, were not very highly prized, nor taken care of half as well as they ought to have been. Still they learned that it was the sacred Book and when one after another left school most of them possessed a Bible. I had not been here long when an Indian bought one, and, having had the family record of a white friend of his written in it, he presented it to the man, who had none. It caused some comment that an Indian should be giving a Bible to a white man. When the first apprentices received their first pay, a good share of their earnings were invested in much better Bibles than they had previously been able to buy.

The following item appeared in *The San Francisco Pacific* in March, 1880 : —

"LO, THE POOR INDIAN!

" The following facts speak volumes. Let all read them. — [Chaplain Stubbs, Oregon Editor.]

"During 1879 I acted as agent of the Bible Society for this region. The sales amounted to over twenty-two dollars to the Indians, out of a total of thirty-two dollars. Of the seventy-five Bibles and Testaments sold, thirty-nine were bought by them, varying in price from five cents to three dollars and thirty cents. These facts, with other things, show that there is some literary taste among them. Not many of the older ones can read, hence do not wish for books ; but many have adorned their houses with Bible and other pictures, twenty of them having been counted in one house, nearly all of which were bought with their money. In the house of a newly married couple, both of whom have been in school, are twenty-seven books, the largest being a royal octavo Bible, reference, gilt. *The Council Fire* is taken here. In a room where four boys stay, part of whom are in school, and the rest of whom are apprentices, — none of them being over seventeen years old, — will be found *The Port Townsend Argus* and *The Seattle Intelligencer.* On the table is an octavo Bible, for the boys have prayers every evening by themselves, and two of them have spent about five dollars each for other books, "Christ in Literature" being among them. At another house are three young men who have twenty volumes. One of them has paid twenty dollars for what he has bought ; Youmans's Dictionary of Every-day Wants, Webster's Unabridged, Moody's and Punshon's Sermons being among them. He was never in school until he was about twenty-two years old and nine months will probably cover all the schooling he ever had. Here will be found *The Pacific.* In another house the occupant has spent about fifty dollars for books, and his library numbers thirty volumes. Among them will be found an eighteendollar family Bible, Chambers's Information for the People, ".Africa," by Stanley, Life of Lincoln, and Meacham's Wigwam and Warpath. Here also, is *The Pacific, The West Shore Olympia Courier, The Council Fire,* and *The American Missionary.* This man never went to school but two or three weeks, having picked up the rest of his knowledge. When Indians spend their money thus, it shows that there is an intellectual capacity in them that can be developed."

It has been, however, and still is, somewhat difficult to cultivate in many of them a taste for reading, so as to continue to use it when older. This is not because of a want of intellectual capacity, but for three other reasons. First, as soon as they leave school and go back among the uneducated Indians, there is no stimulus to induce them to read. The natural influence is the other way, to cause them to drop their books. Second, like white people who remain in one place continually, they are but little interested in what is going on in the outside world. Third, in most books and papers there are just enough large difficult words which they do not understand to spoil the sense, and thus the interest in the story is destroyed. Yet notwithstanding these discouragements, the present success together with the prospect that it will be much greater in the future, as more of them become educated, is such as to make us feel that it pays.

XXXVI.

BIBLE PICTURES.

IT is very plain that Indians who can not read, and even some who can read, but only a little, need something besides the Bible to help them remember it. Were white people to hear the Bible explained once or twice a week only, with no opportunity to read it, they would be very slow to acquire its truths. It hence became very plain that some good Scripture illustrations would be very valuable. I could not, however, afford to give them to the Indians, nor did I think it best, as generally that which costs nothing is good for nothing. But to live three thousand miles from the publishing-houses and find what was wanted was difficult, for it was necessary that they should be of good size, attractive, and cheap. For eight years I failed to find what was a real success. Fanciful Bible-texts are abundant, but they convey no Bible instruction to older Indians. Small Bible pictures, three or four by four or six inches are furnished by Nelson & Sons, and others, but

they were too small to hang over the walls of
their houses and they did not care to buy them.
I often put them into my pocket, when visiting,
and explained them to the Indians, and so made
them quite useful. The same company furnished
larger ones, about twelve by eighteen inches,
which were good pictures. The retail price was
fifty cents. I obtained them by the quantity at
about thirty-seven cents and sold them for twenty-
five, but they were not very popular. It took too
much money to make much of a show. The
Providence Lithograph Company publish large
lithographs, thirty by forty-four inches, for the
International Sabbath-school Lessons, which were
somewhat useful. I obtained quite a number,
second-hand, at half-price, eight for a dollar, and
often used them as the text of my pulpit preaching, but when I was done with them I generally
had to give them away. They were colored and
showy but too indefinite to be attractive enough
to the Indians to induce them to pay even that
small price for them.

At last I came across some large charts, on
rollers, highly colored, published by Haasis &
Lubrecht, of New York. They were twenty-eight
by thirty-five inches, and I could sell them for

twenty-five cents each, and they were very popular. They went like hot cakes — were often wanted faster than I could get them, although I procured from twenty to forty and sometimes more at once. Protestant and Catholic Indians, Christians and medicine-men, those off the reservation and on other reservations as well as at Skokomish, were equally pleased with them, so that I sold four hundred and fifty in twenty-one months. They were large, showy, cheap, and good, care being used not to obtain some purely Catholic pictures which they publish.

"The Story of the Bible," "Story of the Gospel," and "First Steps for Little Feet in Gospel Paths," also have proved very useful for those who can read a little but can not understand all the hard words in the Bible. Their numerous pictures are attractive, and the words are easy to be understood.

XXXVII.

THE SABBATH-SCHOOL.

FROM the first a Sabbath-school has been held on the reservation. Previous to the time when Agent Eells took charge, while Mr. D. B. Ward and Mr. W. C. Chattin were the school-teachers, they worked in this way. But there was no Sabbath-school in the region which the Indians had seen ; the white influences on the reservation by no means ran parallel with their efforts, and it was hard work to accomplish a little. In 1871 Agent Eells threw all his influence in favor of it before there were any ministers on the reservation or any other Sabbath service, with the agent as superintendent. After ministers came, it was held soon after the close of the morning service. The school-children and whites were expected to be present, as far as was reasonable, and the older Indians were invited and urged to remain. Sometimes they did and there was a large Bible class, and sometimes none stayed.

A striking feature of the school has been the

effort made to induce the children to learn the lesson. Sometimes they were merely urged to, and sometimes the agent compelled them so to do, much as if they were his own children. Six verses have usually been a lesson — sometimes all of them being new ones, and sometimes three being in advance and three in review. Those who committed them all to memory were placed on the roll of honor, and those who had them all perfectly received two credit-marks; so that if there were no interruption on any Sabbath in the school, 104 was the highest number that any one could obtain. During 1875 the record was kept for fifty Sabbaths, and the highest number of marks obtained by any of the Indian children was forty-eight, by Andrew Peterson. Eighty-eight were obtained by each of two white children, Minnie Lansdale and Lizzie Ward. Twenty of the Indian children were on the roll of honor some of the time. During 1876 Miss Martha Palmer, an Indian girl, received eighty-six marks out of a possible hundred. The next highest was a white girl, then a half-breed girl, then an Indian boy, and then a white boy. During 1877 the same Martha Palmer received ninety-six marks, the highest number possible that year, there having been no school on four Sabbaths. In 1878 Martha Palmer and Emily Atkins each committed the six verses to memory and recited them perfectly at the school during forty-nine Sabbaths, there having been no school on three Sabbaths. That was the best report during the ten years. The highest number in 1883 was by Annie Sherwood, but the number of credit-marks was only forty-eight.

Sometimes we followed the simplest part of the Bible through by course and sometimes used the International Lessons. The former plan was in many respects better for the scholars, as the International Lessons skipped about so much that the children often lost the connection; they were sometimes not adapted for Indians, and the children would lose the quarterlies or their lesson-papers. The latter plan was for some reasons better for the teachers, as they could get helps in the quarterlies to understand the lesson which they could not well get elsewhere. Sabbath-school papers with a Bible picture in them and an explanation of it were valuable. Such at last I found in *The Youth's World* for 1883. Once a month, while I had them, I gave the papers to the teachers the Sabbath previous and told the scholars to learn a few verses in the Bible about the picture. Then every child received the paper on the Sabbath, and the story was explained.

At first nearly all the teachers were whites ; but in time, as the whites moved away and the young men and women became older and more competent, they took up the work. About half of the teachers during the last two years were Indians. Agent Eells was superintendent of the school from its beginning in 1871 until 1882, when his head-quarters were removed to another reservation, since which time I have had charge. When the agent left he received from the school a copy of Ryle's Commentary on John, in three volumes, which present was accompanied by some very appropriate remarks by Professor A. T. Burnell, then in charge of the school.

"Sanctify them through thy truth : thy word is truth," said Christ, and we found this to be true; the committing to memory of so many verses produced its natural effect. The seed sown grew. Eighteen Indian children out of the Sabbath-school have united with the church.

The average attendance on the school at Skoko-mish has varied. From June, 1875, to June, 1876, it was eighty-five, and that was the highest.

From June, 1881, to June, 1882, it was forty-seven, which was the lowest. The dismissal of employees and their families and the "dark days," of which mention has been made, caused a decrease for a time.

XXXVIII.

PRAYER–MEETINGS.

ANOTHER of the first meetings established on the reservation under the new policy was the prayer-meeting along with the Sabbath-school. To those white people near the reservation who cared but little for religion, and who had known the previous history of the reservation, a prayer-meeting on a reservation! ah, it was a strange thing, but they afterward acknowledged that it was a very proper thing for such a place. That regular church prayer-meeting has been kept up from 1871 until the present time, varied a little at times to suit existing circumstances. The employees and school-children were the principal attendants, as it was too far away from most of the Indians for them to come in the evening. But few of the children ever took part. Too many wise heads of a superior race frightened them even if they had wished to do so. The average attendance on it has varied from twenty-two in 1875 to thirty-eight in 1880. Previous to 1880, it ranged below thirty — since then above that number.

To suit the wants of the children we had boys'
prayer-meetings and girls' prayer-meetings. Sometimes these were merely talks to them, and sometimes they took part. In the summer of 1875 the
white girls first made a request to have one. I
had been to our Association and on my return I
reported what I had heard of a children's meeting
at Bellingham Bay. Two of the girls were impressed with the idea and made a request for a
similar one. Indian girls were soon invited to
come and more or less took part. It was not long
before from its members some came into the
church. For a long time my mother had charge
of this. She died in 1878, after which my wife
took charge. The white girls at last all left and
only Indian girls remained in it. They have often
taken their turn in leading the meeting.

Although for two or three years I had asked a
few boys to come to my house from time to time
to teach them and try to induce them to pray, yet
they never did any thing more than to repeat the
Lord's Prayer, until February, 1877. Then three
boys came and asked for instruction on this subject, and soon we had a prayer-meeting in which
all took part. Previous to that school-boys had
seemed to be interested in religion, but when they

became older and mingled more with the older
Indians they went back again into their old ways;
but none ever went as far as these did then —
none ever prayed where a white person heard them
or asked to have a prayer-meeting with their minister. During that summer the interest increased
and it grew gradually to be a meeting of twenty
with a dozen sometimes taking part, but all were
not Christians. After a few months of apparent
Christian life, some found the way too hard for
them and turned back, yet a number of them came
into the church.

But all of these meetings did not reach the
older Indians. They were too far away to attend,
and, had they been present, the meeting was in an
unknown tongue. So in the summer of 1875 I
began holding meetings at their logging-camps.
They were welcomed by some, while with some,
especially those who leaned toward the Catholic
religion and the old native religion, it was hard work
to do any thing. In these meetings I was usually
assisted by the interpreter John Palmer. At our
church services and Sabbath-school it was very
difficult to induce them to sing or to say any thing.
There were enough white folks to carry them and
they were willing to be carried. At our first meet-

ings with them they sang and talked well, but preferred to wait a while before they should pray in
public.   They did not know what to say, was the
excuse they gave.   On reading I found that the
natives at the Sandwich Islands were troubled in
the same way; and I remembered that the disciples said: "Lord, teach us how to pray, as John
also taught his disciples;" so we offered to teach
them how, for they professed to be Christians.
One of us would say a sentence and then ask one
of the better ones to repeat it afterward.   I
remember how something comical struck one of
the Indians during one of these prayers and he
burst out laughing in the midst of it.   Feeling
that a very short prayer would be the best probably for them to begin with alone, I recommended
that they ask a blessing at their meals.   This
was acceptable to some of them.   I taught them
a form, and they did so for that fall and a part of
the winter.   I once asked one Indian if he ever
prayed.   His reply was that he asked a blessing
on Sabbath morning at his breakfast.   That was
all, and he seemed to think that it was enough.

When winter came the logging-camps closed
and they went to their homes.   They were too far
off to hold evening services with them, because of

the mud, rain, and darkness, and, as they had but little to do, I took Tuesdays for meetings with them. About the first of December we induced four of them to pray in a prayer-meeting without any assistance from us. This meeting was three hours long. It seemed as if a good beginning had been made, but Satan did not propose to let us have the victory quite so easily. In less than a week after this the Indians were all drawn into a tribal sing tamahnous, and all of these praying Indians took some part, though only one seemed to be the leader of it. That was the end of his praying for years. The agent told him that he had made a fool of himself and he said that it was true. In 1883 he was among the first to join the church and since then he has done an excellent work. Still I kept up the meetings during the winter. The Indian, however, is very practical. His ideas of spiritual things are exceedingly small. His heaven is sensual and his prayers to his tamahnous are for life, food, clothes, and the like. So when they began to pray to God, they prayed much for these things, and when they did not obtain all for which they asked, they grew tired. Others then laughed at them for their want of success. I talked of perseverance in prayer.

Not long after this the trouble with Billy Clams and his wife, as already related under the head of marriage, occurred. He escaped at first, but others were put in jail for aiding him. At one of the first meetings after this trouble began, I asked one to pray, but he only talked. I asked another and he said "No," very quickly, and there was only one left. Soon after this, they held a great meeting to petition the agent to release the prisoners. The only praying one prayed earnestly that this might be done. The petition was rightfully refused. The other Indians laughed at him for his failure, and that stopped his praying in public for a long time, with one exception. Once afterward we held a meeting with them and after some urging a few took part, but it was a dying affair. Notwithstanding all that they had said about being Christians, the heart was not there, and until 1883 hardly any of the older uneducated Indians prayed in public in our meetings. Of those four, one left the reservation and became a zealous Catholic ; one has apparently improved some ; one was nearly ruined by getting a wife with whom he could not get along for a time, and at last became a leader in the shaking religion ; and one, as already stated, has done very well.

The next summer, 1876, I visited their logging-camps considerably, and was well received by some, while others treated me as coldly as they dared, doing only what they could not help doing. But they did not take as much part in the meetings as they had done the previous summer, talking very little and praying none. Their outward progress toward religion had received a severe check. As has been the case with some other tribes, Satan would not give up without a hard struggle. Like some of the disciples, they found the gospel a hard saying, could not bear it, and went back and walked no more with Christ.

The business of logging was overdone for several years, and during that time I was not able to gather them together much for social meetings. I worked mainly by pastoral visiting. In the winter of 1881–82 some of them went to the Chehalis Reservation and attended some meetings held by the Indians there and were considerably aroused. They again asked for meetings and I held them, but while they were free to talk and sing, they were slow to pray. Logging revived, and I held meetings quite constantly with them during the next two years.

At that time four of them professed to take a

stand for Christ. Gambling was a besetting sin of
some of them, but with some help from the school-
boys, who had now grown to be men, they passed
through the Fourth of July safely, although there
was considerable of it on the grounds, and two of
them were strongly urged to indulge. The other
two were absent. But in the fall there was a big
Indian wedding with considerable gambling and
horse-racing, and then two fell. Another did a
very wrong thing in another way and was put in
jail for it, and that stopped his praying for a time,
though he has since begun it again. The other
was among the first of the older Indians to join
the church in 1883, and he has done a firm good
work for us since.

In other camps I was welcomed also, but it has
ever been difficult to induce them, even the Christians, to pray or speak much in public. Those
prayer-meetings have usually been what I have
had to say. Occasionally they speak a little; but,
not being able to read, their thoughts run in a
small circle, and they are apt to say the same
things over again, and they tire of it unless something special occurs to arouse them. "You
speak," they often say to me, when I have asked
them to say something. "You know something

and can teach us ; we do not know any thing and we will listen." It is a fact that what we obtain from the Bible is the great source of our instruction for others ; still if we are Christians and know only a little, the Spirit sometimes sanctifies that even in a very ignorant person so that he may do some good with it.

The Clallam prayer - meetings at Jamestown have been different. They began them when I visited them only once in six months, hence they had to take part or give them up. They were not willing to do the latter, therefore they have had to do the former. Sometimes eight or ten take part. They seem to expect that if a person join the church he will take part in the prayer-meeting, and the children of thirteen or fourteen years of age do so with the older ones. Thrown on their own resources in this respect, as well as in others, it has had its advantages.

XXXIX.

INDIAN HYMNS.

OUR first singing was in English, as we knew
of no hymns in the languages which the
Indians could understand. In the Sabbath-school
prayer-meeting and partly in church we have continued to use them, as the children understand
English, and it is best to train them to use the
language as much as possible. "Pure Gold" and
the Gospel Hymns and Sacred Songs, as used by
Messrs. Moody and Sankey, have been in use
among the Indian children for the last twelve
years. Two or three of the simplest English
songs which repeat considerably have also been
learned by many of the older Indians, who understand a little of our language, as: "Come to
Jesus!" and "Say, brothers, will you meet us?"
Yet all these did not reach the large share of
the older Indians as we wished to reach them.
"What are you doing out here?" "Why do you
not go to Sabbath-school?" were questions which
were asked one Sabbath by the wife of the agent

to an Indian who was wandering around outside
during that service. His reply was that as the
first part of the exercises and the singing were in
English they were very dry and uninteresting to
him. Only when the time came for singing the
Chinook song was he much interested. That was
in 1874, and there was only one such song, which
the agent had made previous to my coming; but
the want of them, as expressed by that Indian,
compelled us to make more. The first efforts
were to translate some of our simpler hymns into
the Chinook language, but this we found to be
impracticable, with one or two exceptions. The
expressions, syllables, words, and accent did not
agree well enough for it; so we made up some
simple sentiment, repeated it two or three times,
fitted it to one of our tunes, and sang it. In the
course of time we had eight or ten Chinook songs.
They repeated considerably, because the older
Indians could not read and had to learn them
from hearing them, somewhat after the principle
of the negro songs. Major W. H. Boyle visited
us in 1876, and was much interested in this singing. He took copies of the songs and said he
would see if he could not have them printed on
the government press belonging to the War

Department, at Portland, free of expense; but I presume he was not able to have it done, as I never heard of them again.

In my visits among white people and in other Sabbath-schools I was often called upon to sing them, and was then often asked for a copy; so often was this done that I grew tired of copying them. Encouraged by this demand and by Major Boyle's interest in them, I thought I would see if I could not have them published. I wrote to several other reservations, asking for copies of any such hymns which they might have, hoping that they also would bear a share of the expense of publishing them; but I found that most of them had no such songs, and, to my surprise, some seemed to have no desire for them. So I was compelled to carry on the little affair alone. I was unable to bear the expense, but fortunately then Mr. G. H. Himes, of Portland, consented to run all risks of printing them, and so in 1878 a little pamphlet, entitled "Hymns in the Chinook Jargon Language," was printed, and it has been very useful. The following, from its introductory note, may be of interest:—

"These hymns have grown out of Christian work among the Indians. . . . The chief peculiarity which I have noticed in making hymns in this language is that a large proportion of the words are of two syllables, and a large majority of these have the accent on the second syllable, which renders it almost impossible to compose any hymns in long, common, or short metres."

The following remarks were made about it by the editor of *The American Missionary :* —

"It is not a ponderous volume like those in use in our American churches, with twelve or fifteen hundred hymns, but a modest pamphlet of thirty pages, containing both the Indian originals and the English translations. The tunes include, among others, 'Bounding Billows,' 'John Brown,' and 'The Hebrew Children.' The hymns are very simple and often repeat all but the first line. The translations show the poverty of the language to convey religious ideas. . . . It is no little task to make hymns out of such poor materials. Let it be understood that these are only hymns for the transition state — for Indians who can remember a little and who sing in English as soon as they have learned to read. This little book is a monument of missionary labor and full of suggestion as to the manifold difficulties to be encountered in the attempt to Christianize the Indians of America."

Since then I have made a few others which have never been printed, one of which is here given. The cause of it was as follows: One day I asked an Indian what he thought of the Christian religion and the Bible. His reply was that it was good, very good, for the white man, but that the Indian's religion was the best for him. Hence in this hymn I tried to teach them that the Bible is not a book for the white people alone, but for the whole world — an idea which is now quite generally accepted among them. In all we now have sixteen hymns in Chinook, five in Twana, five in Clallam, and two in Nisqually.

Tune, " Hold the Fort."

(1)   Sághalie Tyee, yáka pápeh,
        Yáka Bíble kloshe,
        Kópa kónoway Bóston tíllikums
        Yáka hías kloshe.

CHORUS.

Sághalie Tyee, yáka pápeh,
Yáka Bible kloshe,
Kópa kónoway tíllikums álta,
Yáka hías kloshe.

(2)   Sághalie Tyee, yáka pápeh,
        Yáka Bible kloshe,
        Kópa kónoway Síwash tíllikums
        Yáka hías kloshe.

CHORUS.

Sághalie Tyee, etc.

(3)   Sághalie Tyee, yáka pápeh,
       Yáka Bible kloshe,
       Kópa kónoway King George tíllikums
       Yáka hías kloshe. — *Cho.*

TRANSLATION.

(1)   God, His paper —
       His Bible is good;
       For all American people
       It is very good.

CHORUS.

God, His paper —
His Bible is good;
For all people now
It is very good.

(2)   God, His paper —
       His Bible is good;
       For all Indian people
       It is very good.

(3)   God, His paper —
       His Bible is good;
       For all English people
       It is very good.

By changing a single word in the third line to
Pa sai ooks (French), China, Klale man (black
men, or negroes), we had other verses.

In time I, however, became satisfied that the Indians would be better pleased if they could sing a few songs in their native languages ; but it was very difficult to make them, as I could not talk their languages, and so could not revolve a sentence over until I could make it fit a tune. The Indians, on the other hand, were too young or too ignorant of music to adapt the words properly to it for many years. I had, however, written down about eighteen hundred words and sentences in each of the Twana, Clallam, and Squaxon dialects of the Nisqually language, for Major J. W. Powell at Washington, and could understand the Twana language a very little, and this knowledge helped me greatly. Some of the older school-boys became interested in the subject, and so we worked together. After some attempts, which were failures, we were able in 1882 to make a few hymns which have become quite popular. Some the Indians themselves made, and some they and I made. The following samples are given of one in each language : —

TWANA.

Tune, " Balerma."

(1)   Se-seéd hah-háh kleets Badtl Sowul-lús!
      Se-seed hah-háh sa-lay!

Se-seéd hah-háh kleets Badtl Sowul-lús!
Se-seed hah-háh sa-láy!

(2) O kleets Badtl Wees Sowul-lús,
Bis e-lál last duh tse-du-ástl
A-hots ts-kai-lubs tay-tlía e-du-ástl;
Bis-ó-shub-dúh e du-wús!

TRANSLATION.

Great Holy Father God!
Great Holy Spirit!
Great Holy Father God!
Great Holy Spirit!

O our Father God,
We cry in our hearts
For the sins of our hearts;
Have mercy on our hearts!

CLALLAM.

Tune, "Come to Jesus!"

(1) N ná a Jesus
A-chu-á-atl.

(2) Tse-íds kwe nang un tun
A-chu-á-atl.

(3) E-yum-tsa Jesus
A-chu-á-atl.

(4) E-á-as hó-y
A-chu-á-atl.

TRANSLATION.

(1) Come to Jesus
Now.

(2) He will help you
Now.

(3) He is strong
Now.

(4) He is ready
Now.

SQUAXON DIALECT OF THE NISQUALLY.

Tune, " Jesus loves me."

The following is a translation of our hymn, "Jesus loves me, this I know," so literally that it can be sung in both languages at the same time. The other two verses have also been likewise translated.

(1) Jesus hatl tobsh, al kwus us hai-tuh,
Gwutl te Bible siats ub tobsh:
Way-so-buk as-tai-ad seetl,
Hwāk us wil luhs gwulluh seetl as wil luhl.

CHORUS.

A Jesus hatl tobsh,
Gwutl ti Bible siats ub tobsh.

(2) Jesus hatl tobsh, tsātl to át-to-bud
Guk-ud shugkls ak hāk doh shuk,
Tsātl tloh tsa-gwud buk dzas dzuk
Be kwed kwus cha-chushs atl tu-us da.

As an illustration of the difficulty I had, the following is given. I wished to obtain the chorus to the hymn, " I 'm going home," and obtained the expression, " I will go home," in Clallam, in the following seven different ways. The last one was the only one that would fit the music.

> O-is-si-ai-a tsa-an-tok^{hu}.
> Ku-kwa-chin-is-hi-a tok^{hu}.
> Ho-hi-a-tsan-u-tok-^{hu}.
> Tsā-ā-ting-tsin-no-tok^{hu}.
> U-tsā-it-tok^{hu}.
> U-its-tla-hutl tok-^{hu}.
> To-kó-tsa-un.

As a literary curiosity I found that the old hymn, " Where, oh, where is good old Noah ? " to the tune of " The Hebrew Children," could be sung in four languages at the same time, and this was the only English hymn that I was ever able to translate into Chinook jargon, thus : —

Chinook Jargon. — Kah, O kah mit-lite Noah álta?
Twana. — Di-chád, di chád ká-o way klits Noah?
Clallam. — A-hín-kwa, a hín chees wi-á-a Noah?
Far off in the promised land.

CHORUS.

By-and-by we 'll go home to meet them.

Chinook Jargon. — Alki nesika klatawa nánitch.
Twana. — At-so-i-at-so-i hoi klis-há-dab sub-la-bad.
Clallam. — I-á che hátl sche-túng-a-whun.

LITERAL TRANSLATION.

Chinook Jargon. — Where, oh, where, is Noah now?
Twana. — Where, oh, where, is Noah?
Clallam. — Where, oh, where, is Noah now?
Far off in the promised land.

CHORUS.

By-and-by we 'll go home to meet them.

Chinook. — Soon we will go and see [him].
Twana. — Soon we will go and see him.
Clallam. — Far off in the good land.

These sentences can be mixed up in these languages in any way, make good sense, and mean almost precisely the same. I found no other hymn in which I could do likewise, but the chorus to " I 'm going home " can be rendered similarly in the English, Twana, and Clallam.

Clallams are much more natural singers than the Twanas. For this reason, and also because there have never been enough whites in church to do the singing for them, there has never been any difficulty in inducing them to sing in church. But for very many years it was different with the

Twanas. When the services were first begun among them the singing was in English and they were not expected to take part in it. When hymns were first made in the Chinook jargon there were so many whites to sing in church, that the Indians did not seem to take hold. They would sing well enough at their camps, the boys would sing loud enough when alone at the boarding-house or outdoors, but when they came to church they were almost mum. The whites and the school-girls did most of it. It is only within the past year or two that a perceptible change has been made for the better.

XL.

NATIVE MINISTRY AND SUPPORT.

BUT little has been done in these respects except to sow the seed, but if the work shall continue another ten years I trust that more will be accomplished. Since I have been here I have worked with the idea that in time the Indians ought to furnish their own ministers and support them. It will, however, naturally take more time to raise up a native ministry than a native church, native Christian teachers than native Christian scholars. These must come from our schools after long years of training. Owing to a lack of early moral training among them, — the want of a foundation, — the words of Paul on this subject have appeared to me to have a striking significance, more so than among whites, although they are true even among them : "Not a novice, lest being lifted up with pride he fall into the condemnation of the devil."

All people are tempted to be proud, but owing to this lack of foundation, Indians are peculiarly so. A little knowledge puffeth up, and, to use a common expression, they soon get the "big-head." That spoils them for the ministry. My first hope of this kind was that John Palmer would turn his attention to the subject, but he had a family before I knew him, and I never could induce him to look much in that direction. In the spring of 1882 two young men who had been in school from childhood took hold well. They began to talk with the Indians, to assist me in holding meetings, and to take charge of them in my absence. I felt that they were too young, — less than twenty-one, — and yet at times I could see no other way to do; but I had reason to fear that both felt proud of their position. During the next summer one of them, in getting married, fell so low that we had to suspend him from the church for almost a year, and the other for a time went slowly backward. Both have come up again considerably, and the latter has done quite well for the last year in holding lay-meetings. I pray "the Lord of the harvest, that he will send forth laborers into his harvest."

As to the support of the ministry, I always felt a delicacy in speaking of the subject, because I was the minister. For several years, as long as

very few of the older Indians were members of
the church, and the ones who were members were
scholars without money, it was difficult to say
much.   As soon as some of the school-boys were
put to work as apprentices, I broached the subject
to them, talked about it, and gave them something
to read on it.   While they were apprentices and
employees most of them gave fairly.   The agent
urged them to do so, but compelled none, and a
few refused entirely.   But when they left the government employ and the agent moved away, they
stopped doing what they had never liked to do.

The older Indians, when they did come into the
church, were hardly prepared for it.   The Catholic
set said that if the people joined them they would
have nothing to pay.   One of the Catholics told
me that the only reason why I wanted to get him
into the church was to obtain his money.   It had
been revealed to them that it was wrong to sell
God's truth.   These arguments, somewhat similar
to those used years ago by some of the more ignorant people in the Southern and Western States,
coupled with the natural love of money, has made
it very difficult to induce even the members of
the church to contribute for the support of their
pastor.   One of them once almost found fault

with me for taking the money contributed at a collection by whites at Seabeck, where I often preached, and he thought I ought not to do so.

The Indians at Jamestown have done somewhat differently. In their region, when there has been preaching by the whites, generally a collection is taken. Noticing this, of their own accord, in 1882 when I went to them, they passed around the hat and took up a collection of three dollars and forty-five cents, and they have sometimes done so since.

XLI.

TOBACCO.

THE use of tobacco is not as excessive among the Twanas as among many Indians — not as much so as among the Clallams. Seldom is one seen smoking or chewing, though a large share of the Indians use it a little. Yet not much of a direct war has been waged against it. There have been so many greater evils against which it seemed necessary to contend that I hardly thought it wise to speak much in public against it. Still a quiet influence has been exerted against it. The agent never uses it, and very few of the employees have done so. This example has done something.

The following incident shows the ideas some of them have obtained. About 1876 the school-teacher heard something going on in the boys' room. He quietly went to the key-hole and listened to see if any mischief were brewing. The result was different from what he had feared. The boys were holding a court. They had their judge and jury, witnesses and lawyers. The culprit was charged with the crime of being drunk. After the prosecution had rested the case, the criminal arose and said about as follows: "May it please your honor, I am a poor man and not able to pay a law- yer, so I shall have to defend myself. There is a little mistake about this case. My name is Cap- tain Chase [a white man of the region]. I came to church on Sunday; the minister did not know me. I was well dressed, and the minister mistook me for another minister. So when he was done, he asked me to say a few words to the Indians. I was in a fix, for I had a large quid of tobacco in my mouth. I tried to excuse myself, but the min- ister would not take no for an answer. So at last I quietly and secretly took out the tobacco from my mouth [suiting his words with a very apt illus- tration of how it was done], threw it behind the seat, and went up on the platform to speak. But I was not sharp enough for the Indians. Some of them saw me throw it away, *and they thought a minister had no business with tobacco*, and that is why I am here; besides I was a little tipsy." I have enjoyed telling this story to one or two tobacco-using ministers.

Somewhat later a rather wild boy wrote me, asking me to allow him to enter the praying band of Indian boys. He promised to give up his bad habits ; and among others he mentioned the use of tobacco, which he said he would abandon.

Within the past year a number of the older Indians have abandoned its use. I have a cigar which was given me by one man. He said that when he determined to stop its use, he had a small piece of tobacco and two cigars, and that for months afterward they lay in his house where they were at that time, and he gave me one of them. Most of those who stopped using it belonged to the shaking set. It was one of the few good things which resulted from that strange affair. But they have been earnestly encouraged to continue as they have begun in this respect.

A white man who has an Indian woman for a wife told me the following. For years both he and his wife used tobacco, himself both chewing and smoking. When she professed to become a Christian, she gave up her tobacco and tried to induce him to do the same, and at last he did so far yield as to stop smoking ; but he continued to chew. All her talk did not stop him. But he saw that when he had spit on the floor and stove, she would get a paper or rag and wipe it up, and hence he grew ashamed and stopped chewing in the house, using only a little — when he told me — in the woods when at work.

XLII.

SPICE.

A^N experience which is not very pleasant comes from the vermin, especially the fleas — not a refined word; but the most refined society gets accustomed to it here because they *have to do so*, and the more so the nearer they get to the native land of these animals — the Indians. I stood one evening and preached in one of their houses when I am satisfied that I scratched every half-minute during the service; for, although I stood them as long as I could, I could not help it. I would quietly take up one foot and rub it against the other, put my hand behind my back or in my pocket, and treat the creatures as gently as I could, and the like, so as not to attract any more attention than possible.

But then Indian houses are not their only dwellings. At one place I once stayed at a white man's house, who was as kind as he knew how to be: but backing for twenty years with very few neighbors except Indians is not very elevating; it is one of

the trials of the hardy frontiersman. I tried to
go to sleep — one bit; I kicked — he stopped; I
shut my eyes — another wanted his supper; I
scratched; and so we kept up the interminable
warfare until three o'clock, when sleep conquered
for two hours. The next day, on the strength of
it, I preached twice, held a council, tramped five
miles, and talked the rest of the time. That
night mine host, having suspected something, proposed that we take our blankets and go to the
barn. I was willing, and we all slept soundly;
but the hay was a year old, and in that region
sometimes innumerable small hay-lice get on it —
a fact of which I was not aware. They did not
trouble us during the night; but when we arose
the next morning our clothes, which had lain on
the hay, were covered with thousands of them.
Every seam, torn place, button-hole, and turned-
over place was crowded with the lilliputians. It
took me three quarters of an hour to brush them
from my clothes. However, it did not hurt the
clothes or me. My better two-thirds would have
said that they needed brushing.

Twice while traveling to Jamestown have I
been obliged, when within twenty miles of the
place, to stop all day Saturday because of heavy

head-winds, when I was exceedingly anxious to be at Jamestown over the Sabbath. That day was consequently spent not where I wished to be. It seemed to me to be a strange Providence; but I have since been inclined to believe that my example in not traveling on the Sabbath, when the Indians knew how anxious I was to reach the place, was worth more than the sermons I would have preached.

The following appeared in *The Child's Paper* in January, 1878 : —

"In the school on the Indian reservation where I live twenty-five or thirty Indian children are taught the English language. At one time a new boy came who knew how to talk our language somewhat but not very well. Soon after he came he was at work with the other boys and the teacher, when, in pronouncing one English word, he did not pronounce it aright. He was corrected but still did not say it right. Again he was told how, but still it seemed as if his tongue were too thick; and again, but he did not get the right twist to it. At last one of the scholars thought that he was doing it only for fun and that he could pronounce it correctly if he only would do so, so he said: 'O boys, it is not because his tongue is crooked but because his ears are crooked!'"

Query: Are there not some others who have crooked ears?

What does Paul say? "Five times received I forty stripes save one." Well, I have never been treated so, for the people are as kind as can be. "Shipwrecked"? No, only cast twice on the beach by winds from a canoe. "A night and a day in the deep"? No, only a whole night and a part of several others on the mud-flats, waiting for the tide to come. No danger of drowning there. So I have determined to take more of such spice if it shall come.

XLIII.

CURRANT JELLY.

THERE is, however, another side to the picture, more like currant jelly. The people generally are as kind as they can be. "We will give you the best we have," is what is often told me, and they do it. Here is a house near Jamestown, where I have stopped a week at a time, or nearly that, once in six months for about six years, and the people will take nothing for it. For seventy-five miles west of Dunginess is a region where a man's company is supposed to pay for his lodgings at any house. I meet a man, who offers to go home, a half a mile, and get me a dinner, if I will only accept it. A girl, with whose family I was only slightly acquainted, stood on the porch one day as I passed, and said : "Mister, have you been to dinner? You had better stop and have some." A hotel-keeper, who had sold whiskey for fifteen years, put me in his best room, one which he had fitted up for his own private use, and then would take nothing for it. The Super-

intendent of the Seabeck Mills, Mr. R. Holyoke,
invited me to go to his house whenever I was in
the place, and would never take any thing for it.
It amounted to about four weeks' time each year
for five or six years, and yet he would hardly allow
me to thank him.   Others, too, at the same place,
have been very kind.   The steamer *St. Patrick*
for two years and a half always carried myself and
family free, whenever we wished to travel on it,
and during that time it gave us sixty or seventy-
five dollars' worth of fare.   Captain J. G. Baker,
of the *Colfax*, said to me, six or seven years ago:
"Whenever you or your family, or an Indian whom
you have with you to carry you, wish to travel
where I am going, I will take you free."   He has
often done it, sometimes making extra effort with
his steamer in order to accommodate me.   The
steamers *Gem* and *McNaught* also made a rule to
charge me no fare when I traveled on them.

Indians, too, are not wholly devoid of gratitude.
It is the time of a funeral.   They are often accustomed at such times to make presents to their
friends who attend and sympathize with them.
"Take this money," they have often said to me at
such times, as they have given me from one to
three dollars.   "Do not refuse — it is our custom;

for you have come to comfort us with Christ's words." At a great festival, where I was present to protect them from drunkenness, and other evils equally bad, they handed me seven dollars and a half, saying, "You have come a long distance to help us ; we can not give you food as we do these Indians, as you do not eat with us ; take this money, it will help to pay your board." But when I offered to pay the gentleman with whom I was staying, Mr. B. G. Hotchkiss, he too would take nothing for the board. The good people of the Pearl Street Church in Hartford, Connecticut, sent us a barrel of things in the early spring of 1883, whose money value I estimated at considerably over a hundred dollars, and whose good cheer was inestimable in money, because it came when our days were the darkest.

God has been very good to put it into the hearts of so many people to be so kind, and not the least good thing that he has done is that he has put that verse in the Bible about the giving a cup of cold water and the reward that will follow.

XLIV.

CONCLUSION.

DR. H. J. MINTHORNE, superintendent of the Indian Training School at Forest Grove, Oregon, once remarked to me, "that, in the civilization of Indians, they often went forward and then backward; but that each time they went backward it was not quite so far as the previous time, and that each time they went forward it was an advance on any previous effort." I have found the same to be true. They seem to rise much as the tide does when the waves are rolling — a surge upward and then back; but careful observation shows that the tide is rising.

There is much of human nature in them. In many respects — as in their habits of neatness and industry, their visions, superstitions, and the like — I have often been reminded of what I have read about ignorant whites in the Southern and Western States fifty years ago, and of what I have seen among the same class of people in Oregon thirty years ago.

Soon after I came here, an old missionary said to me: "Keep on with the work; the fruits of Christian labor among the Indians have been as great or greater than among the whites." I have found it to be in some measure true. Something has, I trust, been done; but the Bible and experience both agree in saying that "God has done it all." I sometimes think I have learned a little of the meaning of the verse, "Without me ye can do nothing," and I would also record that I have proved the truth of that other one, "I am with you alway," — for the work has paid.

I went to Boise City, in Idaho, in 1871, with the intention of staying indefinitely, perhaps a lifetime, but Providence indicated plainly that I ought to leave in two and a half years. When I came here, it was only with the intention of remaining two or three months on a visit. The same Providence has kept me here ten years and I am now satisfied that his plans were far wiser than mine. So "man proposes and God disposes." The Christians' future and the Indians' future are wisely in the same hands.

THE END

www.ingramcontent.com/pod-product-compliance
Lightning Source LLC
Chambersburg PA
CBHW062156270326
41930CB00009B/1554